The
Practical Bee Guide

A Manual of Modern Beekeeping

By
The Rev. J. G. Digges, M.A.

ELEVENTH EDITION
FIFTY-SIXTH THOUSAND

British Library Cataloguing-in-Publication Data
A catalogue record for this book is available from the
British Library

Bee Keeping

Beekeeping (or apiculture, from Latin: *apis* 'bee') is quite simply, the maintenance of honey bee colonies. A beekeeper (or apiarist) keeps bees in order to collect their honey and other products that the hive produces (including beeswax, propolis, pollen, and royal jelly), to pollinate crops, or to produce bees for sale to other beekeepers. A location where bees are kept is called an apiary or 'bee yard.' Depictions of humans collecting honey from wild bees date to 15,000 years ago, and efforts to domesticate them are shown in Egyptian art around 4,500 years ago. Simple hives and smoke were used and honey was stored in jars, some of which were found in the tombs of pharaohs such as Tutankhamun.

The beginnings of 'bee domestication' are uncertain, however early evidence points to the use of hives made of hollow logs, wooden boxes, pottery vessels and woven straw baskets. On the walls of the sun temple of Nyuserre Ini (an ancient Egyptian Pharo) from the Fifth Dynasty, 2422 BCE, workers are depicted blowing smoke into hives as they are removing honeycombs. Inscriptions detailing the production of honey have also been found on the tomb of Pabasa (an Egyptian nobleman) from the Twenty-sixth Dynasty (c. 650 BCE), depicting pouring honey in jars and cylindrical hives. Amazingly though, archaeological finds relating to beekeeping have been discovered at Rehov, a Bronze and Iron Age archaeological site in the Jordan Valley, Israel.

Thirty intact hives, made of straw and unbaked clay, were discovered in the ruins of the city, dating from about 900 BCE. The hives were found in orderly rows, three high, in a manner that could have accommodated around 100 hives, held more than 1 million bees and had a potential annual yield of 500 kilograms of honey and 70 kilograms of beeswax!

It wasn't until the eighteenth century that European understanding of the colonies and biology of bees allowed the construction of the moveable comb hive so that honey could be harvested without destroying the entire colony. In this 'Enlightenment' period, natural philosophers undertook the scientific study of bee colonies and began to understand the complex and hidden world of bee biology. Preeminent among these scientific pioneers were Swammerdam, René Antoine Ferchault de Réaumur, Charles Bonnet and the Swiss scientist Francois Huber. Huber was the most prolific however, regarded as 'the father of modern bee science', and was the first man to prove by observation and experiment that queens are physically inseminated by drones outside the confines of hives, usually a great distance away. Huber built improved glass-walled observation hives and sectional hives that could be opened like the leaves of a book. This allowed inspecting individual wax combs and greatly improved direct observation of hive activity. Although he went blind before he was twenty, Huber employed a secretary, Francois Burnens, to make daily observations, conduct careful experiments, and keep accurate notes for more than twenty years.

Early forms of honey collecting entailed the destruction of the entire colony when the honey was harvested. The wild hive was crudely broken into, using smoke to suppress the bees, the honeycombs were torn out and smashed up — along with the eggs, larvae and honey they contained. The liquid honey from the destroyed brood nest was strained through a sieve or basket. This was destructive and unhygienic, but for hunter-gatherer societies this did not matter, since the honey was generally consumed immediately and there were always more wild colonies to exploit. It took until the nineteenth century to revolutionise this aspect of beekeeping practice – when the American, Lorenzo Lorraine Langstroth made practical use of Huber's earlier discovery that there was a specific spatial measurement between the wax combs, later called *the bee space*, which bees do not block with wax, but keep as a free passage. Having determined this bee space (between 5 and 8 mm, or 1/4 to 3/8"), Langstroth then designed a series of wooden frames within a rectangular hive box, carefully maintaining the correct space between successive frames, and found that the bees would build parallel honeycombs in the box without bonding them to each other or to the hive walls.

Modern day beekeeping has remained relatively unchanged. In terms of keeping practice, the first line of protection and care – is always sound knowledge. Beekeepers are usually well versed in the relevant information; biology, behaviour, nutrition - and also wear protective clothing. Novice beekeepers commonly wear gloves and a hooded suit or hat and veil, but some experienced beekeepers elect not to use gloves because they inhibit delicate manipulations. The face and neck are the most important areas to protect (as a sting here will lead to much more pain and swelling than a sting elsewhere), so most beekeepers wear at least a veil. As an interesting note, protective clothing is generally white, and of a smooth material. This is because it provides the maximum differentiation from the colony's natural predators (bears, skunks, etc.), which tend to be dark-coloured and furry. Most beekeepers also use a 'smoker'—a device designed to generate smoke from the incomplete combustion of various fuels. Smoke calms bees; it initiates a feeding response in anticipation of possible hive abandonment due to fire. Smoke also masks alarm pheromones released by guard bees or when bees are squashed in an inspection. The ensuing confusion creates an opportunity for the beekeeper to open the hive and work without triggering a defensive reaction.

Such practices are generally associated with rural locations, and traditional farming endeavours. However, more recently, urban beekeeping has emerged; an attempt to revert to a less industrialized way of obtaining honey by utilizing small-scale colonies that pollinate urban gardens. Urban apiculture has undergone a renaissance in the first decade of the twenty-first century, and urban beekeeping is seen by many as a growing trend; it has recently been legalized in cities where it was previously banned. Paris, Berlin, London, Tokyo, Melbourne and Washington DC are among beekeeping cities. Some have found that 'city bees' are actually healthier than 'rural bees' because there are fewer pesticides and greater biodiversity. Urban bees may fail to find forage, however, and homeowners can use their landscapes to help feed local bee populations by planting flowers that provide nectar and pollen. As is evident from this short introduction, 'Bee-Keeping' is an incredibly ancient practice. We hope the current reader is inspired by this book to be more 'bee aware', whether that's via planting appropriate flowers, keeping bees or merely appreciating! Enjoy.

THE PRACTICAL BEE GUIDE

A MANUAL OF MODERN BEEKEEPING

CONTENTS

PREFACE TO ELEVENTH EDITION.

FIFTY-ONE THOUSAND copies of previous editions having been sold out and the demand for the book steadily increasing, this eleventh edition of 5,000 copies has been prepared.

The GUIDE is still the old book in so far as it retains that which by its nature is unchanging in apiculture; but it is also completely modern in that it incorporates in its pages all the latest knowledge regarding the nature of bee diseases and their cure, the newest methods of feeding and handling bees, and full descriptions as to hiving, marketing, rearing and breeding.

Where necessary new illustrations have replaced those which had become obsolete and a certain number of revisions have been made through the text where this was deemed advisable in the light of new developments and research.

The GUIDE as it now appears will enable the beginner to make a success of his beekeeping from the very start, and also shows how honey production may be a very paying proposition.

The commercial beekeeper, on however large a scale he operates, will find, we trust, that he must include this book in his library, and it is hoped that it retains with its scientific accuracy its old charm which is witnessed to by the generous approval of correspondents from all parts of the world.

This GUIDE consists of Three Parts. Part I. (pp. 1-55), deals with the History and Anatomy of the Bee, and with Bee Products: Part II. (pp. 56-101), describes the Hives and Appliances in general use: Part III. (pp. 102-299), consists of Practical Directions for Management, with instruction for exhibitors and judges of Bee Products and a concluding chapter on Bee Flowers and Plants. The GUIDE is arranged in numbered and titled paragraphs. Where, in any paragraph, reference to subjects dealt with in other portions of the book is desirable, the paragraph numbers are inserted in brackets, thus obviating the necessity for frequent examination of the Index, and facilitating reference to the subjects required. Of the illustrations in the GUIDE, many are from original photographs by the author, and pen-and-ink sketches drawn specially for this work.

We gratefully acknowledge indebtedness to the following for permission to publish illustrations:—Messrs. Burtt and Son, J. T. Burgess and Sons, Robert Lee, R. Steele and Brodie, E. H. Taylor Ltd., Dadant and Sons, G. B. Lewis

Co., A. I. Root Co., A. G. Woodman Co., Dr. John Anderson, Messrs. R. W. Frow and J. Tinsley. Illustrations (after Barbo) are published by agreement with M. Ulrico Hospli, and (after Witzgall) by permission of M. Ulgen Ulmer.

Also to Mr. L. Upcott Gill for allowing free use of the work of the late F. R. Cheshire; to Dr. R. F. Caird for help in the Anatomy Section; to Professor Hambleton, U.S.A., for foul brood plates; to Mr. E. G. Burtt, Miss A. D. Betts, B.Sc., Dr. H. L. A. Tarr, Mr. A. H. Bowen, and to Mr. A. S. Rowse.

And to Mr. R. O. B. Manley for the great trouble he has taken in revising this book and for bringing it up to date where needed, so that the matter embodies the most recent knowledge in connection with bees and beekeeping, both scientific and commercial.

THE·PRACTICAL·BEE·GUIDE

PART I.

THE HONEY BEE

CHAPTER I.

THE OCCUPANTS OF THE HIVE.

Kingdom—Animal. *Sub-Kingdom*—Annulosa. *Division*—Arthropoda.
Class—Insecta. *Order*—Hymenoptera. *Family*—Apidæ.
Genus—Apis. *Species*—Mellifica.

> " Therefore doth heaven divide
> The state of man in divers functions
> Setting endeavour in continual motion;
> To which is fixed, as an aim or butt,
> Obedience; for so work the honey-bees;
> Creatures that by rule in nature, teach
> The act of order to a peopled kingdom."
>
> SHAKESPEARE *(Henry V, act I, sc. 2.)*

1. It is natural that a guide to beekeeping should begin with a description of the bees that are to be kept. And it is very necessary that everyone who desires to derive either pleasure or profit from the keeping of bees should know something of the bees which he proposes to keep—of their habits, their requirements, of the laws which govern their actions, and of the objects to which their marvellous energies and intelligence are devoted.

2. Therefore, this guide begins with a description of the occupants of the hive, namely, the Queen, the Workers, and the Drones.

3. **The Occupants of the Hive.** In the summer months the hive of a prosperous colony of bees will be found, upon

examination, to contain a queen, from 30,000 to 60,000 workers, and from 300 to 400 drones.

QUEEN.   WORKER.
                           Fig. 1.

4. **The Queen** (Fig. 1) is not the sovereign ruler of the bee kingdom, as her name might imply. She is neither daughter, wife, nor widow of a king. She is obedient rather than commanding; and yet a queen in her own right; born to the purple; pre-eminent and distinguished above all others; the abundant  mother, carrying in her prolific womb the creation and hope of unnumbered millions of her race. Hers is the longest life, extending to several years. Her very movements are queenly, the stately pace among her children marking her out to the observant as distinct from other occupants of the hive. In size, and form, and colour she is unique; longer, and more delicately moulded; often darker in hue in the black races, more golden in the yellow and less hairy in all. Her mission is to propagate; and for that most holy office nature endows her richly. Mated once for all, her strength, her life to it are unceasingly devoted. Within the hours that make a day and night 3,000 eggs from her teeming flanks may fall; and this prodigious labour will cease only with exhaustion of fecundity or approach of death. (45).*

5. **The Workers** (Fig. 1) are the smallest bees in the colony; females, like the queen, but undeveloped. Theirs is a brief life, full of toil, of work so incessant that in the full flow of summer activity it yields to the pressure of exacting duty; and within a few weeks they drop and die, sacrificed to the demands of destiny, martyrs to the common good. (200). If born in the

---

* The figures in brackets, thus (45), refer to the paragraphs bearing the numbers indicated.

autumn months they can survive the winter time of rest, and with the opening spring begin the work which unborn generations are to take up and carry to completion. Their responsibility is exceeding great; their labour is magnificent. They are the gatherers who, when Nature decks the country-side with fresh beauties, sally forth, and hurrying ever from flower to flower, collect the nectar, and pollen with which to feed the young, and propolis to fill up cracks and make the hive more homely. They manufacture wax, and with it build the combs which serve as cradles of the race and larders for the store of honey. They feed the queen, nurse the young, cleanse the hive, and set up portal-guards to defend from all aggression the citadel that holds the secret of their destiny—the treasure of their faithful hearts. Fearless, surpassingly diligent, beautifully unselfish, their marvellous intelligence fits them for that stupendous enterprise to which their lives are devoted and for which they gladly die. **(15)**.

6. **The Drones** (Fig. 1) or male bees, are thick and bulky, not so long as the queen, but longer than the workers. These are the oft-maligned, noisy, buzzing bees,

" The lazy yawning drone "

of Shakespeare, and the harmless, innocent butts for the gibes of modern critics. Theirs is a life of brief dependence and submission. They gather no stores; Nature has not fitted them to do so. The one object of their existence is to inseminate the young queens. To that end they are born, are tolerated in the colony, and are allowed free access to the honey cells. Theirs, also, is the sacrifice of life to duty; and such of them as survive to the close of autumn are driven out of the hive to end, in cold and hunger, a life which, if seemingly idle or useless, was, at least, inoffensive, and full of possibilities whose vastness fills with awe and amazement every thinking mind. **(43)**.

CHAPTER II.

THE BEE IN SPRING.

7. **Signs of Survival.**—Throughout all the long winter-time, the living mass clinging to the hive-combs has maintained life and warmth. The bees of the cluster have been steadily changing places; those on the outside passing to the centre of the sphere, their places taken by those within in steady rhythm. Now, with the lengthening of the days, as the sun, in genial humour, peeps through the open door and gives to the long-imprisoned inmates assurance of kindlier conditions without; the bee-man, watching for signs of survival, delights to see first one, and then another, and presently many of his little pets appear upon the alighting board. Discreet in their new-found joy, they risk no long excursion, nor venture over much. Scenting the freshness of the air, they seem to revel in it, and in the heat and light which stir the life in them. They move about the entrance; examine the doors and porch; meet and salute each other; and rising, fly for a moment in front of the hive. A gladsome hour this for the bee-man also; an infectious happiness. He knows now that snow and storms, and all the frost and cruel winter hardships, have failed to work their devastation within the little home which his fore-sight and loving care secured and sheltered before the falling leaves had left the branches bare. With each succeeding sun the bees in larger numbers move abroad—creatures " fanatically cleanly," who will suffer much and long and yet refuse to sully the purity that their incessant care preserves within the hive (413).

8. **Breeding Begins.**—In this, the new year's opening month, begins that wondrous work on which the thoughts, and energies, and hopes of all the colony are concentrated (196). The queen, stirring in the centre of the cluster, communicates to all around her that the hour has come for which, through the long months of winter, they have lived and waited; and activity spreads throughout the hive. From cell to cell, within a small circle, she passes, examining each, and depositing therein a tiny egg. Upon it nurse bees will lavish most tender care. During three days they will hatch it; and then, the grub appearing, it shall be fed for three days with specially secreted larval food produced by the nurse bees in certain glands, and

after that for two days more shall be added food of the sweetest and purest—honey and pollen drawn from the flowers of the previous summer and stored for this same purpose in adjacent combs. Then shall the cell be sealed, still warmed by the clustering nurses, until the larva, transformed into a nymph, shall, twelve days later, emerge a perfect bee to share the labours and to participate in the busy, and often hazardous enterprises of the colony. (214).

9. Work Out of Doors commences.—Meanwhile the queen has enlarged the circles of her brood and has ventured upon fresh combs. Her downy progeny are bursting their cells on every side; the population is increasing, and the temperature in the hive rises rapidly. Outside, a spirit of resurrection has entered into nature, in whose scenes of progressive loveliness everything that moves experiences a new joy.

> " The softly warbled song
> Comes from the pleasant woods, and coloured wings
> Glance quick in the bright sun that moves along
> The forest openings."

Advancing spring has rescued from the embrace of winter the purple anemone and yellow crocus, fresh as the morning dew and lovelier than the robe of Solomon in the days of his glory; gorse has made the hill-sides golden; hazel, and salex, and dandelion open their attractions around the fields. And from out the hive come the busy workers to gather in the stores kind Nature has provided, and in turn, to render her good offices by transfer of the fertilising dust from flower to flower (79). Where nectar is, they sip it; where pollen, their feathery hairs collect it, and in the little baskets (*corbiculæ*) with which their hindmost legs are furnished (34) they bear it home to feed the larvæ. Water also they will find, for breeding cannot progress without it; and propolis to fasten joints and to exclude unwelcome draughts (80). These safely delivered up to those who work within, they start afresh, nor cease their eager gathering until the fading light, or cooling atmosphere, warns them that the life required to-morrow must not be sacrificed to-day.

10. Wax Production and Comb Building.—Within the hive there is proceeding a work most truly marvellous. Those bees whose part it is to supply material for the building of the combs, have fed themselves from stores of honey, and, clinging one to the other in shape of festoons first, to thus facilitate the climbing of the rest, have formed in compact cluster (67).

There, motionless, during many hours they hang, retaining and increasing the heat within the mass until a high temperature is attained; when upon the ventral plates, or pockets, under the abdomen appear clear scales of wax (37). First transferring these to the mouth for preparation, they hand them over to the builders, who, taking them in their mandibles, construct with them the comb—the masterpiece " that touches absolute perfection," by which the bees have taught a lesson to the highest human intelligence, and have applied the shape and form which give the greatest capacity and strength with least expenditure of material, time, and labour. (73).

11. Sanitation in the Hive.—Other bees fulfil a lowlier task and undertake the cleansing of the hive. The winter's dead they carry out for burial. The brood which, immature and chilled and lifeless, occupy cells that missed the cluster's nursing warmth, are seized and dragged away to safer sepulture lest they infect the living and render unavailing the anxious labours of the colony. The floor board, littered with particles of broken comb, and pollen pellets, and dust from two hundred thousand tiny, restless feet that come and go unceasingly, is swept and cleaned. For, nothing that can be moved or torn asunder, and that is not sweet and pure like bees themselves and like the largess of the open flowers, may linger long among those cheerful toilers who, if cleanliness be next to godliness, are, of all the insect class, nearest heaven.

12. Guarding the Portal.—Others still, placed about the portal, keep guard upon the treasury. Their watchful office is to see that all who seek an entrance have lawful business there. These are the sleepless sentinels, well-armed, who pounce at once upon stranger bees and drive them off; or with their poison-stings make execution upon such as, intent on robbery, are bold enough to risk a conflict. (343).

13. Approach of Summer.—And the patient, earnest queen—a slave to duty and willing minister of all, encouraged by the steady flow of honey, puts forth her best endeavours. Comb after comb is filled from top to base with honey sealed, and hatching brood, and larvæ pearly white, and eggs like bits of silken thread upon the bases of the cells. (192). Beneath the porch two ceaseless streams of merry bees pass and return; for, currant, thorn, and sycamore have hurried into bloom, and summer, with its happy song and gladsome days, is near at hand.

> " Fresh flow'rs shall fringe the wild brink of the stream,
> And with the songs of joyance and of hope
> The hedgerows shall ring loud."

CHAPTER III.

THE BEE IN SUMMER.

14. A Crisis.—About the time that sees the nectar-yielding flowers coming into full blossom, affairs within the hive approach a crisis. Fifty-thousand gatherers, speeding upon the fragrant breezes through every sunny hour of spring, have carried home great quantities of nectar to fill to overflowing each vacant cell. The queen, who, possessed of an insatiable desire for reproduction and in the full flow of maternal vigour, has increased by thousands daily the number of her children, now finds herself encroached upon in her domain. The little bands of " fanners " at the door exhaust themselves in vain endeavours to ventilate their over-heated home (63). The bees returning from the fields loiter at the entrance, and hesitate to add their presence to the close-packed mass within. Some will cluster there, victims of a strange inertia;

" The slow hours measuring off an idle day."

Within a week the hatching brood will add a new congestion. Plainly a crisis has arrived! Something must be done, and done at once; for, in bee life, except in winter, inactivity is the extreme vice that merits naught of mercy.

15. The Mysterious Influence.—Now that subtle, mysterious Influence which governs the whole life of the bee from the moment in which she struggles from her uncapped cell, a downy, awkward infant, until worn out with strain of excessive industry she drops from some pink heather bell, in the autumn evening, to rise no more: that silent, persistent, irresistible Influence which orders the economy of the hive; inspires each tiny occupant with courage of a hero; makes all instinct with uniformity of splendid purpose; and endows them with glorious spirit of self-sacrifice above all human imitation—a willingness to leave all, to lose all, and to bear all that may be, for love of the race and reverence for its destiny—asserts itself. A tremor passes through the bees, and an entirely new emotion seizes them. That love of others which recks not of personal suffering; that awe of the future which counts not of present perils; that infrequent exaltation which beautifies self-abnegation, idealizes the Unknown, and yields up life itself for others —possesses them. Their patient, untiring labours have secured for them supreme success: now they will forfeit all. They have reached the highest point of affluence: now they will renounce their wealth and fall to poverty. Their home is furnished through, and stored with food abundantly: now they will leave to others the fruits which their energies have borne, forsake their home, and rush out, wildly exuberant of happiness, to build again their fortune, or in houseless cold and hunger to die. (218).

16. **Indomitable Spirits.**—Not, however, without their queen. She shall accompany them. It is not meet that they should too far court disaster (219). Without her, they must inevitably perish. With her, they shall die indeed, yet live again in their successors. Nor will their indomitable spirits contemplate extinction. Let but some friendly nook be found —some cavity in a spreading tree whose advancing age provides a cradle for a new-born race (218); there combs will form again, and eggs be tended, and every passer-by shall hear the humming music of the bees, down by the river side where

> " the curling waves
> That break against the shore, shall lull the mind
> By one soft impulse saved from vacancy."

17. **Queen Rearing.**—However, one all-important preparation must first be made. The bees will stay behind to nurse the growing brood must have a queen to raise the colony to strength again when the enthusiastic swarmers shall have carried off the venerated mother bee. This, by one stupendous miracle of nature, shall be accomplished. Not one, but many queens shall be provided, lest any untoward accident should mar the great design. The workers, eager to enter on their new adventure, construct some special cells—cells larger and with thicker walls. In them the queen, with that sublime indifference to personal advantage which at the moment actuates her, deposits eggs. These, which in ordinary course of nature would produce but worker bees—females undeveloped, incapable of impregnation (210)—shall be supplied with richer food, and in more abundance; shall have their cells enlarged yet more, and strengthened, and made to hang, in shape like acorns, between the combs (Figs. 2, and 26, p. 50); until the cells are capped, and the royal princesses are left to spin their silken veils and, eight days later, to emerge as perfect virgin queens.

18. **The Swarm—A Deliberated Sacrifice.**—Meanwhile restlessness seizes the old queen, who sees that the fulfilment of

her maternal duty has been applied to raise, within the kingdom which she alone has peopled, rival claimants to her throne. She is not satisfied. She hurries from comb to comb, vainly endeavouring to assert an authority long subordinated to the requirements of her children. She even threatens the young princesses in their waxen nurseries. Wild excitement results among the little citizens. The palace of peace and home of steady labour is thrown into confusion. It is all so novel, this mad disorder and revolution of which no drone or worker has had experience previously. It is the perplexing acceleration of deliberated sacrifice, coming suddenly, rushing headlong, like the bursting of a mountain torrent that cannot by any means be stayed. The vats of honey are opened, and multitudes are feeding eagerly; for, suspected

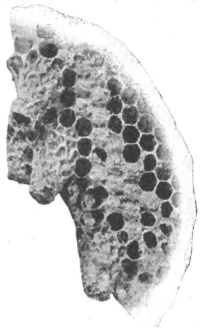

Fig 2. QUEEN CELLS.

danger always leads the bees to lay in store for quick emergencies (176). The queen and all her people realize that the moment has arrived for the inevitable reckless sacrifice which, in its ready willingness to give up all for the future of the race, invests the swarm with that uncommon glory which, during long ages, has been recognized and admired by astonished man.

19. The Swarm—An Ecstasy.—Pouring from the insufficient opening they come, in bewildering haste; a riotous throng, rapturously jubilant, in the very ecstasy of extravagant emotion; harmless, too, in their design, and in their exaltation so sweetly amiable that he who will may handle them in safety (175). A vast multitude it is, rushing hither and thither, with great noise of humming, which presently begins to gather in a cluster upon some neighbouring tree where it is joined by the queen when the whole swarm gathers round her—in very numbers assuring her timid heart, unaccustomed to rough

exposure and risk of outer dangers—and form a cluster with the faithful mother, so still that any passing traveller may hardly notice them. Now let the watchful owner hive them without delay, and set them to work in a new home, or they will rise and, following their scouts sent out before to find a dwelling, will settle in some distant tree or chimney, or will invade the ruined tower upon the neighbouring hill, and so be lost to useful purpose. (218).

20. **The Virgin Queen.**—The now depleted stock, deprived of more than half its numbers by that most boisterous exodus which robbed it also of its queen, presents once more a scene of peaceful labour. As if no mighty revolution had just disturbed their order, the bees pursue their avocations, apparently oblivious of the strange events which, but an hour ago, had shaken their kingdom to its foundations. A few days later the oldest of the young princesses is heard piping in her cell, as if conscious of the high importance of the position that awaits her, and impatient to attain it before her hatching rivals can intervene. The apex of her cell the workers have thinned and smoothed in order to assist her exit. Presently she will cut the capping and, pressing against it, force it open like a round, hinged lid (Fig. 26, A, p. 50), and step out upon the comb. The nearest honey cell shall have her first attention; and then she who shall give life to unnumbered thousands, will devote her first active hours to massacre. Reaching the other queen cells she will endeavour to tear them open at the sides and to slay her rivals (209). If this be not permitted, she will stay, and watch her opportunity to wage a battle-royal with any young princess who ventures abroad among the combs; or she will lead off an after-swarm (224), thus abdicating the position which, for so short a time and anxious, she occupied, and seeking peace in some new home where she may fulfil her task unhindered. But if the hive economy require no further division of the forces, the royal cells will be attacked (Fig. 26, B, p. 50), and the occupants, astounded at this violent assault upon their privacy, be destroyed. " One queen, one kingdom," is, as in the domain of man, a law of bee life admitting few exceptions.

21. **The Queen's Wedding.**—So, in fifteen days from the depositing of the egg, a virgin queen has opened her astonished eyes upon the hive which is to be her home; upon the restless workers who come and go, and hurry back well laden; upon the drones, those bulky, strong-winged males whose lives, though short and helpless, are not devoid of joy; upon the

combs that hold the nectar stores, and gilt-capped cells of
hatching nymphs whose vacant places, when they emerge, she
must occupy with living germs that shall produce a multitude, renewing month by month the population wasted by
excessive toil.   But this, not yet.   So far she moves about
unnoticed, in constant exploration that knows no instant's rest,
and preparation for that wondrous incident which shall entitle
her to claim the homage of her people, and to her queenly title
add the higher, and more sacred name of " Mother."   So
far she has not felt the glow of sunshine, nor filled her tracheæ
(36) with the breath of heaven.   The eventful hour has not
arrived.   She must wait a few days more before she stakes
herself, and all the secret of the future, upon the hazard of a
flight.   Then she approaches the entrance, inspecting everything, but not daring to venture farther.   Again she appears,
and hurries up and down; excited; impelled by that mysterious
exaltation which Nature pours out lavishly when great ends
are to be accomplished by perilous enterprises.   She spreads
her wings and rises, quickly noting every little thing that
marks the outworks of her citadel, and most careful in this
precaution, because of her exceeding value who carries in her
person the hope and destiny of all.   Pursuing wider circles she
surveys the site until its every feature becomes familiar.
Meanwhile, on the wing, are countless drones, observing, each
with his magnificent eyes of 26,000 hexagonal lenses (30), the
timid virgin's movements.   Soon the loud humming of the
full-fed males attracts the young queen, and as she enlarges
the circles of her flight and passes over them, instantly they
are in full pursuit.   Here may be observed wise Nature's
regulation that gives the battle to the strong, and to the brave
the fair.   The agile lover; he whose self-restraint has dipped
with temperate appetite into the honey vats, and whose quick
power of flight, not lessened by emasculating idleness, is
trained and strengthened by sufficient exercise, is first to reach
the queen, and in brief ecstasy of that embrace gives all his
vigour to the making of a hardy race; and, giving all, he
dies.   (42).

22. Parthenogenesis.—Thus mated once for all, the queen
returns and meets a welcome from her people.   Never will she
leave the hive again, unless the swarming of the colony compel
her, or some unusual need, or incident, require.   She will take
up the task of supplying the vacant cells with eggs.   Generation after generation shall live and die, and leave her still
fulfilling her calling.   Nor will several years exhaust the
25,000,000 spermatozoa which one short intercourse supplied

(43). Just here is disclosed another marvellous feature in the life of the bee. The drone which inseminated the queen; himself fatherless, the product of an unimpregnated egg, becomes the father of countless thousands of worker bees, and of many fully-developed queens. The queen with which he mated can, at will, lay eggs of either sex. Passing across the comb from cell to cell she will deposit in one an egg from which will hatch a female (worker), and in an adjoining cell, built larger to accommodate a drone, she will lay an egg that shall produce a male; the former impregnated as it passes the spermatheca (45), the latter, not. Strange, also, that from the egg which the queen by movement of a muscle has impregnated with element of the male, the workers can, at will, hatch out an undeveloped female like themselves, or a fully developed queen to carry on the reproduction of the species (207). And strange, that eggs laid by a queen who never has been mated, or by a worker who sometimes will rashly take upon her the functions of a queen (210), will hatch out drones, and fecundation follow upon parthenogenesis. (44).

23. A Splendid Example.—The queen, now in " full use," rapidly occupies the cells with eggs, of which from 2,000 to 3,000 may be deposited in one day (4). The population rises. The bees, encouraged by increasing quantities of brood, and urged on by the hunger-want of growing larvæ, search the country-side and carry in rich stores of nectar; still looking to the future; labouring for others; setting a splendid example of diligence, and perseverance, and foresight. Summer will not last for ever. They know it, these patterns of hopeful industry, whose message to the world is wise: Improve the shining hour, for time in its passing waiteth for none.

CHAPTER IV.

THE BEE IN AUTUMN AND WINTER.

" Morn on the mountain, like a summer bird,
Lifts up her purple wing; and in the vales
The gentle wind, a sweet and passionate wooer,
Kisses the blushing leaf, and stirs up life
Within the solemn woods of ash deep crimsoned,
And silver beech, and maple yellow leaved,
Where Autumn, like a faint old man, sits down
By the wayside a-weary."

24. The Death of the Drones.—As autumn with its chill nights and shortening days advances, the supply of nectar rapidly diminishes in the plants. It is an anxious time for the bees. Stores are not accumulating. The colony has suffered serious losses. From time to time the white-sealed combs of honey—the fruit of many days of earnest labour, have been removed, stolen by some dexterous hand. And daily in the combs to which the queen is wedded fresh mouths cry out for food. It is necessary for the survival of the colony that a limit be set to the consumption of stores. The drones—always heavy feeders, and for whom Nature has now no sphere of usefulness, have become, by reason of their appetite, the most immediate danger. They have had their day of indulgence, and sunny idleness. Their continued presence in the hive; their death within its portals when the cold of winter should make their removal impossible and render their decaying bodies a source of peril—must be prevented. The time has come for them to share that sacrifice to the future which is the lot of all alike in the community of high ideals to which they belong. In this is no special injustice. Nor can one say, with any degree of certainty, that in this laying down of life for the sake of others there is none of that glorious spirit of love which has inspired the workers to give themselves and all their energies and endurance, even unto death, in faithful adherence to their purpose. The slower intelligence of the drone may not realize at once the need that has arisen; and the life of pampered idleness to which, in the nature of things, he has been condemned, may unfit him for the display of voluntary self-abnegation so remarkable in the other sex. Many, however, leave the hive at noon, never to return. Others, " infirm of purpose," seek to share, for one night more, the comforts of the hive; but sentries at the entrance forbid it and drive them off.   Others still, fearful of destiny, have clung to the combs, with weak love of life exceptional in such a race and feeble efforts to resist expulsion to the inhospitable fields without.   On them the workers pour the vials of their wrath, and the helpless victims, left by Nature defenceless among a multitude of pitiless enemies, succumb to their wounds, or are driven out to join their comrades in misfortune.   As the sun sinks and twilight gathers round the scene, the chill of the autumn evening settles upon the vanquished, and all that army of males, once so gay and careless, lies motionless and dead.

25.   The Approach of Winter.—That awful tragedy over, the workers return to their more peaceful duties.   Blackberry, heather, and ivy, still offer their sweets, and much remains to be done before sufficient stores can be collected and sealed to supply the colony with food for winter and early spring. But foraging becomes a more precarious task.   The days in which a bee may work out of doors grow shorter.   Rain and high winds claim their victims.   The strength of the stock diminishes rapidly.   And the queen gradually ceases to lay, well knowing that presently the task of the nurse bees will have become impossible.   For autumn, with its harvest song and glory tints, is passing, and

> " The leaves are falling, falling,
>   Solemnly and slow ;
> ' Caw ! caw ! ' the rooks are calling,
>   It is a sound of woe,
>   A sound of woe ! "

Presently silence reigns in the hive.   The bees have collected upon the centre combs, clustering closely,

> " Insensibly subdued to settled quiet."

There they will hang together until, the frosts and storms of winter passed, spring shall visit the earth again, and the morning sun, shining through the entrance of their citadel, shall woo them to the work and adventures of another year.

> " Every winter,
> When the great sun has turned his face away,
> The earth goes down into a vale of grief,
> And fasts, and weeps, and shrouds herself in sables,
> Leaving her wedding-garlands to decay—
> Then leaps in spring to his returning kisses."

CHAPTER V.

ANATOMY OF THE BEE.

26. A Bee Guide would be far from complete if it failed to supply such information as may appear to be necessary for all who desire to take an intelligent interest in the management of bees. Within the limits of such a work as this, however, it is not possible to enter at any great length into the subject of bee anatomy; nor, indeed, would it be desirable, for, as Hunter has said—

" Of the natural history of the bee more has been conceived than observed. It is commonly not only unnecessary to be minute in our description of parts in natural history, but in general improper. Minutiæ beyond what is essential, tire the mind, and render that which should entertain along with instruction, heavy and disagreeable."— *Phil. Transactions*, 1792.

Those who are anxious to study a subject so interesting, may find all that they require in the various books which deal with it more fully.

27. External Skeleton.—The external skeleton of the bee is composed of chitin, covered for the most part with hairs of the same substance, which have their special uses, some as organs of touch, some as brushes, others as gatherers of pollen or as clothing, protectors, or ornaments. A glance at the illustrations (Figs. 8 and 14) will show that the body of the bee is made up of three distinct parts, viz.—the head, the thorax, and the abdomen.

28. Head.—The head (Figs. 3, 4, 5, 6) consists of several parts, among which are included the simple eyes; the compound eyes; the antennæ or feelers; and the organs of the mouth.

29. Simple Eyes.—The three simple eyes (*ocelli* or *stemmata*), of which only one is visible in the illustration (Fig. 3), are arranged in triangular form upon the vertex in the queen and worker, and in the front of the face in the drone (Figs. 4, 5, 6).

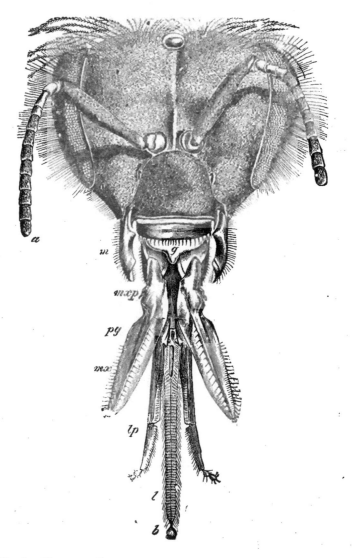

Fig. 3. HEAD AND TONGUE OF WORKER BEE (*Magnified sixteen times*).

a, Antenna, or Feeler ; *m*, Mandible, or Outer Jaw ; *g*, Epipharynx, or Gum Flap ; *mxp*, Maxillary Palpus ; *pg*, Paraglossa (shown above the Lingua, opposite *pg*) ; *mx*, Maxilla, or Inner Jaw ; *lp*, Labial Palpus ; *l*, Lingua, or Tongue ; *b*, Bouton, or Spoon.

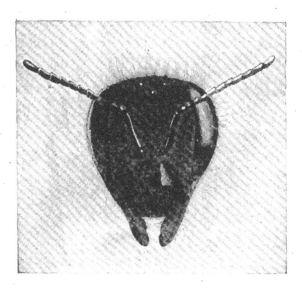

Fig. 4. HEAD OF WORKER (*Magnified*).

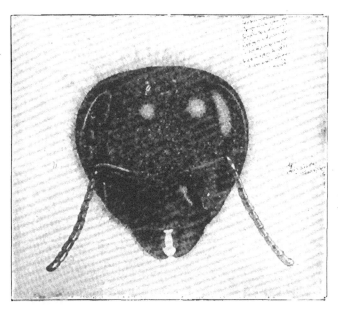

Fig. 5. HEAD OF QUEEN (*Magnified*).

30. Compound Eyes.—The two compound eyes, placed one on each side of the head (Fig. 3), are largest in the drone,

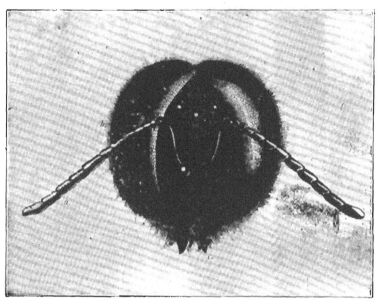

Fig. 6. HEAD OF DRONE (*Magnified*).

and smallest in the worker. They are made up of a number of separate eyes united together and containing in the drone

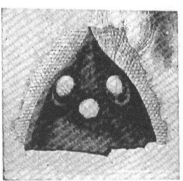

Fig. 7.
SIMPLE EYES OF DRONE (*Magnified*).

about 13,000, in the queen, 5,000, and in the worker 6,000 hexagonal lenses or facets to each eye. These, pointing in almost every direction, give to the bee an exceedingly wide range of vision, wider far than would have been possible with a fixed, simple eye.

31. Antennæ. — The Antennæ, or feelers (Fig. 3, *a*) are cylindrical organs inserted close to each other in the front of the head. They are covered with hairs and, articulated to the head by a hemispherical joint controlled by four muscles, they can be moved about rapidly in every direction. They are made up of twelve joints each in the worker and the queen, and of thirteen joints in the drone (Fig. 9.) The antennæ give to the bee a power akin to that of speech and, by their

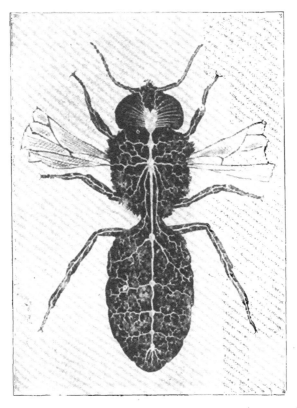

Fig. 8. NERVOUS SYSTEM (*Magnified*).

motions, form a language in which wants and desires can be communicated.

32. **Organs of Mouth.**—The organs of the mouth include the following:—The *mandibles* or jaws (Fig. 3, *m*) situated one on either side of the labrum. Their movement is lateral. They are provided with hairs, are exceedingly powerful, and, in the queen and drone only, are rough and notched. The *labrum* or upper lip (shown above *g*, Fig. 3), moves vertically. The *epipharynx*, or gum flap (*g*) has a covering of white membrane exceedingly delicate, and is brought into use when liquids are being taken up by the tongue, as explained below.

The *maxillæ*, or second jaws (*mx*, and Fig. 10, *c*) are hollowed out, are supplied with very stiff hairs, and, in conjunction with the *labial palpi* (*lp* and Fig. 10, *b*), form a tube in which the tongue works; they bear a short pair of *maxillary palpi*,

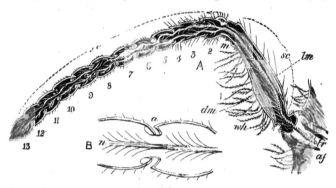

Fig. 9. LONGITUDINAL SECTION OF DRONE ANTENNA.

Nerve Structures removed (*Magnified twenty times*).

A, *sc*, Scape; *fl*, Flagellum; 1, 2, 3, *etc.*, No. of Joints; *af*, Antennary Fossa, or Hollow; *tr*, Trachea; *m*, Soft Membrane; *wh*, Webbed Hairs; *lm*, Levator Muscle; *dm*, Depressor Muscle. B, Small portion of Flagellum (magnified sixty times)—*n*, Nerve; *a*, Articulation, or Joint.

or feelers (*mxp*). A third pair of jaws—*second maxillæ*, are fused together so as to form a *labium*, or under lip, beneath the opening of the mouth, consisting of a basal *mentum*, paired *paraglossæ* (shown opposite *pg*), by which liquids reach the front of the tongue for swallowing; and *labial palpi* (*lp* and Fig. 10, b), each consisting of four joints, the two terminal joints being very small and supplied with sensitive hairs. These palpi embrace the tongue behind, as the maxillæ embrace it before, and together form a tube surrounding the tongue, as stated. The *lingua*, or tongue (*l* and Fig. 10, *a*) is connected at its roots with the mentum, and is stretched out or withdrawn by the action of the *protractor linguæ* and *retractor linguæ* muscles. Covering it is a sheath clothed with hairs some of which are sensitive. At the extremity of the tongue is the spoon (*b*), which is provided with delicate hairs. When liquid is taken up, the tongue, sweeping backwards and forwards by means of a highly elastic rod running through its centre, gathers the liquid upon its hairs; the maxillæ and the labial palpi form a tube around it; and the front of the epipharynx being lowered to close the space above the maxillæ, the tube is completed to the œsophagus or gullet (38), and the

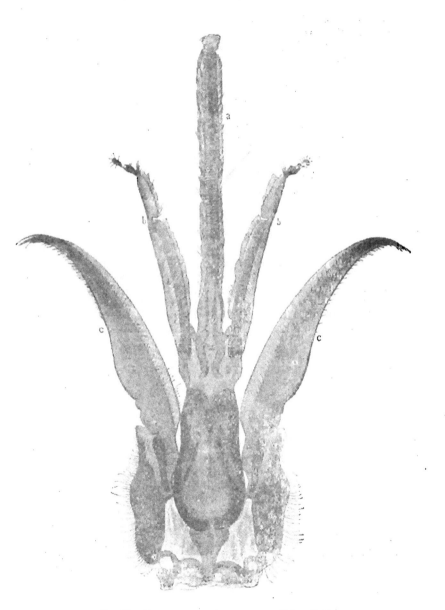

Fig. 10. TONGUE AND APPENDAGES (*Magnified*).

a, Tongue ; *b*, Labial Palpi ; *c*, Maxilla.

liquid is taken up. The tongues of the queen and drone are shorter than that of the worker, the last, only, of the three having had laid upon her the duty of gathering nectar from the flowers.

33. **Thorax.**—The thorax (Fig. 14, p. 26) consists of the three segments below the head, and styled the *pro-thorax*, next the head, and bearing the front pair of legs (34), the *meso-thorax*, in which are articulated the second pair of legs and the first pair of wings (35), and the *meta-thorax*, which carries the third pair of legs and the second pair of wings, and has the first segment of the hind body, or abdomen (37), fused with it. The thorax is covered with hairs, long and feathered in the worker for the collection of pollen, and in the drone short and spiny, but unsuited to the gathering of pollen. The queen is comparatively bare, her mission being confined, chiefly, to the hive.

" A little device will make the bees our assistants in studying their thoracic and leg structure. Take a thin string, about a foot long, and at each end fix a dead bee, by tying round the neck. Drop the suspended ' culprits ' between the frames of a stock, so that the middle of the string rests like a saddle on the top bar. In a couple of days, every hair will be cleaned from the ' gibbets,' and their bodies polished like those of beetles, so that the attachment of the wings, the spiracles, the lines dividing pro-, meso-, and meta-thorax, the actual form of the leg joints, and the character of their articulations, with many other interesting points, will be clearly visible."--*Cheshire.*

34. **Legs.**—Three pairs of legs originate in the thorax—the anterior legs in the pro thorax; the intermediate legs in the meso-thorax; the posterior legs in the meta-thorax. The anterior leg has the curry-comb—a semi-circular toothed recess, and a *velum*, or sail, by which the antennæ are combed, the legs being moved to the front of the head, and then drawn outwards, cleaning the antennæ which have dropped into the recesses. The intermediate leg is furnished with a spur which has been supposed to act as a lever to remove the pollen balls from the corbicula, but the precise use of which is still a subject of controversy. The posterior, or hind leg of the worker (Fig. 11), consisting of nine joints, is provided, as to the upper joints, with stiff, bristling hairs, by which pollen and propolis are collected. The *tibia* (*ti*) and the *planta* (*p*) are articulated at the inner angles of the joints, and, as they move, the parts opposite *wp* open and shut like jaws, the upper one having a supply of teeth which close upon the lower, flattened surface. These jaws are not used for the removal of the plates of wax

from the abdomen as was at one time thought probable; but are, in fact, a press by which the pollen is pushed from below into the pollen baskets. (Snodgrass, quoting Sladen and Casteel).

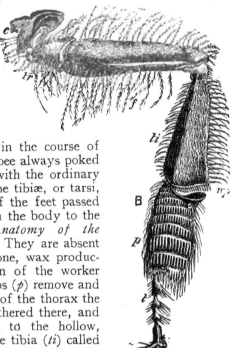

Snodgrass says that in the course of his observations, the bee always poked the wax plates loose with the ordinary hairs, or spines, of the tibiæ, or tarsi, and then by means of the feet passed them forward beneath the body to the mandibles—"*The Anatomy of the Honey Bee*," p. 68. They are absent in the queen and drone, wax production being a function of the worker only. The stiff combs (*p*) remove and collect from the hairs of the thorax the particles of pollen gathered there, and these are transferred to the hollow, fringed portion of the tibia (*ti*) called the *corbicula*, or pollen basket, the combs on the left leg supplying the right corbicula, and those on the right acting similarly towards the left basket. These baskets, with their loads of varied-coloured pollen, are familiar objects to all who have watched bees alighting at their hives

Fig. 11. THIRD RIGHT LEG OF WORKER.
Side next the body.
(*Magnified ten times*).
c, Coxa ; *tr*, Trochanter ; *ti*,Tibia; *wp*,Wax Pincers; *p*, Planta ; *t*, Tarsus.

in the breeding season (79). Corbiculæ do not appear on the posterior legs of either the queen or the drone, the duty of collecting and carrying pollen being assigned to the worker only. The queen, a great walker, has the largest legs, and the drone has the smallest. The *tarsus*, or foot (*t*) has five joints, the terminal joint being furnished with two *unguiculi*, or claws, of great strength, which can be turned up or down as required. These claws enable the bees to cling to their combs, to fix themselves securely to other substances, and also to suspend themselves to the hive-top, or to each other in festoons (10) or clusters. Between the claws is the *pulvillus*, or cushion, which secretes an oily, sticky substance that enables the bee to move about upon, or to adhere to, glass and other smooth surfaces.

35. Wings.—The wings (Fig. 12), which also originate in the thorax, are four in number—the anterior pair and the posterior pair, articulated into the meso-thorax and the meta-thorax respectively. The upper and outward margin of the posterior wing has a number of hooklets (B, *e*, *f*), and the lower and inner margin of the anterior wing is folded in a plait (A, *c*, *d*). As the anterior wing is raised for flight, its folded plait passes over the hooklets of the posterior wing and is caught by them (C, and D. *p*, *h*), so that the two wings

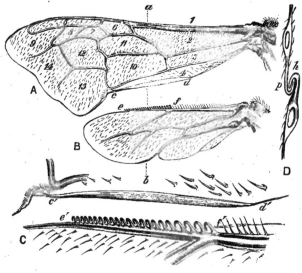

Fig. 12. WINGS OF THE BEE.—NERVURES, CELLS, AND DETAILS.

A and B, Anterior and Posterior Right Wings of Worker (under side), magnified eight times—1 to 14, Cells ; *c*, *d*, Plait ; *e*, *f*, Hooklets. C, Plait and Hooklets, magnified twenty-five times—*c′*, *d′*, Plait ; *e′*, *f′*, Hooklets. D, Cross Section (through line *a*, *b*) of *p*, Plait, and *h*, Hooklet, locked together

act together as one wing, thus, on the principle—" Unity is strength," adding power and speed to the flight. When the bee alights, the wings become free, and lie closely over the abdomen, thus permitting the insect to enter comb cells, which, otherwise, would be impracticable. The wings of the drone are the largest, and those of the workers the shortest. The vibrations, when in flight, have been calculated by Marey and Landois at 190 and 440 per second respectively; but modern research appears to show that about 260 is more clearly correct, and this figure is that now commonly accepted. Bees can fly backwards, and, even when in full flight, can stop very suddenly,

When leaving the hive to collect food they will fly at the rate
of from fifteen to twenty miles an hour; but, when returning
heavily laden, their speed is much less, varying from five to
twelve miles an hour. The author's experiments with bees
of several colonies returning empty to their hives gave an

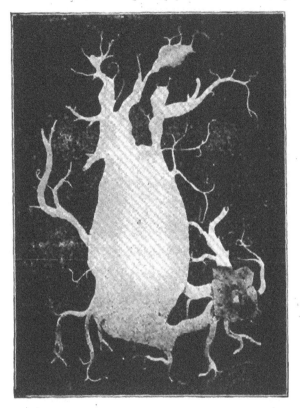

Fig. 13. TRACHEAL BAG—AIR⁻SAC (*Magnified.*)

average flight of 15⅔ miles. The limit of their usual flight
from the hive on foraging duty may be taken as two miles.
They have, however, been known, in exceptional circumstances,
to travel as far as seven miles in search of food. For the
practical purpose of the honey-producer, however, except in
very fine weather, it is probable that the effective range of an
apiary is not really much over a mile.

36. Spiracles and Tracheæ.—The breathing of the bee
is carried on through the *spiracles*, or openings, in the sides of

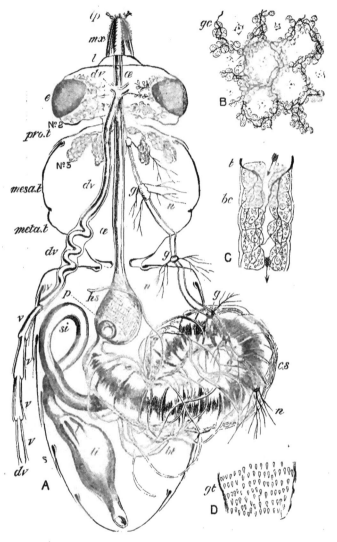

Fig. 14. DIGESTIVE SYSTEM OF BEE. (*Magnified ten times*).

A, Horizontal Section of Body—*lp*, Labial Palpus ; *mx*, Maxilla ; *e*, Eye ; *dv*, Dorsal Vessel ; *v*, Ventricles ; Nos. 1, 2, 3, Salivary Gland System; *œ*, Œsophagus ; *pro.t*, Prothorax ; *mesa.t*, Mesathorax ; *meta.t*, Metathorax ; *g.g*, Ganglia of Chief Nerve Chain ; *n*, Nerves ; *hs*, Honey Sac ; *p*, Stomach-mouth ; *cs*, Chyle Stomach ; *bt*, Biliary or Malpighian Vessels ; *si*, Small Intestine ; *l*, Lamellæ ; *li*, Large Intestine. B, Cellular Layer of Stomach— *gc*, Gastric Cells (magnified 200 times). C, Biliary Tube—*bc*, Bile Cells; *t*, Trachea. D, Inner Layer, carrying *gt* Gastric Teeth.

the body (Fig. 14, *s*) which can be opened or closed at will. These spiracles admit air to the tracheæ, or tubes, which, as shown in the illustration, ramifying in countless numbers throughout the body—" thus virtually making a lung of the entire body "—(*Snodgrass*)—convey the necessary oxygen to the various organs. The tracheæ communicate, in addition, with numerous air-sacs in the thorax and abdomen. Immersed in liquid, breathing through the spiracles is stopped and the insect dies.

37. **Abdomen.**—Joined to the thorax by a short tube (the *petiole*), is the abdomen (Fig. 14). The worker's is enclosed by six visible rings, or segments, of chitin, each of which is constructed of two plates—the *dorsal* plates on the back, and the *ventral* plates on the lower side. Those shown (Fig. 15) are the ventral plates (10) where the wax scales are found (67). The abdomen of the queen is longer and more pointed than that of either the worker or the drone (Fig. 1), but only in the worker are the secreting membranes present on which wax is produced.

38. **Honey Sac.**—The honey sac (Figs. 14, *hs* and 16, c) is situated in the abdomen, and is connected above with the *œsophagus*, or gullet (*œ* and Fig. 16, b), running through the thorax to the mouth (62), and below, with the *chyle stomach* (*cs* and Fig. 16, d), beneath which are the *ileum*, or small intestine (*si* and Fig. 16, f) and the large intestine (*li* and Fig. 16, g) or *colon*. Between the honey sac and the chyle stomach is the stomach mouth (*p*) by which, at the will of the bee, the contents of the honey

Fig. 15. UNDER SIDE OF WORKER BEE, SHOWING WAX SCALES.

(Magnified three times).

sac may be admitted to, or excluded from, the chyle stomach (62). The nectar carried in the honey sac may be, by contraction of the muscles there, transferred as honey through the œsophagus and mouth to the comb cells, or may be admitted through the stomach mouth to the chyle stomach for digestion. The honey sac can hold one-third of an ordinary drop; but the usual load of a foraging bee is only one-firth. The author (" *Irish Bee Journal,*" Nov. 1907) calculated the weight of nectar per load as .333 of a grain, and Dr. Millar (in " *Gleanings* "), pointed out that this agreed virtually with .350 grains calculated by Professor

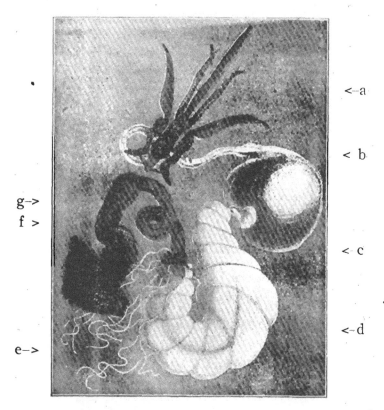

Fig. 16. DIGESTING APPARATUS (*Magnified*).

a, Tongue ; *b*, Œsophagus ; *c*, Honey Sac ; *d*, Stomach ; *e*, Malphigian Tubes ; *f*, Small Intestine ; *g*, Large Intestine.

Koons, whose figures were confirmed by Professors Gilette and Lazenby working in chemical laboratories with delicate balances.

39. Sting.—The sting (Figs. 17 A and 18) consists of a horny sheath (*sh*) terminating in a sharp toothed edge, and guiding the lancets, or darts (*d, d'*). The lancets have barbed edges (*b, b*), and are connected above, at *c, c'*, with the compound levers (*i, k, l,* and *i', k', l'*), by which the sting may be

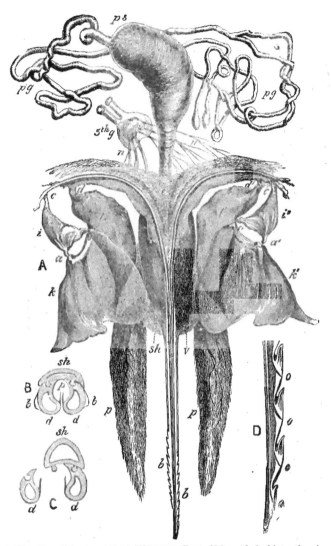

Fig. 17. STING OF THE WORKER BEE (*Magnified thirty times*).

A, Sting separated from its Muscles—*ps*, Poison Sac ; *pg*, Poison Gland.
5th *g*, Fifth Abdominal Ganglion ; *n, n*, Nerves ; *e*, External Thin Membrane
joining Sting to last Abdominal Segment ; *i, k*, and *l*, and *i′, k′*, and *l′*, Levers
to move Darts ; *sh*, Sheath ; *v*, Vulva ; *p*, Sting Palpus, or Feeler ; *b*, Barbs.
B and C, Sections through Darts and Sheath, magnified 300 times—*sh*, Sheath ;
d, Darts ; *b*, Barbs ; *p*, Poison Channel. D, Termination of Dart, magnified
200 times—*o, o*, Openings for Poison to escape into Wound.

forced into comparatively tough substances.   When the bee is
about to sting, the muscles of the compound levers contracting
revolve the latter round the points *f*, *f'*, and, pressing upwards
against the curved arms of the lancets at *c*, *c'*, the levers drive
them down with the sheath, and beyond it deeper into the
wound.   The contents of the poison sac (*ps* and Fig. 18, b)
which is supplied by the poison glands (*pg* and Fig. 18 c) are
discharged down the hollow poison canal formed by the sheath
and lancets, by means of a pumping mechanism actuated by
the movement of the lancets, the poison ultimately escaping
into the deepest part of the wound, until (if the sting be not
removed at once), the poison sac is emptied.   The barbs of the

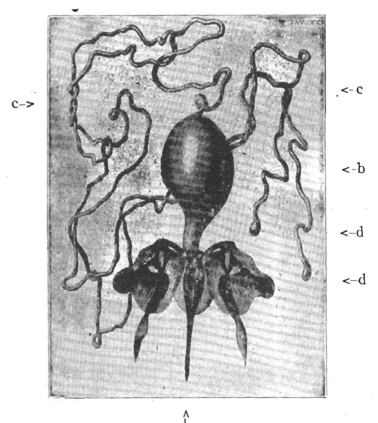

c->

.<- c

<-b

<-d

<-d

∧
⋮
a

Fig. 18.   STING OF WORKER BEE (*Magnified*.
a, Sting ;   *b*, Poison Sac ;   *c*, Poison Gland ;   *d*, Secreting Bag.

lancets fasten them into the object stung; and although, if left undisturbed, the bee is able, by working it round after the manner of a screw, to withdraw the sting (as one might withdraw a gimlet), the pain caused by the injection of the poison generally causes an immediate assault upon the offender, which is knocked away and the sting left in the flesh, and, attached to it, the poison sac and gland. More frequently than not, however, even if unmolested after stinging, the bee will tear herself away, leaving her sting in the wound. When left in this way, movement of the lancets continues, reflexly, and poison is injected into the wound for some time afterwards if the sting is allowed to remain.

40. Palpi, or Feelers.—Quick as is the bee in her attack, she will not proceed to sting until she has examined the surface of the object to be pierced. For this she is provided with the *palpi*, or feelers (Fig. 17, A, *p*, *p* and Fig. 18), which have sensitive hairs and delicate nerve points, enabling the insect to discover whether the particular spot selected for assault is capable of being pierced.

41. Queen's Sting.—The sting of the queen (Fig. 19) is longer than that of the worker, and is curved. As already stated **(21)**, the mother bee appears to realize the exceeding value of her life to the colony, and to be unwilling to risk the loss of her sting by incautious use. Unless in very exceptional circumstances, it is not used by her as a weapon of offence or defence, and then only, or chiefly, as against rival queens **(20.)** The drone has no sting, the sting being an essentially female structure—in reality, a highly modified ovipositor, or egg-laying apparatus.

42. Organs of Drone.—The organs of the drone include two *testes* (Fig. 20, A, *t* and Fig. 21, a) in communication, by means of the two tubes—*vasa deferentia* (*vd*) with two seminal vesicles (*vs*). These vesicles discharge at the base of two mucous glands into the *ductus ejaculatorius* (*de*), at the end of which is found the organ of generation (*o* and Fig. 21, *e*, and Fig. 22). The *spermatozoa* (B) originates in the testes. As they mature they pass into the *vesiculæ seminales* (*vs*) and, mingled with mucus from the glands (*mg* and Fig. 21, *b*), proceed continually through the ductus ejaculatorius (*de* and Fig. 21, *c*) into the *bean* (*b*) and, in mass, are called the *spermatophore* (Fig. 22). Coition takes place on the wing **(21)** when the pressure of air in the tracheæ and air vessels (*h*) assists the abdominal muscles in extruding the organs.

Fig. 19. STING OF QUEEN BEE (*Magnified*).

With the expulsion of the spermatophore (43) the organs are ruptured, and the drone dies. The queen, having now within her "the potency of the two sexes," returns to the hive carrying, as an appendage, part of the male organs—a sure sign of impregnation.

43. **Organs of the Queen.**—The organs of the queen include the *ovaries* (Fig. 23, O.O.) in which the eggs are developed; the *oviducts* (*od*), the *spermatheca* (*s*, and Fig. 24), which retains the spermatozoa received from the drone and numbering, according to Leuckart, the enormous quantity of 25,000,000 (22); a duct which joins the spermatheca with the vagina, and which, by opening or closing, permits or prevents the passing of the spermatozoa when eggs are traversing the *common oviduct* (*co, d*); and the *vagina*.

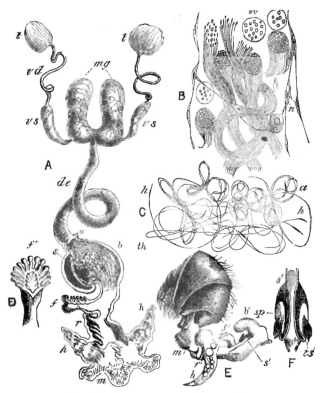

Fig. 20. ORGANS OF THE DRONE BEE.
(Magnified twelve times).

A, Organs Removed from Body, but in true Relative Position—*t*, Testes ;
vd, Vas Deferens ; *vs*, Vesicula Seminalis ; *mg*, Mucus Glands ; *de*, Ductus
Ejaculatorius ; *o*, Termination of Organ ; *s*, Sickle-shaped Scale, beneath
which Spermatophore is formed ; *ts*, Triangular Scale ; *b*, Bean ; *f*, Fan-
shaped Appendage ; *r*, Ridges ; *h*, Horns ; *m*, Masque of Réaumur, or Hairy
Membrane. B, Spermatozoa developing within Spermatic Tubes of Testes
(Magnified 500 times)—*sv*, Spermatic Vesicle ; *n*, Nerve Cells. C, Spermatozoa
as they arrange themselves after removal from the body—*a*, Coiled form ;
h, Head ; *th*, Thread. D, Face View of Appendage *f* in A—*f″*, Fan-like Fringe.
E, Organs Extruded ; lettering as A. F, Front View of portion of Bean
—*s″*, Sickle-shaped Scale ; *sp*, Spermatophore ; *ts*, Triangular Scale.

44. Parthenogenesis.

—In 1845 Dzierzon (85) announced
his discovery of parthenogenesis in bees (22). In 1849 he
wrote : —

" In the copulation of the queen, the ovary is not impregnated, but
this vesicle or seminal receptical (Fig. 24) is penetrated or filled by the

male semen. By this, much, nay all of what was enigmatical is solved —especially how the queen can lay fertile eggs in the early spring, when there are no males in the hive. The supply of semen received

Fig. 21. SEXUAL ORGANS OF THE DRONE BEE
(*Magnified*).

a, a, Testicles ;   *b, b,* Mucous Glands ;   *c,* Seminal
Duct ;   *d.* Triangular Scale beneath which the per-
matophore is formed ;   *e,* Horns and Penis.

during copulation is sufficient for her whole life . . . To lay drone eggs, according to my experience, requires no fecundation at all."

Later on he wrote :—

" All eggs which come to maturity in the two ovaries of a queen-bee are only of one and the same kind, which, when they are laid without coming in contact with the male semen, become developed into male Bees, but, on the contrary, when they are fertilized by male semen, produce female Bees,"

45. Fertilization of the Egg.—The queen can, at will, fertilize the egg as it passes the entrance to the spermatheca, or can allow it to pass unfertilized: in the former case it will produce a female bee; in the latter, a male. It follows that if a queen be mated with a drone of a different race the workers

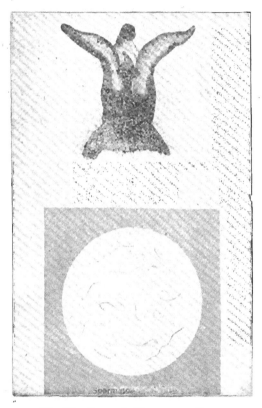

Fig. 22. DRONE'S HORNS AND PENIS.
BELOW—SPERMATOZOA (*Magnified*).

produced by the queen will exhibit characteristics of both parents, while the drones will partake of the nature of the queen only. Siebold proved the existence of seminal filaments in thirty of fifty-two female eggs examined, while in twenty-seven drone eggs similarly examined he found not one seminal filament.—"*A True Parthenogenesis*," 1857, pp. 88, 90. The supply of spermatozoa, decreasing as the fertilization of her eggs proceeds, fails and becomes exhausted usually at the end of three years; but, even at the close of her second year a queen, under the "forcing" methods of modern beekeeping, ceases to be profitable, in consequence of the enormous drain upon her resources (294).

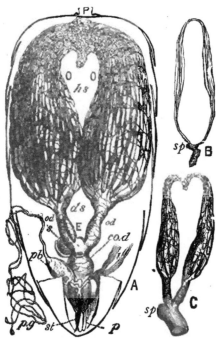

Fig. 24. SPERMATHECA. (*Magnified forty times*).

a, Space filled by clear fluid; *b*, Mass of Spermatozoa; *c*, Spermathecal Duct; *d, d*, Spermatozoa in activity.

Fig. 23. ORGANS OF THE QUEEN, etc.

A. Abdomen of Queen, under side (magnified eight times)—P, Petiole; O, O, Ovaries; *hs*, Position filled by Honey Sac; *ds*, Position through which Digestive System passes; *od*, Oviduct; *co.d*, Common Oviduct; E, Egg passing Oviduct; *s*, Spermatheca; *i*, Intestine; *pb*, Poison Bag; *pg*, Poison Gland; *st*, Sting; *p*, Palpi. B, Rudimentary Ovaries of Ordinary Worker—*sp*, Rudimentary Spermatheca. C, Partially developed Ovaries of Laying Worker —*sp*, Rudimentary Spermatheca. (See also Fig. 104b, page 147).

" A prolific queen will lay, during her life, 1,500,000 eggs—a number so vast that the eggs, lying in contact, end to end, would stretch about one and three-quarter miles. A good queen is able to furnish to the cells an average of two eggs per minute for weeks in succession. Taking the lowest estimate, she then yields the incredible quantity of twice her own weight daily, or, more accurately, four times, since at this period more than half her weight consists of eggs."—*Cheshire*.

Charles Dadant reported many queens laying 73,500 eggs in twenty-one days—"*American Bee Journal*," August, 1920,

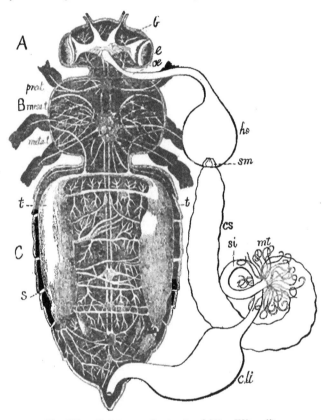

Fig. 24b. INTERNAL ORGANS. (*After Witzgall*).

A, Head—*b*, Brain ; *e*, Eye ; *œ*, Œsophagus, or Gullet. B, Thorax—*pro.t.*, Pro-thorax ; *meso.t.*, Meso-thorax ; *meta.t.*, Meta-thorax· C, Abdomen—*hs*, Honey Sac ; *sm*, Stomach Mouth ; *cs*, Chyle Stomach ; *si*, Small Intestine ; *mt*, Malphigian Tubes ; *c*, *li*, Colon, or Large Intestine ; *t*, Tracheæ, or Large Air Vesicles ; *s*, Spiracle.

p. 265. This works out at the rate of 3,500 eggs per day. A queen that has not been mated within twenty-one days of her birth usually becomes incapable of impregnation and a drone-breeder (198). Recent work, however, has shown that the daily rate of laying is normally much below this figure and is probably rarely over 2,000 at the peak of laying.—(*Snodgrass*).

CHAPTER VI.

DIFFERENT RACES OF BEES.

46. The Hive-Bee.—The only species of the genus Apis which concerns the beekeeper is *A. mellifica.* The reason for this is that this species has quite a unique method of passing through the winter; for, while all other insects either hibernate in a mass, as do some ants, or else perish with the exception of the pregnant females, which hibernate individually, the hive-bees lay up a great store of honey during summer and cluster in a dense mass upon that hoard during winter, and survive by maintaining the heat of their cluster through assimilating the honey. It is this fact that gives this insect its great value to mankind, for the storing instinct is diverted to our advantage, and we supply our tables with the honey which our bees have stored for their winter support. There are many varieties or races of honey-bees which are native to different territories and have, each of them, their peculiarities of character. All, however, readily interbreed, and to keep any of these races pure, unless isolated in their own country, is virtually impossible.

47. Black, or Native Bees—sometimes described as " German "—were, until the beginning of the present century, the most familiar honey-bees in these Islands. For many centuries our ancestors used these bees alone, and none thought of the possibility of importing foreign bees. About seventy years ago, however, foreign bees were first brought in, but remained little more than curiosities for years; but during the first quarter of this century, the widespread havoc of " Isle of Wight " disease (398) reduced the numbers of Native bees very greatly, and led to heavy importation of foreign varieties, with the result that, for good or ill, to-day the original Native Blacks are rare in the pure state. In appearance these bees differ little from other black bees such as French, German or Dutch. The body is black, as the name denotes, with some inconspicuous grey hairs on the abdomen. They are less prolific than are some other races; but they are hardy and adapted to our climate. They begin working and breeding early in the spring. They are excellent comb builders, their cappings being white, and their comb honey is specially attractive when placed on the market side by side with sections from some other varieties of bees. They cannot always be relied upon to be docile, and easily handled; but they have none of the wickedness of the Cyprian, Syrian or French Black bees. The queens of this race are dark in colour, with no distinctive feature to catch the eye readily, and are thus difficult to see when it is necessary to find them; the drones are always black.

48. **Carniolan Bees** are natives of the Austrian Alpine districts and take their name from Carniola, in Austria. They differ in appearance from Black bees, having broad, whitish bands on the abdomen which make them appear larger. Their queens are somewhat distinctive in colour, being of a brown shade with darker bands, and are much more easily seen on the combs than are the queens of Blacks. The drones are black. These bees use propolis most sparingly, and build beautifully white combs; their comb honey being exceptionally fine. They winter well, begin work early in spring, and, although very gentle, are stout defenders of their homes. Most amiable bees, manipulations can be carried on with ease and confidence, and on this account they are suitable for beginners (189). The objection to them is that they are inveterate swarmers, especially so when kept in small hives; but this objection may not weigh with those who are capable of exercising due control over the swarming propensity. There are some strains of this variety, however, in which this propensity is too strong for control, and the wise beekeeper will make trial of one colony before deciding to adopt Carniolans.

49. **Caucasian Bees** are natives of the Caucasus, in South Russia. The typical grey Caucasian bee with its beautiful, broad bands of soft greyish white, is one of the most beautiful of the honey-bees. It inhabits that district nearest to the central and higher parts of the great Caucasus mountain range. To the north, as the mountains are left, the bees approach more and more to the type of the common black bees of central Russia, and to the south the grey gradually merges into the Italian type. The typical central Caucasian bee is a very distinct race, both in habit and appearance. Like the Carniolan, it appears large on account of the wide grey bands. It is said to have the longest tongue of any hive-bee, which must give it special value where certain plants with long corolla tubes are grown, such as red clover. It is the gentlest of all the honey-bees, and may frequently be manipulated without either veil or smoke when weather is suitable. Caucasians are excellent cappers of comb-honey, though somewhat reluctant

builders of comb. They are great workers and usually store weights of honey equal to any, and exceeding most races. They are by no means excessive swarmers, and belief to the contrary has probably arisen from confusion with Carniolans which they somewhat resemble in appearance.   Their queens are prolific and early breeders, and have the very distinctive habit of stopping breeding much earlier in the autumn than any other race.   In wintering they consume a very small quantity of stores; but breeding very rapidly in spring, they require an ample supply at that season.   Their queens are dark in colour and somewhat inconspicuous and hard to find; their drones are black.   Their faults are three.   They build a great deal of brace comb between the frame top-bars and between the brood and super frames; they gather great quantities of propolis towards the close of summer, and with it build a rampart at the hive entrance, often accumulating such a mass here that, if the frames are not arranged to hang an inch from the floor, they are fastened down and can sometimes only be removed by breaking; they do not, however, over-use propolis elsewhere.   They have a curious tendency to concentrate their stores in as few combs as possible, often finishing and sealing half the combs in a super while completely neglecting the rest.   This last trait leads to ultra-heavy storage in the brood-chamber as it combines with early cessation of breeding.   On the whole, it appears that this race is an excellent one, and with selective breeding, may rival the Italian race, especially in such climates as ours.   It is greatly superior to the Italian in wintering, for it not only requires less stores, but usually comes out stronger in spring.

50. **Dutch Bees.**—These are a sub-variety of the common European black bee and are probably derived from an admixture of South European blood. They often have three tan-coloured bands on the first three segments of the abdomen, the remaining segments being brown or black; in fact, in appearance, some of them are indistinguishable from many mongrel bees.   Dutch beekeepers encourage swarming, and their bees respond, often refusing to adapt themselves to modern methods. Like admitted mongrels, however, some of them are excellent bees, and many beekeepers have praised them highly, both in Great Britain and Ireland, and, no doubt, with a suitable strain, much may be done by correct management.   These bees appear to succeed best in those parts of these countries where white clover is the principal honey plant and where it yields late in the year, and some beekeepers in Southern Ireland speak of them with enthusiasm. Dutch

Bees, like most blacks, cap their combs well and are usually good-tempered and as easy to handle as average blacks or cross-breds. Many thousands of colonies of these bees were brought to these Islands when the " Isle of Wight " disease (398) was raging, in the hope of counteracting the effects of that disease. It was erroneously believed at the time, that Dutch bees were immune to the scourge.

51. French Blacks.—A variety native in the South of France, these bees have been imported during the last ten years or so in the form of " package bees " (161). They are similar in appearance to Native Blacks, but are much more prolific. They are excellent workers and store good weights of honey; build comb well and cap honey attractively. Bees from certain parts of France are reported to be rather vicious in temper, but those from other parts have proved quite manageable and as easy to work as any other race of bee. These " package bees " form a reliable source of supply of early bees which is of the greatest value to honey-producers in this country.

52. Italian, or Ligurian Bees.—This is, at present, the most important of pure races. Originating in Italy, they have spread throughout the beekeeping world and, apart from cross-breeds, probably they gather more honey than any other variety, at all events in the world's commercial apiaries. Here in the British Isles nearly every professional queen-rearer is engaged upon breeding Italians, and it is probably largely owing to its combining excellent characteristics as a honey-getter with distinctive colouring, that this is so. It is easy to recognize cross-bred bees from this race. A pure Italian queen mated to a drone of any black variety will produce workers, some of which will be like their male parent. Italian bees are always distinguished by not less than three bands of a yellow shade which may vary from a golden colour to a deep tan. Some strains are produced by careful breeding for colour, which have four or five yellow bands, and such are known as " Goldens." The late Mr. F. W. Sladen made quite a stir some thirty years ago, by breeding Golden bees in Kent. These bees, both queens and workers, were almost entirely yellow except for the head and tip of the abdomen. Goldens are beautiful bees, but it must be owned that they are not entirely desirable for use in our climate. " Handsome is as handsome does," says the adage, and it is certain that for honey-production in this country the " leather "-coloured or

" three-banded " Italian is superior, if of good strain, to any other yellow breed. In fact it is very doubtful if a really good strain of these bees can be beaten as honey producers. Italian bees require much more stores for winter than do most black races, and this must not be forgotten by those who decide to try them for the first time. They breed rather late in the autumn. They do not use much propolis and, in contra-distinction to Caucasians, they tend to spread their stores, as gathered, over a large area of comb and are apt to leave more honey unsealed at the end of the season than are other races. In colour they vary, as has been shown; but the queens are nearly always conspicuous and· are by far the easiest to find of all the bee varieties of importance. They are lighter in colour and without bands. The drones vary greatly in colour from almost pure golden to black. Originally, the Italians were very poor bees for comb-honey production, for their cappings were apt to be dull and unattractive. Most black bees cap their honey cells with wax before they have quite filled them, thus leaving a clear space between the cap and the honey, which permits the wax covering to remain dry and white; but some Italians and a few other yellow races com-pletely fill the cells so that the wax caps are in actual contact with the contents which imparts a dull, wet look which quite spoils the appearance of the finished product. However, most breeders of Italians have now completely overcome this difficulty by selective breeding, and their bees may usually be relied upon to furnish sections of excellent quality. Italians are usually easy bees to handle and, if allowed sufficient room in their hives to accommodate their extremely prolific queens, are not excessive swarmers. These bees are often more inclined to commence robbing than many races, and they are certainly very apt to " drift " or stray into the hives of other colonies and remain there permanently, which may assist the spread of Acarine disease (399).

53. **Cross-bred Bees and Mongrels.**—The races described in the foregoing paragraphs are those which merit attention by the prospective beekeeper, and of them it may be said that the Italian is, at present, by far the most important. The Caucasian race may in time, after sufficient experiment, be found to be of equal or superior merit in this climate, and is sufficiently distinctively coloured to afford some hope of successful breeding as a pure race; but that time is not yet. Carniolans are, at present, too great swarmers for the average beekeeper to tolerate, and the other dark-coloured races, such as Dutch, Natives or other Northern European types, can

hardly be described as pure varieties at all except, perhaps, in the case of the genuine Native British Bee, if anywhere it still survives uncrossed. The great majority of the bees in the British Isles are, at the present time, of mixed blood—in most cases very mixed indeed. And the bulk of our honey is produced by these cross-bred or mongrel tenants of our hives. Much has been said and written to the disadvantage of these bees; but the fact must be faced that it is virtually impossible, short of regular importation and continual re-queening, to maintain any apiary in a pure state in these countries for twelve months. Some first crosses are among the best of all honey-bees; but the product of cross-bred parents on both sides are apt to be much less desirable. In considering this, it must not be forgotten that the drone is produced by parthenogenesis (44), and that, consequently, the sons of all pure-bred queens will be pure themselves no matter how their mother mated and, if all queens in a district or isolated apiary be pure-bred, all the drones will be also pure. Therefore it seems that the ordinary beekeeper will be wise to try to breed a few queens from his best stock, headed by a pure-bred queen, and use them to re-queen other colonies as required. Cross-bred bees are often very apt to be bad-tempered, and this is a great disadvantage. It is believed, however, that disposition is inherited from the male parent, and much may be done by trying to have plenty of drones of some pure and gentle race in the apiary and by eliminating as far as possible all queens whose bees are vicious, whether such queens be old or young, or whether their bees are good in other respects or not. Caucasians are extremely gentle; yet a queen of that race mated with a French Black drone will usually produce extremely bad-tempered offspring; while a French virgin mated to an Italian has been found to produce quite mild-mannered bees. First crosses derived from the mating of a Caucasian queen with an Italian drone are often bees of great merit, as also are bees from the crossing of an Italian drone with a Black queen; but the latter cross reversed often gives a bad-tempered colony.

54. Cyprian Bees have at times been introduced to these countries from the island of Cyprus. They are very handsome in appearance, having small pointed bodies with yellow bands. They are prolific and good workers. Their comb-honey is of very inferior quality as they leave no air-space under the cappings. They are extremely prone to produce laying workers (210) and they use propolis lavishly. They are of an excessively vicious temperament, and it may be said that their faults so far outweigh their virtues, in this climate, at any rate, that they are best avoided.

55. **Egyptian Bees** resemble Italians in appearance, but are much smaller. In our climate they are very bad-tempered, stinging furiously on slight provocation. The cappings of their combs are unsightly. They produce laying workers in abundance. They do not form a proper winter cluster, and, in short, they are worthless to beekeepers of these countries.

56. **The Syrian, or Holy Land Bees** are also similar in appearance to Italians, but are otherwise very different. They swarm excessively and build large numbers of queen cells which gives them a certain value for queen-rearing purposes. They are vicious and difficult to handle. Dr. E. F. Phillips tells us that—

" Many virgin queens go with after-swarms and do not kill each other until one is mated. Young queens lay drone eggs in the first month."

57. **Tunisian, or Punic Bees.**—Natives of the north coast of Africa, these bees are black in colour and "black" in temperament. They are easily provoked and extremely irritable and revengeful. They give trouble also by their persistent use of propolis. Unaccustomed to winter—

" They breed all the year round at the expense of large consumption of stores and bees."—*G. W. Bullamore.*

They have met with little favour, and there seems no reason to suppose that they have any future here.

58. **The Common East Indian Bees** (*A. indica*), though of a different species from the hive-bees, build wax combs in which they store, and in their native land some small amount of honey is harvested. They are, however, interesting to beekeepers in these countries, only as curiosities. These bees are considerably smaller than the bee of Europe, and there is in the same territory an even smaller bee which collects honey. This is the *Dwarf East Indian Bee*, which is so small that the cells of the single comb, which it attaches to a twig of a small tree, are not much more than one-eighth of an inch in diameter.

59. **Giant Bees** (*A. dorsata*) are found in India and Ceylon, China, and eastwards to Java. They build single combs, five or six feet long by three or four deep, on high trees or rocks.

Little is known of them, and it appears certain that, even were it proved that they were workable under domestication as are our honey-bees, they would be quite unfit to survive in a temperate climate.

60. Other Bees.—There are vast numbers of bees of various kinds which are of great interest to the entomologist; but they have nothing to do with the honey-bees. The familiar humble bees in their varied colours; the leaf-cutters; the masons and a host of others are fully described in the works of many naturalists, such as Fabre, Sladen and others, whose writings those interested are recommended to consult.

60A. Strain.—In considering the merits of the various varieties of hive-bees, it should always be borne in mind that the question of strain is of very great importance; more so, in fact, than that of race. There are Italians and Italians; Blacks and Blacks; Cross-breeds and Cross-breeds. We find this matter of strain running across the breeding of all domestic stock. Certain good or bad characteristics will show themselves in our bees as well as in other stock, and the wise bee-man will try as far as possible to perpetuate the strains that show the good and eliminate those that show the detrimental characters. Dr. Miller's dictum still stands: " Breed from your best queens "; but that is not the whole story. It does not always follow that the best queens will produce the best queens. Probably an even safer plan would be, in view of the fact of male parthenogenesis in the honey-bee, to *breed from those queens whose daughter queens have proved their worth.* That is to say, when we have found a queen whose daughter queens, generally speaking, give better than average results, we should try to keep that queen going as long as possible and breed from her as many young queens as we possibly can. More ideal still would be to find two of these good breeding mothers; breeding queens from the one and a mass of drones from the other.

CHAPTER VII.

BEE PRODUCTS. HONEY COMB, etc.

61. Honey.—It is a common error to suppose that honey is gathered by bees from flowers. Honey is the product of the nectar secreted in the nectaries of flowers and subjected to a chemical change in the honey sac (38) of the bee, the cane sugar of the nectar being converted into the grape sugar of honey by its mixture with the secretion of certain glands in the insect. Speaking generally, nectar may be said to contain from 50 *per cent.* to 80 *per cent.* of water (63), according to the flowers from which it is collected and to the state of the atmosphere as damp or dry. Some flowers—the fuschia, for example, secrete nectar which has a much smaller percentage of water. The secretion is Nature's provision for securing the fertilization of plants by inducing the visits of insects, notably of the bee, in order that pollen, the fertilizing dust, may be carried from flower to flower (79). It is affected by temperature, and by the state of the weather. It is lessened by continued drought, and increased by gentle rain accompanied by heat. Usually it is greatest in the morning, decreasing in the afternoon. Every beekeeper knows what it is to have his bees idle during days of sunshine, although situated in the midst of honey-producing plants and flowers, when long absence of rain and dew has retarded the secretion of nectar.

62. Gathering and Storing Honey.—When bees visit the flowers, they suck the nectar by means of the spoon (32) and groove and, passing through the œsophagus or gullet, it enters the honey sac (38). Below the honey sac is situated the stomach mouth which the insect can, at will, open to admit the honey to the

(*Photo by J. G. Digges*).

Fig. 25. BEE ON CLOVER.

chyle stomach as food, or close when the honey is intended
to be stored (38). In the latter case the muscles of the honey
sac are brought into play, and the fluid is forced out of the
mouth and deposited in the comb cells. The existence of the
honey sac and stomach mouth explain various phenomena in
the life of the bee—how, when swarming, she can carry from
the hive sufficient honey to serve as food for a considerable
time, and even for the production of wax in her new home (18);
how, in the winter season, she can feed from the contents of the
honey sac during several days without having recourse to the
comb-cells.

63. Water in Honey.—When nectar, thus converted into
honey, has been deposited in the cells, it becomes necessary to
evaporate from it a quantity of water. Dr. Smyth says:

" In order to complete a pound of sealed honey in their comb-cells
the bees must evaporate at least half a pound, and frequently a pound
of water from the cells, and out of the hive."—*Irish Bee Journal.*

Root, in the " *A. B. C. of Bee Culture*," estimates the water
in honey, after evaporation, as from 15 to 30 *per cent*. John
H. Lovell says:

" The average moisture of honey is 17.59 *per cent.*, while that of
nectar is not far from 75 *per cent.*, so that the weight of the nectar
would exceed that of the honey fourfold."—*The Flower and the Bee*,
p. 116.

The evaporation is effected by raising the temperature of the
water and of the interior of the hive, and by fanning (14) the
moist and heated air out through the doors. On occasions
of extreme humidity of the atmosphere outside, evaporation
within the hive becomes arrested and the gathering of nectar
ceases for a time. When a cell is almost filled with honey,
it is sealed with a capping of wax, and in that condition the
honey will keep indefinitely in a warm, dry place.

64. Honey as Food.—As an article of food, honey is very
valuable. It is a pre-digested food which passes integrally
into the blood, not requiring to undergo in the stomach the
process of invertion without which industrial sugar is not
assimilable by our organisms. Those who desire to follow a
perfect, and at the same time a palatable regimen, are wise in
selecting honey as a permanent element of their daily food.
The role of honey will become a more honoured one when the
vigour and vitality represented by its properties become a
familiar fact, not only to an *elite* of doctors and dietists, but

also to the public generally. It is to be noted that at a temperature above 145° Fahr. ferments loose their valuable qualities, and that boiling honey—which is sometimes recommended—destroys many of the good qualities, such as aroma and flavour, as well as the ferments which it contains. The value of these digestive ferments is somewhat doubtful, however, and with care, honey may be heated sufficiently for commercial purposes without undue injury to either aroma or flavour (325). It is sometimes stated that honey is merely a form of sugar; but the inverted sugars, levulose and dextrose, of which it is largely composed, are very different from the sugar of commerce, to say nothing of minute but valuable traces of various minerals such as iron, phosphorus, manganese and, indeed, almost all the mineral elements found in the human body (Root). There are also various aromatic oils and resins which play a large part in its varied flavours and render it so palatable a table delicacy. In short, the age-old dictum holds good to-day just as it did in ancient times when the Hebrew sage wrote: " My son, eat thou honey because it is good, and the honey-comb which is sweet to thy taste."

65. Adulteration of Honey.—When honey has been adulterated with glucose, the presence of glucose may be recognized if a little of the mixture be slowly poured into a glass containing absolute alcohol, and if the alcohol then shows turbid, or milky, having a gummy substance at the bottom.

66. Honey Dew.—An unpleasant, dark, rank-flavoured substance called honey dew, is sometimes gathered by bees, much to the annoyance of their owner. During a spell of hot, dry weather, with absence of moisture and rain, this objectionable deposit may be seen upon the trees, and the bees eagerly gather it. Its name is due to an erroneous opinion by which it was described as a dew of honey falling upon the leaves. Investigation, however, has shown that the substance is a discharge from the bodies of aphides, which suck the sap of certain trees and discharge it continuously as a saccharine, viscous fluid. In the absence of rain to wash it off, it adheres to the leaves and is resorted to by both bees and ants. Ants (424) are particularly fond of it, and may often be seen literally milking the aphides. It is stated by Lubbock, who made a special study of the subject, that certain species of ants " farm " aphides in their nests, feeding them with the leaves required, and enjoying the saccharine produce of these " milch cows." Honey dew is sometimes produced without any action of aphides, as an exudation (Miellée) from the leaves.

67. Beeswax.—Beeswax has a specific gravity of between .960 and .970, and will melt at 144° to 148° Fahr. It is a natural secretion, produced in a liquid state by the wax glands in the body of the bee, and moulded, in the shape of tiny scales, in the wax pockets under the ventral plates (37). (Fig. 15). From these pockets the scales are transferred to the mouth, to be made flexible previous to being used in comb building (10. 34.) The wax scales are " so thin and light that one hundred of them hardly weigh as much as a kernel of wheat."—(*Dubini.*) For the secretion of wax, bees require a temperature of from 90° to 95° Fahr. They feed liberally, and then form in clusters, remaining inactive in a high temperature until, after about twenty-four hours, the honey, converted into wax, appears as described above (10).

68. Honey used in Wax Production.—As to the quantity of honey that is required by clustering bees for the production of wax—it is not possible, with our present knowledge, to state definitely. Opinions upon this subject vary considerably. Until further discoveries have been made, it may be taken as a fairly accurate estimate that, according to the conditions existing in the hive, from 6 lbs. to 15 lbs. of honey are consumed by bees in the production of 1 lb. of wax. An experiment conducted by Mr. S. Simmins and described in his book, *A Modern Bee Farm*, appeared to show fairly conclusively that estimates have usually been greatly exaggerated and that the normal amount of honey consumed in wax-production during a honey-flow (when wax is most generally produced) is probably only about 5 lbs. or 6 lbs. per 1 lb. of wax. Nevertheless, if honey be valued at 8d. per lb.—a low estimate—and wax at 1s. 6d., it is readily seen that the production of beeswax is costly and that the work of the bees might be more profitably expended in other ways. Allowing that, on average, about eight or ten pounds of honey is consumed to produce 1 lb. of wax, it follows that the wax so produced must cost many times its own value. (78).

69. Paraffin Wax and Ceresin Wax are mineral products, unsuitable for bee hives. They are sometimes used for the adulteration of beeswax by manufacturers of foundation, but, being of a lower specific gravity than that of beeswax, their presence as adulterants may be easily detected (122).

70. Honey Comb.—The combs of a hive at swarming time will be found, on examination, to contain four distinct kinds of cells, viz.—Worker cells; Drone cells; Transition cells; and Queen cells (192).

71. Worker Cells (Fig. 26, G), in which worker bees are reared, are about ½″ deep, and ⅛″ wide; so that five cells measure about 1″, and from twenty-seven to twenty-nine go to the square inch (197).

72. Drone Cells (Fig. 26, F), in which drone bees are reared, are about ¾″ deep, and ¼″ wide; so that four cells measure about 1″, and from sixteen to eighteen go to the square inch (204).

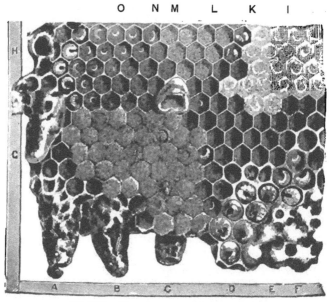

Fig. 26. HONEYCOMB. (*Natural size*).

A, Queen Cell, from which Queen has hatched, showing lid ; B, Queen Cell torn open ; C, Queen Cell, cut down ; D, Drone Grub ; E, Drone Cell, partly sealed ; F, Drone Cells, sealed ; G, " False " Queen Cell, and beyond— Worker Cells, sealed, and Bees emerging from cells ; H, Old Queen Cell ; I, Sealed Honey ; K, Fresh Pollen Masses ; L, Cells nearly filled with Pollen ; M, Aborted Queen Cell on face of Comb ; N, Bee biting its way out of Cell O, Eggs and Larvæ in various conditions.

73. Hexagonal Cells.—Both worker and drone cells are six-sided, or hexagonal, a shape which, as Charles Darwin explained, is consequent upon the building of a number of cells in contact, and the result of this construction is that the bee-comb has the greatest capacity and strength, with the least expenditure of material and labour. Being hexagonal, the cells approximate to the shape of the bees, avoid waste of space, and so support each other that they can be constructed of the lightest material, and of exceeding delicacy, for

" Walls so thin, with sister walls combined;
Weak in themselves, a sure dependence find."
—EVANS.

74. Transitional Cells, irregular in shape—better called Intermediate or Accommodation Cells—are constructed to connect worker and drone, or queen, cells.

75. Use of Cells for Storing.—The three kinds of cells— Worker, Drone and Transitional, may be used for storing honey and pollen. They slope upwards from the base, thus being easier to fill, and safer as receptacles for honey than if built horizontally.

76. Queen Cells (Fig. 26, A, B, C) are solidly built of almost pure beeswax except at the tips, where pollen is introduced to render them porous (206). They are like waxen thimbles, about an inch long when sealed, and tapering downwards (17). Being built separately and not in contact with the rest of the comb, except at their bases, they are round instead of hexagonal. Unlike the ordinary brood cells, queen cells are not used a second time, but are cut down by the bees (Fig. 26, C, H) soon after the emergence of the queens.

77. Cappings.—Cells occupied by brood have a porous capping of wax and pollen; those which contain honey are capped with wax.

78. Value of Combs.—The wax employed in the combs of 11 " standard " frames (104) weighs about two pounds. We have seen (68) that this wax is very costly, both in honey consumption and also in loss of time by the bees while producing it. Comb is, therefore, a thing too valuable to be wasted; the more use the beekeeper can take out of his combs, and the more economically he can have them built, the more profitable will his industry be (121). It must, however, be stated that combs should not be used indefinitely for breeding purposes, because the portions of the cocoons left in the cells by hatching bees (200) may eventually reduce the size of the cells so appreciably as to render them unfit for brood-rearing (201).

79. Pollen.—Pollen is the fertilizing dust of flowers, and for bees, an indispensable food. On examination of a typical flower (Fig. 27, B) it is found to be composed of four whorls, or sets of organs on the same plane with one another and distributed in a circle about an axis. These organs are:—(1) The outer whorl, or *calyx* (*a*): (2) the second whorl, or *corolla* (*b*): (3) a whorl of parts alternating with the corolla, and called the *andrœcium* (*c*): and (4) the inner whorl, or *gynœcium* (*d*). Nos. 1 and 2 are the floral envelopes, or coverings. No. 3— the *andrœcium*—is made up of a series of leaves, or stamens (A): these are the male organs, and have at their summits

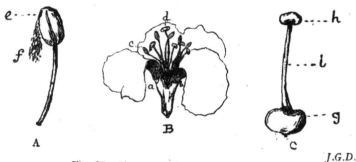

Fig. 27. FLOWER : STAMEN : AND PISTIL.

A, Stamen, *e*, Anther ; *f*, Pollen. B, Sketch of Typical Flower, *a*, Calyx :— Sepals; *b*, Corolla :—Petals; *c*, Andrœcium :—Stamens; *d*, Gynœcium (Pistil):— Carpels. C, Pistil, *g*, Ovary; *h*, Stigma ; *i*, Style.

the anthers (*e*) which contain the fertilizing dust (*f*). No. 4 —the *gynœcium*, or *pistil* (C)—is the female sexual organ, situated in the centre of the flower and containing the ovary (*g*) and stigma (*h*). For the production of a perfect seed it is necessary that the germs of the pistil be fecundated by the pollen of the stamen. When the pollen grains are ripe they are shed by the anthers. Some flowers are bisexual, or herma-phrodite, having both male and female organs, but these are rarely self-fertilized, Nature having provided against it: as, for example, in the primula, in which occur long stamens and a pistil with a short style, or short stamens and a pistil with a long style. Fertilization is commonly effected by insects and, to encourage their visits, the perfume, nectar, and gay colours of the flowers are developed (61). Bees are among the most useful workers in this field of nature's economy. They enter the flowers (9), gather their loads of pollen, even roll themselves in the rich dust, fill with it their baskets (*corbiculæ*) (34), carry home their provender and deposit it in the cells. Thus the pollen is carried from stamen to pistil, and from flower to flower, and fruits and flowers become fertilized which, but for the visits of the insects, would remain barren. Bees have long been recognized as valuable fellow-labourers with the horticulturist and agriculturist, and many cases are on record in which fruit trees have ceased to bear, or have borne but indifferently, when bees had disappeared from the neighbourhood. When pollen arrives at the hive, it is packed in cells, is often covered with honey, and is sealed over with wax.

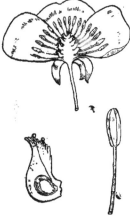

BEE PUBLICATIONS

Fig. 27b.
BUTTERCUP AND PARTS.

" Perhaps there may be some reader of this who has never studied how flowers are fertilized, and has, therefore, never realized how much the beauty of the world is due to the agency of insects, more especially of the bee. I have, therefore, made a drawing which will show the comparatively simple manner in which fertilization takes place in a butter-cup. I have drawn the buttercup as it appears if cut in two through the centre. First, there are the little leaves hanging down over the stalk, then the cup of beautiful glossy yellow leaves, next a circle of a number of little stalks with heads. On the right-hand side, beneath, I have drawn one of these very large indeed, so that one may see plainly the head which, when it is ripe, opens full of tiny balls of yellow dust (Fig. 27, A), which are the grains of pollen so beloved by the bee, and so essential to the fertilization of the flower. They, when they fall on the innermost circle of closely packed heads, fertilize the seed. On the left-hand side I have drawn some of the grains of pollen having fallen on the moist top of the seed. Here it remains, until it sends down a tiny thread which, penetrating into the very heart of the seed, awakes it to life and growth. Perhaps some may wonder what use is the bee to the plant. Cannot the pollen simply fall on the seed, and nothing more be required ? But even the dim consciousness of the flower is aware that no plant can be perpetually self-fertilized, and that those which are content through long ages, first to deteriorate, and then to vanish from the earth, are those which have not striven with all their power to gain the help of some carrier, who will carry the grains of pollen to another flower which awaits them, and bring back to it another flower's pollen, and lay it down exactly on the right place. The problem for the flower to solve is how to find a carrier, and having found one, to make him carry his burden to the right destination and put it, so to speak, in the right letter-box. For postmen, the flower choses insects. If the flower grows in an open, sunny place, it attracts the bee by colour. If the flower grows in a shady place it attracts by scent as well as by the bait of nectar."— A. BEATRICE RAMBAUT, in the *Irish Bee Journal*.

" Having gone to visit the bees of a lady friend living within six miles of Dublin, we first went to look at her fine peach house. She pointed out to me how badly the blooms had set on a tree that was not easy to fertilize, and said that the gardener had been complaining that the bees had not helped him as much as usual this spring by visiting and fertilizing the blooms. A look at the hives soon explained this, all the combs, except the outside ones, being a compact mass of rotten foul brood, a very few live bees being left in one hive."— M. H. READ, in *Irish Bee Journal*.

" A land flowing with milk and honey is the classical description of a bounteous agricultural tract; but whilst the production of milk has grown into a large and specialized industry, beekeeping has remained a very minor adjunct to general agriculture and horticulture. Yet there is much truth in the old description. The farmer who neglects beekeeping pays a penalty. The part played by bees in the fertilization of useful farm crops is an important one. Cases are on record in which the yield of clover seed has been greatly enhanced by the presence of a colony of bees in the field; whilst instances of the beneficial effect of bees on the yield of fruit trees and orchards are numerous . . . The economic value of beekeeping to the fruit farmer or to the general farmer is not therefore restricted to the value of the honey produced, but is often to be found to a still greater extent in more copious crops of fruit and pasture. This is important because it is the realization of a full average yield which frequently determines whether the farmer's undertaking in a given year has been worth while or not."—*Report of The Imperial Economic Committee*. London, 1928.

80. **Propolis.**—Propolis is a resinous, sticky substance, gathered from pine, horse chestnut, and other trees, and carried by the bees, as they carry pollen, on their hind legs. It is used for filling up cracks, to exclude draughts, and to make the hive watertight. It is applied also, much to the bee-keeper's regret, to fasten together the frames, and other parts of the hive furniture (183). When hives are situated under high trees, the vibration, caused by the roots as

" Through woods and mountain passes
The winds, like anthems, roll,"

is felt at once by the bees, who endeavour to modify it as far as possible, by fixing their combs and frames in the hive with propolis (9). Occasionally bees will use propolis to defeat their natural enemies, or to fix and render harmless unwelcome intruders. The term, " Propolis," signifies " before the city," " an outwork "; the use of the substance in the defence of the hive having been observed. Huber describes the construction of barricades of wax and propolis in the hive entrance, to exclude the Death's Head Moth (*Sphinx Atropos*), while giving passage to the workers. Reaumur observes that a snail having gained admission to one of his hives, the bees, being unable to remove it, promptly arrested its progress by fastening it down with propolis. Maraldi relates a somewhat similar occurrence, his bees having covered all over with propolis a large slug which they had been unable to dislodge. It is quite a common practice with bees in modern hives to attach pieces of Naphthaline (381) to the floorboard, and even to enclose them in a case of propolis to overcome the objectionable smell. Sometimes bees collect their "propolis" from the bitumen used on roads, roofs, etc.; this material tends to stain the wood of frames and sections, but is otherwise harmless.

PART II.

HIVES AND APPLIANCES

CHAPTER VIII.

HIVES AND FRAMES.

81. Ancient Hives.—Beekeeping as an industry is ancient. It is certain that from a very early period a high value has been set upon honey as an article of food, and that, long centuries ago, bees were kept for profit in manufactured hives. Virgil, who wrote B.C. 70, describes the hive in use in his day. It was constructed of plaited osiers and bark, and was plastered with mud to make it waterproof. Pliny tells us that when the spring flowers in the Italian valleys had failed, the bees, in their hives, were carried at night up the rivers in boats in search of better pasturage. In parts of Asia hives of pottery were used and were built into the walls of the houses. The osier hive of Virgil was, probably, somewhat like the old-fashioned straw skep with which we in this country are so familiar.

82. The Skep (Fig. 28) is made of straw, bound with cane or other pliable material. It has its uses (83); but as a permanent home for bees its defects are too many and serious

Fig. 28. THE SKEP.

to admit of its adoption by anyone who desires to keep bees for profit and upon humane principles. It does not permit proper management. It does not allow that perfect control of the bees and their work which is essential to success. Although its cost may not exceed a couple of shillings, it is expensive, because it precludes the use of foundation (118) which, in the modern hive, effects so large an economy. It is dangerous, because, not open to examination by the owner, it may harbour disease without his knowledge, and may spread infection far and near (363). And, associated as it is with the hateful sulphur pit, by which our forefathers, for want of a better method, obtained the honey harvest by sacrifice of the bees who gathered it (151), it is not to be encouraged as an adjunct of modern beekeeping, except within certain limitations.

Fig. 29.

THE SKEP. FLAT TOP FOR SUPERING.

83. Uses of Skeps.—Bees crowded in skeps are likely to give off early swarms, and with that object in view, stocks in skeps may often be turned to good account. Skeps are useful for carrying swarms (162), and in the operations of driving (169) and hiving (245). They may be used, to some extent, for the production of surplus honey in supers (284). For this purpose the skep is made with a flat top (Fig. 29) having a hole in the centre of the crown.

84. The Skep Replaced by the Movable-Comb Hive.—But modern beekeeping encourages more intelligent management, and aims at higher success than can be hoped for by the use of the straw skep which, except in a limited number of cases, chiefly in remote rural districts where some cottagers still retain it, has now given place to the hive with movable frames (86), which has effected a revolution in beekeeping by admitting adequate supervision over the work of the colony, by facilitating the harvesting of larger quantities of honey, and by rendering unnecessary, indeed inexcusable, the destruction of the bees. (151).

85. Genesis of the Movable-Comb Hive.—Towards the close of the eighteenth century, Huber (151), the blind Naturalist, who was born in Geneva in 1750, constructed a hive in shape like a book, each leaf containing a comb, and by this means he was able to arrive at the discoveries which have made his name famous. In 1838, Dzierzon, a German, and the discoverer of parthenogenesis of bees, *i.e.*, reproduction without fecundation (44), began the use of hives in which the combs were attached to top bars. This was improved upon in 1851 by Langstroth, "the father of American apiculture," who invented the hive opening at the top, and with combs in movable, suspended frames.

86. Advantages of the Movable-Comb Hive. — To this invention modern bee-keeping owes the rapid progress it has made in the past half century. The movable frame gives free access to all parts of the hive, and admits of the various operations by which control is exercised over the bees, and their labour turned to the best account (151). The condition

Fig. 30. The " C.D.B." Hive.

of the colony may be thoroughly inspected (363); bees and combs may be changed from one hive to another as required (264); queen rearing (299) and artificial swarming (233) may be practised; natural swarming controlled (226); honey extracted without destruction of the combs (289); and such intelligent management can be pursued as may produce the best results.

87. Hives in General Use.—The modern movable comb hives in general use may be said to fall roughly into four classes. The old-style " single-walled " hives; the " W.B.C." hives; the British-American type of single-walled hives; and the American hives, pure and simple. The great majority of hives used in the British Isles belong to one of the first two classes, the " W.B.C." hive being especially popular in England, while the other kind is more used in Scotland and Ireland. In the latter country the " C.D.B." (Congested Districts Board) hive (Fig. 30) is very popular. In England and Scotland very similar hives are in general use. In all these hives the principle is the same; their frame-holding bodies are as illustrated in Figure 32, there being inner walls on two sides only, where they are required to form the rabbet upon which the frames rest. The " W.B.C." hive consists of a complete set of outer cases which are simply a shell which covers and contains the frame-holding bodies. It is illustrated in Fig. 36. The third style of hive is based upon a compromise between the American hives (97, 98) and the ordinary British and Irish hives. It differs from the latter in having no porch and no plinths or any overlapping structure, and in having an inner cover or crown-board of wood instead of " quilts " of textile material. From the American hives it differs in having the bee-space

Fig. 31. THE " FEDERATION " HIVE.

between the bodies of frames provided under instead of above the frames; that is to say, the hive walls are so constructed that their upper edges are flush with the frame tops, whereas, in the American hives, the walls rise a bee-space above the frames. This class of hive, having become increasingly popular among beekeepers, has now been standardised under the auspices of the Ministry of Agriculture in London as the " National " hive (96). The external measurements of hives may, if uniformity is no object, vary to any extent; but the internal measurements of the frame-holding bodies (91) must be such as will with the utmost accuracy suit the measurements of the frame to be used, and must provide such bee-space (88) as careful observation of the natural instincts of the bees has shown to be desirable. This may appear too obvious to require explanation; yet some unfortunate mistakes have been made by inexperienced persons in manufacturing hives to a given external measurement, only to find that the frames could not be worked in them.

88. Internal Measurements.—The internal measurements of a modern hive are too exact to admit of slipshod carpentry. A 1-16th of an inch, one way or another, may make or mar a hive; an inaccuracy of a nature so trifling that it would be quite inconsiderable in the case of a piano or of a wooden leg, may render a hive utterly useless for the keeping of bees upon modern principles. A movable-comb hive is such only when its combs are movable; and it is found that if the spaces between the ends of the frames (104) and the inner walls of the body box (91) are less than $\frac{1}{4}$-inch, the bees, being unable to pass, will fasten the frames to the body box with propolis, while if the spaces are more than $\frac{3}{8}$-inch, the bees will build brace comb there. There is, therefore, a safe space from $\frac{1}{4}$-inch to $\frac{3}{8}$-inch, and if this be increased or diminished the frames are liable to be fastened to the body box, in which case manipulations of the hive will involve unnecessary exasperation of both the bees and their keeper. As to the respective advantages of the $\frac{1}{4}$-inch and the $\frac{3}{8}$-inch spaces, some difference of opinion exists among experienced beekeepers. All, however, agree that where bees are found to respect the $\frac{3}{8}$-inch space, that space offers very important advantages in the greater facility with which frames may be moved, and the minimising of the risk of crushing bees, and even of killing queens, during manipulations (191). Between the bottom bars of the frames and the floor board (90) a space of not less than $\frac{1}{2}$-inch should be left. It follows from what has been said that accuracy in the making of hives is essential. If it be desired to manufacture hives at home, one good hive, as a pattern, should be procured, and the measurements of that hive, so far as the internal dimensions are concerned, should be followed with the utmost exactness. The timber should be of good quality and thoroughly seasoned. American seasoned pine is largely used in the manufacture of the best hives. All wooden hives require to be kept well painted externally to protect the timber from the effects of the weather.

89. The Single-walled Hives.—Figs. 30, 31 and 32 give a good idea of the appearance and construction of this type of hive when used for the production of comb honey. As illustrated they consist of four parts, viz.:—Floor-board and legs (A); Body-box, or Brood-chamber (B); Lift or Riser (C), and Roof (D). Additional space for supers may, if necessary, be provided by the use of an extra lift. When used for the production of extracted honey, instead of the lift as illustrated, a second body of the same kind as the brood-chamber is used, and this may be made to hold either the same sized frames or shallower ones. These latter are very extensively used by those who work for extracted honey. There are standard

frames $5\frac{1}{2}$ inches deep, but the same length as the brood frames.
Such bodies, either deep
or shallow, may be tiered
upon one another to any
desired extent. They are
often used with wider
spacings which are pro-
vided by the use of extra
wide metal ends (104) so
that eight will fill the same
space as ten ordinarily
spaced frames. In the
next four paragraphs are
given the exact measure-
ments for making a
typical single-walled hive
for use in the production
of comb honey.

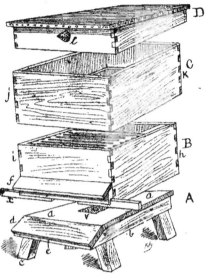

Fig. 32. THE " FEDERATION " HIVE.
(The Parts Separated).

90. The Floor Board
(Fig. 32, A) is made of
two pieces of timber
(a,a) $16\frac{7}{8}''$ × $11''$ × $\frac{7}{8}''$,
rabbeted $\frac{1}{2}''$ and nailed or
screwed to two rails (b) $23\frac{1}{2}''$ × $2''$ × $\frac{7}{8}''$, to which rails the
legs (c) $8\frac{1}{4}''$ × $3''$ × $2''$, are fastened. The rails are chamfered
to $20\frac{1}{2}''$ at the front ends, and on the chamfers is nailed the
alighting board (d) $16\frac{7}{8}''$ × $4\frac{1}{2}''$ × $\frac{7}{8}''$, the upper edge
chamfered to an angle of 60°, and the lower edge rabbeted
$\frac{3}{8}''$ × $\frac{3}{8}''$ (e) to form a rest for a hiving board (244). In the floor
board a round hole $2''$ in diameter is cut as a ventilator (v and
Fig. 33), and is covered on the upper side with perforated
zinc, the under side having a piece of wood $7''$ × $3''$ × $\frac{3}{8}''$
screwed to the floor board, so that it can be revolved to open
or close the ventilator at will (94, 228. Fig. 33).

91. The Body Box (Fig. 32, B) measures, internally, $18''$
in length, $17''$ in width, and $9\frac{1}{2}''$ in depth. This is sufficiently
large to take eleven frames and one dummy, or division board
(100). The sides (h) are $19\frac{3}{4}''$ × $9\frac{1}{2}''$ × $\frac{3}{8}''$, the front (i) is
$17\frac{1}{4}''$ × $8\frac{5}{8}''$ × $\frac{7}{8}''$, and the back, $17\frac{1}{4}''$ × $9\frac{1}{2}''$ × $\frac{7}{8}''$, rabbeted
$\frac{1}{4}''$ × $\frac{1}{2}''$ at the bottom to rest on and overlap the floor board.
These are dovetailed, and are nailed together flush on the
upper edges. If put together with a double rabbet nailed, the
above measurements must, of course, be altered accordingly.

The front and back have two grooves running from top to bottom, $\frac{3}{8}''$ wide $\times$ $\frac{1}{4}''$ deep, beginning $1\frac{1}{8}''$ from the ends. Two inner walls, $18\frac{1}{2}'' \times 8\frac{1}{2}'' \times \frac{3}{8}''$, are fitted into the grooves and are chamfered outwards on the upper edges to carry the frames

Fig. 33.

FLOOR-BOARD VENTILATOR.

(Figs. 34, 56): they are nailed $\frac{1}{2}''$ below the top of the body box, so that when the body box is placed in position upon the floor board the sides and back overlap the floor board, and the front, being only $8\frac{5}{8}''$ deep, leaves a space of $\frac{3}{8}''$ between it and the floor board as an entrance for the bees. The inner walls being $\frac{1}{2}''$ below the level of the sides and back, and $\frac{3}{4}''$ distant from the sides, the frames (104), when in position, are level with the top of the body box, and are prevented by the hive sides from moving latterly (280). It will be seen that the body box measures internally when complete $18''$ $\times$ $14\frac{3}{4}'' \times 8\frac{1}{2}''$. This leaves a space of $\frac{3}{8}''$ between the frame ends and the inner walls of the body box, and a space of $\frac{1}{2}''$ between the bottoms of the frames and the floor board. Four slips, $17\frac{3}{4}'' \times \frac{3}{4}'' \times \frac{1}{4}''$, are nailed between the tops and bottoms of the inner walls and the hive sides, and a space of $\frac{3}{8}''$ is left between the upper slips and the bottoms of the frame shoulders.

The spaces between the inner walls and the hive sides are sometimes filled with cork dust, chaff or sawdust to preserve the heat of the brood chamber. The front (i) has either a $\frac{1}{4}''$ groove in the centre of the bottom, or an arrangement in the porch in which run two doors (x) $8'' \times \frac{1}{2}'' \times \frac{3}{16}''$ so that the entrance may be reduced, or enlarged, or closed, as required. Above the doors a porch (f) is provided to keep off rain from the entrance.

Fig. 34.

CHAMFERED INNER WALL.

92. The Lift or Riser (Fig. 32, C) measures internally $20''$ long, $18''$ wide, and $12''$ deep, and is made of two pieces $20\frac{3}{4}'' \times 12'' \times \frac{3}{8}''$, and two pieces $18\frac{3}{4}'' \times 12'' \times \frac{3}{8}''$ dovetailed together. Four pieces, $3'' \times \frac{3}{8}''$, are screwed to the insides, $\frac{3}{4}''$ from the bottom. When in position the lift overlaps the body box, and in winter it is reversed and telescoped over the body box, thus providing additional walls and assisting to preserve the heat of the brood chamber. The lift, in summer, serves to enclose the supers (107), and allows sufficient space for packing round them. When the lift is reversed for winter, the porch is removed from the body box and is fastened to the lift, in a corresponding position (436 and Fig. 172 *a*, page 290).

93. The Roof (Fig. 32, D) measures internally 19⅞″ long × 18⅞″ wide × 5½″ deep in front, and 4½″ deep at the back. It is made of two pieces, 21⅝″ × 5½″ running to 4½″ × ⅜″ for the sides; one piece, 19⅝″ × 5½″ × ⅞″ for the front; and one piece, 19⅝″ × 4½″ × ⅞″ for the back. The front and back are rabbeted ½″ to overlap the lift. On these are nailed two pieces, 23″ × 10¾″ × ½″, which are covered with zinc, thus making the roof perfectly rain and snow proof. The roof slopes to the back to throw off rain. It makes a convenient table for the smoker, and other appliances when neighbouring hives are being manipulated. When in position the roof overlaps the lift. Two holes, 1½″ in diameter, are cut in the gables; the front hole having two escape cones (*l*) fitted to it, to permit the

Fig. 35. THE "A" ROOF.

exit of bees which otherwise might be imprisoned, and the back hole being covered inside with perforated zinc. These holes act as ventilators, and the cones are sometimes used for the purpose of clearing bees from supers (286). Roofs are also made A-shape (Fig. 35.) In this case the front, back and sides are the same length as the roof described above. Four pieces, 24⅝″ × 6¾″ × ⅝″, feathered to ¾″, form the cover, overlapping each other 1″; and a ridge board, 24⅝″ × 2″ × 1¼″, cut out ₁⅜₆″, is fitted on the top. The objection to such roofs lies in their tendency to open at the joints, and to admit damp. They should be kept well painted.

94. Heather Hives.—These are hives in principle identical with those described in the above paragraphs, but they are specially strongly made so that they shall stand up against rough usage while being transported to the moors and back again, often over extremely rough roads. They are provided with special ventilation devices to enable the bees to be confined during transport without risk of suffocation, and also with facilities for being quickly and securely fastened together so that their various parts shall not be in danger of coming apart while on their annual journeys.

95. The "Standard W.B.C." Hive (Fig. 36).—This hive,

which is very popular in England, consists of the following separate parts, as illustrated:—Floorboard (A); body box (B), to take 10 standard frames and a division board; supers (C) to take 8 broad shallow frames; and/or section crates (D) (111); outer covers (E) to enclose the body box and supers; and roof (F) fitted with cone escape. The hive was originally designed by the late Mr. W. B. Carr, and the Standard W.B.C., which differs from the original in having its outer covers made with sloping sides to shed the rain better, was adopted by a number of Beekeepers' Associations about 1920, and has now almost entirely superseded the original model. The FLOORBOARD measures 27″ × 20″ and is made of two runners 27″ × 3″ × ⅞″, one at each side, with tongued and grooved boards nailed across them. The entrance is provided in the floorboard by

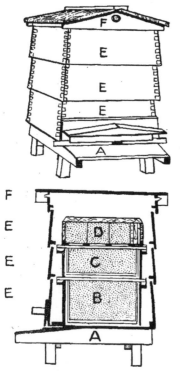

Fig. 36. THE " W.B.C." HIVE.

sloping the runners from 11″ from the back down to the front, making the runner 1½″ wide at the front instead of 3″. Two strips 9¼″ long × 2¾″ wide × ⅞″, tapering to nothing thick, are nailed at the top of the sloping part, one at each side, and a rebate ⅝″ from front to back by ½″ from top to bottom should be cut along the top front edge of each of these strips. When these parts are nailed in position the measurement from the top edge of the rebate to the back of the floor should be 20″. The LEGS, measuring 8″ × 2″ × 2″, are nailed to the floorboard runners and can be stiffened by two strips of wood 20″ long × ⅞″ square (one for each pair of legs) laid across from runner to runner and nailed both to the legs and to the under edge of the runners. The OUTER CASES (or lifts) measure 20″ square outside at the top and 21½″ square outside at the bottom, and are made out of two sides 21½″ at the bottom edge and 20″ at the top edge (sloping equally at each end), by 8″ wide by ⅝″ thick, and two ends cut just like the sides in all respects except that they are $1\frac{1}{4}''$ shorter ($20\frac{1}{4}''$ at the bottom edge and $18\frac{3}{4}''$ at the top edge). The sides are nailed on to the ends, and to prevent each lift from overlapping the next below it too far, strips are nailed all round on the inside and about $\frac{1}{2}''$ from the lower edge. For this purpose will be needed 4 strips $19\frac{5}{8}'' \times \frac{1}{2}'' \times \frac{1}{2}''$. After nailing the lift together it will be found that the top edges slope slightly inwards, and these should be planed level to provide a good bearing surface for the lift above. On the front of the lowest case a porch and entrance slides are fitted as described for the "Federation" Hive (91). The ROOF measures $20\frac{1}{4}'' \times 20\frac{1}{4}''$ inside measurement. It is of the gable type and is made of two gable ends 23" long by $3\frac{1}{2}''$ wide (bevelled from the centre to each end where the width is reduced to $1\frac{1}{2}''$) and $\frac{3}{4}''$ thick; two sides $20\frac{1}{4}'' \times 2'' \times \frac{1}{2}''$; two roof boards $25'' \times 12'' \times \frac{1}{2}''$; and a capping. A hole is drilled in each of the gable ends near the apex of the gable to allow for ventilation over the quilts and is closed by perforated zinc or a cone escape. The gable ends are nailed on to the sides so that the latter are $20\frac{1}{4}''$ apart inside measure, and the tops of the sides are then bevelled to the slope of the gable. The framework so formed is then squared up (until the distance across the two diagonals is equal) and the roof boards are nailed on, being bevelled at the upper edge so that they meet at the ridge. To prevent the roof from overlapping too far, strips are nailed all round on the inside and about $\frac{1}{2}''$ from the lower edge. For this purpose will be needed 2 strips $20\frac{1}{4}'' \times \frac{1}{2}'' \times \frac{1}{2}''$, and two $19\frac{3}{8}'' \times \frac{1}{2}'' \times \frac{1}{2}''$. The INNER BROOD CHAMBER measures $15\frac{5}{8}'' \times 14\frac{1}{2}''$, inside measurement, and is made of two sides $17\frac{1}{16}''$ long $\times 9'' \times \frac{1}{2}''$, and 2 ends $15\frac{5}{8}'' \times 8\frac{1}{2}'' \times \frac{1}{2}''$, or if $\frac{1}{4}''$ metal runners are used the ends should be $8\frac{1}{4}''$ wide. If the side boards do not hold the full 9" a thin strip should be nailed along their bottom edges, to make them up to this width. The sides are nailed on to the ends so that the internal measurement of the brood chamber is $15\frac{5}{8}'' \times 14\frac{1}{2}''$, and the spaces where the lugs of the frames rest are filled by two strips, one $15\frac{5}{8}'' \times \frac{5}{8}'' \times \frac{1}{2}''$, and the other $16\frac{5}{8}'' \times 1\frac{1}{4}'' \times \frac{1}{2}''$. The SHALLOW FRAME SUPER is similar to the brood chamber, but made of boards 6" wide instead of 9" (the ends being $5\frac{1}{2}''$). An EKE can be made if desired and is similar to the brood chamber but only three inches deep, with the ends the same width as the sides and without the strips. It is used either to convert a shallow super into an inner brood chamber, or under the inner brood chamber in winter to give extra space, or over a brood chamber or shallow frame super as a tray to hold quilts or other packing materials. It is held in position by four strips $4'' \times 1'' \times \frac{1}{2}''$ screwed two on each side on the outer surface of the sides, and projecting an inch above their upper edge. Resting on the floorboard and between the inner and outer brood chambers a tunnel strip, or bridge, piece is required, to prevent the incoming bees from entering the space between the two. This measures $19'' \times 1\frac{1}{4}'' \times \frac{7}{8}''$, and if the frames are placed at right angles to the entrance it is rebated to fit between the two projecting sides of the inner brood chamber. If the frames are parallel with the entrance, a plain strip $18\frac{1}{4}'' \times 1\frac{1}{4}'' \times \frac{7}{8}''$ will serve.

96. **The National Hive.**—In Figs. 37, 38 are given illustrations of the National Hive. In paragraph 87, we saw that a class of hives embodying the strict simplicity of design of the American standard hives and the British standard frame, has been coming more and more into use in these countries. A hive of this type was introduced by Messrs. Burtt and Son, Gloucester, some fourteen years ago, and similar patterns were subsequently put on the market by other makers of hives. Recently the Ministry of Agriculture, London, decided to get all makers to agree to manufacture this hive to a standard pattern which should be called the "National Hive," and be

Fig. 37.

NATIONAL HIVE. SHOWING CONSTRUCTION.

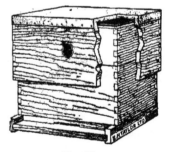

Fig. 38.

NATIONAL HIVE WITH DEEP COVER.

officially recognised as such by the Ministry. The National Hive consists of a floorboard which is reversible, as in the American hives, and gives an entrance of $\frac{7}{8}''$ depth on one side and $\frac{3}{8}''$ on the other. An entrance block is provided with two openings of different sizes which may be used as desired to contract the entrance. The brood chamber is $18\frac{1}{8}''$ square and holds 11 standard frames. The sides are flush with the top bars of the frames. An inner cover, or crown board, may or may not be used, as desired. In the case of hives, such as the " National," the hive walls being flush with the top bars, a rim must be provided to the inner cover to allow a bee-space over the frames. A piece of stout canvas or other suitable material may be used instead of the inner cover, if desired. The cover is flat, as illustrated, and is undoubtedly much better for this climate if deep as in Fig. 38. The extracting super may be either a duplicate of the brood chamber or a shallow body of the same kind. The comb honey super is made to take eight rows of four sections and, if an extracting frame be arranged to take the place of each outer row of sections, results will be more satisfactory. Full particulars of this hive are to be had from the Ministry of Agriculture, London, in Marketing Leaflet N. 79.

97. The "Langstroth" Hive (Fig. 39), popular in America and appreciated in these countries also, has the following measurements: The FLOORBOARD, measures $22'' \times 16\frac{1}{4}''$, is made of $\frac{7}{8}''$ tongued and grooved boards $15''$ long and in sufficient number to make up to $22''$ wide, nailed into the grooves of two runners, each measuring $22'' \times 2\frac{1}{8}'' \times \frac{7}{8}''$, and having the groove $\frac{7}{8}''$ wide and $\frac{1}{4}''$ deep, $\frac{7}{8}''$ from one edge. Back cleats $14\frac{1}{2}'' \times \frac{7}{8}''$ sq. and $14\frac{1}{2}'' \times \frac{7}{8}'' \times \frac{3}{8}''$ are nailed at the top and bottom of the back. The entrance block, which is removable, is a piece $14\frac{3}{8}'' \times \frac{7}{8}''$ sq. slotted to give a beeway $\frac{3}{8}''$ deep and $4''$ to $5''$ in length. The BROOD CHAMBER is $20''$ $\times 16\frac{1}{4}''$ outside and is made of timber $9\frac{9}{16}''$ wide and $\frac{7}{8}''$ thick, finished sizes. From the timber are cut two boards $14\frac{1}{2}''$ long and rebated along one edge $\frac{5}{8}''$ in the depth by $\frac{1}{2}''$ in the thickness, or proportionately deeper if metal runners be used. These two boards form the ends of the brood chamber and the rebates hold the lugs of the frames. The sides measure $20''$ long and are nailed on to the ends. Handholds can be worked in the sides if required. The INNER COVER is made of three tongued and grooved boards $\frac{3}{8}''$ thick and measuring in all $16\frac{1}{4}''$ wide by $20''$ long. Strips $\frac{7}{8}'' \times \frac{5}{16}''$ are nailed on one surface of the inner cover all round the edge to hold the boards together and provide a beeway, and a hole is cut in the centre board large enough to take a Porter Bee Escape. This hole can also be used as a feeding hole in spring or autumn and when not in use it is closed by laying over it a small piece of board or sacking. The SHALLOW FRAME SUPER is identical in size with the brood chamber but $5\frac{3}{4}''$ only in depth. The

ROOF measures $22\frac{1}{4}''$ × $18\frac{1}{4}''$ outside and is made of material $2\frac{1}{2}''$ wide by $\frac{7}{8}''$ thick.   The ends are cut $16\frac{1}{2}''$ long and the sides $22\frac{1}{4}''$ long, the sides being nailed on to the ends.   The framework thus formed is squared up (the test being that the

Fig. 39. LANGSTROTH HIVE.   Fig. 40. MODIFIED DADANT HIVE.

diagonal measure from one corner to the opposite one should be the same for each diagonal) and covered with boards $\frac{3}{8}''$ thick, which are nailed on.   The roof is then covered with sheet zinc which is folded over at least one inch on each side and tacked into place.

98. The "Modified Dadant" Hive (Fig. 40) is much esteemed by some of our most successful beekeepers.   The FLOORBOARD measures $22''$ × $18\frac{1}{2}''$, and is made of $\frac{7}{8}''$ tongued and grooved boards $17\frac{1}{4}''$ long and in sufficient number to make up to $22''$ wide, nailed into the grooves of two runners, each measuring $22''$ × $2\frac{1}{8}''$ × $\frac{7}{8}''$, and having the groove $\frac{7}{8}''$ wide and $\frac{1}{4}''$ deep $\frac{7}{8}''$ from one edge.   Back cleats $16\frac{3}{4}''$ × $\frac{7}{8}''$ sq. and $16\frac{3}{4}''$ × $\frac{7}{8}''$ × $\frac{3}{8}''$ are nailed at the top and bottom of the back.   The entrance block, which is removable, is a piece $16\frac{5}{8}''$ × $\frac{7}{8}''$ sq., slotted to give a beeway $\frac{3}{8}''$ deep and $4''$ to $5''$ in length.   The BROOD CHAMBER is $20''$ × $18\frac{1}{2}''$ outside and is made of timber $11''$ wide and $\frac{11}{16}$ $\frac{7}{8}''$ thick, finished sizes. From the timber are cut two boards $16\frac{3}{4}''$ long and rebated along one edge $\frac{5}{8}''$ in the depth by $\frac{1}{2}''$ in the thickness, or proportion-ately deeper if metal runners be used. These two boards form the ends of the brood chamber and the rebates hold the lugs of the frames. The sides measure 20'' long and are nailed on to the ends. Handholds can be worked in the sides if required. The INNER COVER is made of three tongued and grooved boards $\frac{3}{8}''$ thick and measuring in all $18\frac{1}{2}''$ wide by 20'' long. Strips $\frac{7}{8}''$ × $\frac{5}{16}''$ are nailed on one surface of the inner cover all round the edge to hold the boards together and provide a beeway, and a hole is cut in the centre board large enough to take a Porter Bee Escape. This hole can also be used as a feeding hole in spring or autumn, and when not in use it is closed by laying over it a small piece of board or sacking. The SHALLOW FRAME SUPER is identical in size with the brood chamber but $6\frac{5}{8}''$ only in depth. The ROOF measures $22\frac{1}{4}''$ × $20\frac{1}{2}''$ outside and is made of material $2\frac{1}{2}''$ wide by $\frac{7}{8}''$ thick. The ends are cut $18\frac{3}{4}''$ long and the sides $22\frac{1}{4}''$ long, the sides being nailed on to the ends. The framework thus formed is squared up (the test being that the diagonal measure from one corner to the opposite one should be the same for each diagonal) and covered with boards $\frac{3}{8}''$ thick which are nailed on. The roof is then covered with sheet zinc which is folded over at least one inch on each side and tacked into place. (Illus. pp. 199 and 293.) It is generally found advisable in these Islands to have the roofs of the American style hives made much deeper than shown in the illustration, and a depth of 9 inches is not excessive. The sides may be made of lighter wood, and should be made to fit over the hive very loosely to facilitate removal and to allow a space between roof and hive around the sides. This aids in keeping the hive dry in winter.

99. Observatory Hives.—The "Brice" Observatory Hive (Fig. 41) takes one frame below, and four sections of one shallow frame above. The

Fig. 41. " BRICE " OBSERVATORY HIVE.

sides are double-glazed, and are fitted with baize-covered shutters. A feeding arrangement is supplied at the side.

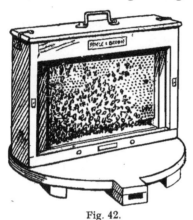

Fig. 42.
"NICOLSON" OBSERVATORY HIVE.

The floor is round, and can be revolved at will to permit dead bees to drop into a receptacle underneath. There are ventilators with shutters which work on pivots, an exit for the bees, and a strong strap with which to carry the hive. The "Nicolson" Observatory Hive (Fig. 42), (manufactured and supplied by Messrs. Steele and Brodie, Wormit, Fife), is made to take one standard frame, with lifts to accommodate a second standard frame or a shallow frame, or three sections. The sides are fitted with baize-covered shutters. Food is given from the top. A removable bottom-panel facilitates cleaning. The hive can be revolved without interfering with the bees' flight, and can be raised from its turnable and carried to another room, or even to a distant show. There are also a special research design which permits access to any part of the comb without disturbing the hive, and a third design to take three frames tiered above one another in summer and alongside one another in winter. Such observatory hives can be had to hold two " standard " frames and six sections. They are very suitable for use at exhibitions and shows, and are most useful to those who desire to study the hive-labours of the bee.

100. The Dummy or **Division Board** (Fig. 43) is made

Fig. 43.
DIVISION BOARD, OR DUMMY.

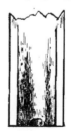

Fig. 44.
ENAMEL CLOTH, FOR END OF DUMMY.

to fit the body-box (91). It consists of a piece, $14\frac{5}{8}'' \times 8\frac{1}{2}''$ $\times \frac{3}{8}''$, with a top bar of $16'' \times \frac{7}{8}'' \times \frac{1}{2}''$, to run on the chamfered tops of the inner walls. It is, therefore, level with the tops of the frames. Two cleats, $8\frac{1}{2}'' \times 1\frac{1}{2}'' \times \frac{3}{8}''$, are nailed to the back to prevent warping. The Dummy is $\frac{1}{8}''$ less than the width of the body-box, and the ends are fitted with two slips of enamel cloth, $1\frac{1}{2}''$ wide, to fill the spaces, and to conserve heat (Fig. 44). The enamel cloth may be folded, and fastened between the plinths and the Dummy. The Dummy is less likely to be fastened at the ends by propolis when enamel cloth is used. Dummies which allow a $\frac{1}{4}''$, or a $\frac{3}{8}''$, space underneath are preferred by some experienced bee-keepers.

101. Use of the Dummy.—Dummies are used for enlarging

or contracting the brood nest as required (247). By their means the hive can be adjusted to the size of the colony, and frames can be removed and replaced with greater ease to the manipulator and with greater safety to the bees (191).

102. "Federation" Dummy.—Dummies can also be used for ventilating the brood nest during very warm weather—a necessary provision when it is desired to control the swarming propensity (228), and also for feeding, comb-cleaning, and other purposes (291). To supply this want, the "Federation" Dummy (Fig. 45) has been devised. It has a piece, $10\frac{1}{2}'' \times 4\frac{1}{2}''$, cut from the bottom. The vacancy may be filled with perforated zinc, or excluder zinc (117) as required. The plinths are rabbeted, and a slide, $11\frac{1}{2}'' \times 5''$, with ends rabbeted to correspond with the grooves in the plinths, slides between the latter, and can be raised, held at any point, and lowered as desired.

103. Sheet and Quilts are required upon the frames or supers to preserve heat, to prevent draught, and to keep the bees from ascending into the roof. The sheet is made of bed ticking or unbleached calico. The quilts should be of felt, carpet, or other warm material. The sheet and quilts should be large enough to cover the interior of the body-box when they are placed upon the frames. From the sheet a circular piece may be all but cut out from the centre so that it can be turned back when feeding is in progress (127) to give the bees access to the feeder; at other times it can be restored to its original position. The sheet, lying as it does upon the frames, should not be made of woollen material, because bees are apt to catch their claws (34) in such stuff, and that irritates them. The sheet will lie flat upon the frames if put on damp in the first instance. In summer, a sheet of American cloth, enamelled side down, may with advantage be used instead of a sheet of ticking; but at other seasons it is advisable that the covering should be of porous material to permit evaporation of the moisture of the hive. Straw mats or chaff cushions are sometimes used on the quilts. In winter, it is useful to cover the brood-nest and quilts with an empty super or other bottomless box, having a piece of canvas or calico tacked underneath, and filled with cork-dust, chaff, or other warm material (434).

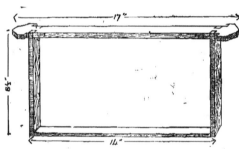

Fig. 46. THE " STANDARD " FRAME.
" ABBOTT " WIDE-ENDED PATTERN.

104. Frames.— The frame which is here described has been, for some years, recognized in these countries as the " standard " frame (Fig. 46). It is made for use in a hive the internal measurements of which have been given above, and in accordance with the known instincts of bees as applied to the building of their combs. We observe that worker comb, i.e., comb in which worker bees are reared, is $\frac{7}{8}''$ thick; the frame is therefore made $\frac{7}{8}''$ wide.

The spaces between sealed brood combs are about $\frac{3}{8}''$ to $\frac{5}{8}''$; the frame is therefore intended to provide a $\frac{5}{8}''$ space between the combs. This is effected by shoulders on the top bars of the frames, or by the use of " metal ends," by which, when the frames are pressed together

Fig. 46a. " W.B.C." METAL END SPACER.

in the hive, the necessary space is provided. The frame measures 14″ long × 8½″ deep. The top bar is commonly made 17″ long × $\frac{3}{8}''$ thick; the side bars are 8½″ long × $\frac{1}{4}''$ thick; the width of all being very usually, $\frac{7}{8}''$; but in Ireland the top bar is generally made ½″ thick. It is quite an advantage in all frames to have the top bars a good deal wider than the $\frac{7}{8}''$, and a width of $1\frac{1}{16}''$ or $1\frac{1}{8}''$ is liked by many bee-keepers. The four pieces are made to dovetail into one another, and are usually sold in the flat. When put together they should be fastened at the corners with four tacks or fine wire nails. Underneath the top bar are two grooves, the centre groove to hold an edge of a sheet of foundation (125), and the side groove to take a thin wedge supplied with the frame, by which the foundation is held in the centre groove. Frames are now sold at prices so low that it is not advisable for beekeepers to manufacture frames for themselves. It is necessary that the frame be put together perfectly square. There are also in use frames having a saw-cut along and through the top bar—a happy home for the worms of wax moth (430)—into which cuts the sheets of foundation are fastened (125), and frames with plain top bars to which the foundation is attached by melted wax (125).

105. Various Sizes of Frames.—Frames are used of larger size for the brood nest by some beekeepers, and it is claimed for the larger frames that they give better results. The practice generally is to use the " standard " frame, as described. It is of importance that, whatever size be adopted, it should be uniformly used in the apiary, because there is a decided advantage in being able to interchange frames In America the popular frame is larger than our standard frame, and many beekeepers at home hold that our standard should be enlarged. The Langstroth frame, in use in America, has the following dimen-sions: Top bar, $19\frac{1}{8}''$ long × $\frac{3}{4}''$ thick; side

Fig. 47.

UPPER : LANGSTROTH FRAME.

LOWER : MODIFIED DADANT FRAME.

bars, $9\frac{1}{8}''$ long × $\frac{3}{8}''$ thick; bottom bar, $17\frac{5}{8}''$ long × $\frac{3}{8}''$ thick. The Modified Dadant frame is similar in all respects to the Langstroth, except that it measures $11\frac{1}{4}''$ in depth and is spaced $1\frac{1}{2}''$ from centre to centre. Super, or " Shallow " frames, for use in extracting supers (116) are in very general use. They differ from the standard frame in being only $5\frac{1}{2}''$ deep, the super being 6″ deep. It is claimed for them that they are more readily taken to by the bees in supers than are standard frames, as they increase the accommodation above the brood nest more

SUNLIGHT AND SHADE. AN OUT-APIARY.

Photo by *A. S. Rowse.*

gradually; but it is an objection to them that they are not interchangeable with standard frames.

106. The "Claustral" Detention Chamber.—This appliance, which was illustrated and described in the *Irish Bee Journal* for October and November, 1906, was devised by M. l'abbé Gouttefangeas, whose book, "Ruche Claustrante et Méthode Claustrale," appeared in the preceding year.

The chamber (as shown p. 74) may be attached to, or may form part of any hive. It is closed by the alighting board which is hinged for the purpose and made to fit perfectly light-proof, forming the dark ante-chamber, or cloister. Two zinc aerating tubes, 1" in diameter and two feet long, with revolving hoods on top and air holes within the chamber, provide sufficient ventilation. The bees, shut in from light and liberty, may be safely confined in winter (435), or during manipulation of other stocks, or when stocks are being moved from place to place (167); bees in nuclei can be retained (303), robbing can be effectually dealt with (344), and the danger of spring or autumn dwindling can be reduced (433). This appliance is now rarely used.

CHAPTER IX.

APPLIANCES FOR SUPERING.

107. Supering.—The term " supering " is applied to the use of sections and frames above the brood nest, in order to

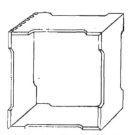

obtain surplus honey (268) of a marketable quality, and free from the mixtures of larval remains and pollen which used to characterize the honey offered for sale before modern beekeeping introduced better methods.

108. The Section (Fig. 48) is a case of bass wood, $4\frac{1}{4}''$ × $4\frac{1}{4}''$ × $1\frac{1}{2}''$ to $2''$ × $\frac{1}{8}''$. It is sold flat, in one piece,

Fig. 48. THE SECTION.

dovetailed at the ends, and with three V-shaped cuts across the wood (Fig. 49) to permit the folding of the section. Beeways are provided by reducing the width of the wood to $1\frac{5}{8}''$, so that when the sections are pressed together in the crate (**111**) the bees can pass in and out of them.

109. Sections of Various Kinds.—Sections are made to hold approximately 1 lb.; that is to say, the completed section is a nominal 1-lb. retail package. It should weigh, wood, honey and wax, as nearly as possible 16 ozs. It has been found that a section measuring $4\frac{1}{4}''$ × $4\frac{1}{4}''$ and $1\frac{7}{8}''$ wide will, if well filled, weigh 1 lb. This is the measurement of the section used all over America and other foreign countries. In Great Britain the $4\frac{1}{4}''$ section is usually made $1\frac{15}{16}''$ wide, and in Ireland a $2''$ section has for long been popular. A "tall" section is also used a little in these countries and is quite popular in America. It measures $5''$ × $4''$ and virtually always made

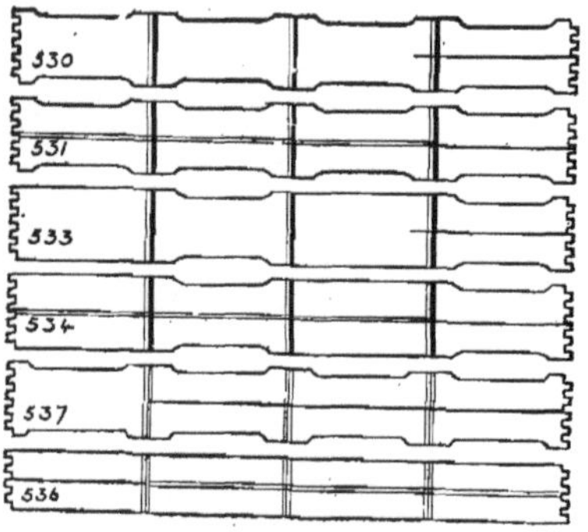

Fig. 49. VARIOUS SECTIONS.

without beeways and 1⅜″ wide. It also holds approximately 1 lb. The 2″ section is definitely too wide as it may weigh as much as 18 or even 19 ozs., and this extra weight has, in practice, to be given away. Sections also differ in the manner in which they are designed according to the method by which the foundation (118) is to be fitted into them. They may be made without any split or groove so that the fixing must be done by melting the edge of the foundation and immediately applying it to the section (270), or one side may have a cut along the centre of the top to grip the foundation when it is inserted; or three sides may be divided in much the same way, so that three sides of the foundation are secured and three sections can be fitted at one operation (271). Sections differ also in the matter of their beeways. There are four-way and two-way sections, which have beeways cut in all four sides (Fig. 48) and in the top and bottom only respectively. There is no perceptible difference in the working of them by bees, but the two-way are greatly to be preferred because they are more easily cleaned and are also more readily wrapped for market (322). Sections without beeways are used; but are not popular in these countries. With them the beeways are provided by the use of a special separator. In England, the section with a groove around inside three of its sides and a split along the top is popular, while in Ireland the three-side-split section is almost universally used.

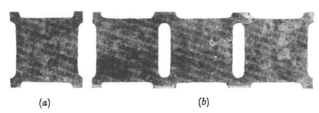

(a)   (b)

Fig. 50. (a) SHORT SEPARATOR. (b) LONG SLOTTED SEPARATOR FOR FOUR-WAY SECTIONS.

110. The Separator is a sheet of zinc, tin, or very thin wood, used between the rows of sections to secure even surfaces to the combs and to prevent the bees from drawing out the cells beyond the edges of the sections. Short separators (Fig. 50, *a*) are 4¼″ × 4¼″ × ⅛″, or 1/16″ *i.e.*, square with the sections. Long separators (Fig. 50, *b*) are 12¾″ × 4¼″ × ⅛″ or 1/16″ covering three sections. There are also separators to cover four sections. Beeways are cut out to permit the bees to pass freely from one section to another. The long separators are easier to handle, and those made of zinc or tin will, with ordinary care, last for many years. Wooden separators, being so thin, require careful handling to avoid breakages.

111. The Comb Honey Super is commonly known as a " Rack " in Great Britain and as a " Crate " in Ireland. It is a bottomless box (Fig. 51) usually constructed to hold 21 $4\frac{1}{4}'' \times 4\frac{1}{4}''$ sections in seven rows of three; but in some hives, including the " National " (96), there are four sections to a row

Fig. 51. SECTION CRATE.

and the super may contain 28 or 32 sections. The latter is the case with the " National " hive. The common 21-section super is made of two pieces $17'' \times 4\frac{3}{8}'' \times \frac{5}{8}''$, and two $14\frac{1}{8}'' \times 4\frac{3}{8}'' \times \frac{5}{8}''$ dovetailed together. Its internal measurements are, therefore, $15\frac{3}{4}'' \times 12\frac{7}{8}'' \times 4\frac{3}{8}''$. The $\frac{1}{8}''$ extra in depth is intended to allow for shrinkage, for it is of great importance that the crate, when in use, should not be in the least degree

shallower than the sections; otherwise, when crates are tiered up on the hives (282), the weight resting upon the lower sections tends to depress the laths on which they stand and to destroy the bee space, thus leading to serious mischief (88). Underneath, a frame

Fig. 52. SECTION CRATE. *(For 28 sections)*.

of $\frac{1}{4}''$ laths is placed. These carry the sections and separators, and when the crate is placed upon the frames, the laths provide the necessary bee space between the frames and the sections. It follows that if the laths are less than $\frac{1}{4}''$ or more than $\frac{3}{8}''$ thick, the bees will fasten the sections to the tops of the frames and serious difficulty will arise when it becomes necessary to remove the crate (282).

112. The Divisional Crate (Fig. 53) consists of three single crates, each holding seven sections. It is used towards the close of the honey flow, to secure the perfecting of unfinished sections, when the bees would not have time, or honey, to fill a larger number (282).

113. Observatory Crates (Fig. 54) are constructed so as to hold sections, separators, and a glass follower, with or without springs. A door is made in the end of the crate, and when it is opened the sections can be seen and an opinion can be formed as to the state of the work in the crate.

Fig. 53. DIVISIONAL CRATE.   Fig. 54. OBSERVATORY CRATE.

114. The Follower is a board 4⅜″ wide by the length of the row of sections. It is inserted in the super immediately after the last row of sections to press them together. It is kept in its place by springs or wedges (Figs. 51, 52 and 53).

115. The Hanging Crate, or section frame (Fig. 55) is used for holding six sections in the body box, or super box

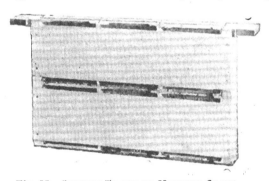

Fig. 55 SECTION FRAME OR HANGING CRATE.

Separators are attached to the frame on both sides to prevent the drawing out of the cells beyond the width of the sections. These crates are used early in the season, near the brood nest, to secure " bait " sections for the first crates, so as to induce the bees to occupy the latter (279). Towards the close of the season, unfinished sections, taken from the upper crates, may be given below in these frames to be completed (282).

116. The Super Box (Fig. 56) is used for holding frames above the body box, or brood chamber. It is a bottomless box, the same width internally as the body box, but varying in length according to the

number, and in depth according to the depth, of the frames to be used in it. If for standard frames (104) it should be 9″ deep; if for shallow frames of 5½″ depth (105), it should be 6″ deep. The sides, to carry the frames, are chamfered in the same way as are the inner walls of the brood chamber (91) and are ½″ shallower than the ends. Two pieces, 2″ × ⅜″, rabbeted 1″ × ¼″, are

Fig. 56. SUPER BOX
WITH " ABBOTT " FRAMES,

nailed, one on each side, their upper edges being level with the tops of the ends of the box. These pieces enclose the ends of the top bars of the frames, preventing them from shifting; they conserve the heat, and are useful also as handles.

117. The Excluder (Fig. 57) is used to prevent the queen from reaching and depositing

eggs in the sections, or frames, placed above the brood chamber, and for shutting off the queen and drones from any part of the hive in which their presence is not desired (102). It is a sheet of zinc large enough to cover the tops of the frames, when used to exclude from the upper storey, and perforated with holes which permit the worker bees to pass, but exclude the queen and drones.

Fig. 57. EXCLUDER.

In practice it is found to offer some obstruction to the workers, and it is rapidly falling into disuse among beekeepers who work for section honey.   But it has still its admirers among experienced apiarists, who claim that the advantage of having

Fig. 57b.   WIRE EXCLUDER.

the sections protected from the queen's attentions more than compensates for any possible obstruction to the workers (281).   Where super boxes (116) with frames are employed for extracting purposes, an excluder below the super box is generally used.   It is important to arrange the excluder with its openings running across, and not parallel with, the frames, thus giving the bees freer access to the supers. New excluders should be rubbed with emery cloth, to remove the rough edges of the openings. The Waldron Wire Queen Excluder (Fig. 57 b), opposing no obstruction to worker bees, has come rapidly into favour. It is framed and provides a bee space by which the whole area of the appliance becomes available, with complete ease of access to the supers.   The wires are firmly soldered to, and securely held by, cross girders, so that no uneven spacings of the wires may permit a queen bee to pass through.

Fig. 57c.   BURGESS WOOD AND WIRE EXCLUDER.

CHAPTER X.

COMB FOUNDATION.

118. Use of Foundation.—No less important than the introduction of the movable frame, the invention of foundation (Fig. 58) marked a distinct advance in the methods of practical beekeeping, simplified the management of frame hives, and effected a substantial economy in the expenses of working. It has already been pointed out (88) that the great advantage

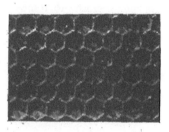

Fig. 58.   COMB FOUNDATION.

of the modern movable-comb hive depends upon its frames, in use, being really movable. If bees are placed in hives fitted with empty frames, they will build their combs in the frames, but at such angles, and in such manner, as frequently to fasten the frames together and to render them immovable in the hive, thus defeating the object in view. If strips of wax, as " starters," be fixed below the top bars of the frames, the bees will begin their combs at the starters, but will sometimes build them so irregularly that, here and there, comb will be joined to comb and only a few, if any, of the combs will be perfectly even and movable. In both cases there will be constructed so large a proportion of drone cells that the drones reared in such cells may be sufficiently numerous to consume an appreciable part of the surplus honey which it is the aim of the beekeeper to secure for himself (205). To obviate those difficulties; to enable the beekeeper to exercise complete control over the work in the hive; and to constitute apiculture as a remunerative occupation, it was necessary that some means should be devised to compel the bees (1) to build straight, separate combs, hanging evenly and parallel, each within its own frame; (2) to construct such cells, worker or drone, and in such proportion, as the owner may desire; and (3) to apply to the manufacture of new combs, wax which had been used for the same purpose again and again, with " cappings " (77) and odd scraps that, otherwise, might be wasted, or sold below their real value, thus preventing an extravagant consumption of honey for the secretion of wax, and an extravagant waste of time on the part of the bees during the processes of wax-secretion and comb building (78).

119. Invention of Foundation.—The application by Lang-stroth, in 1851, of the movable frame principle (85) made the construction of suitable combs more than ever necessary; and, six years later (1857), Mehring, a German, of Frankenthal, produced a sheet of wax on which the shape of cells was stamped, to serve as a "foundation" for the bees to build upon. Improvements upon Mehring's invention were designed to form upon the foundation the beginnings of the cell walls; and, in 1876, A. I. Root, of Medina, Ohio, U.S.A., constructed a roller mill with embossed cylinders capable of turning out foundation in continuous sheets, and with the formation of the cells, as it is now produced. E. B. Weed subsequently devised the rolls which impress the foundation that is called by his name. These rolls are faced with type heads, and give absolute similarity throughout the sheets.

120. Varieties of Foundation.—Foundation is now supplied of various sizes, both of sheets and cells, and of various thicknesses. "Medium brood," and "Thin brood" ("Weed"), in sheets to fit the standard frame, have eight sheets and ten sheets respectively to the pound weight, and are made either with worker or drone cells. "Thin super" (Fig. 59), and "Extra thin super" ("Weed"), in sheets to fill three sections each, have twenty-five to thirty-three and thirty to thirty-six sheets respectively to the pound weight. Brood foundation is used in frames in the brood nest and super box. Super foundation is used in sections, and is made thin enough to avoid, as far as possible, the unpleasantness of a heavy mid-rib in comb which is intended to be eaten (109).

Fig. 59. SUPER FOUNDATION.

121. Advantages of Foundation.—The advantages secured to beekeepers by the use of foundation are many :—(1) When whole sheets are used in frames and sections, the combs built upon them are perfectly straight, so that they can be moved about in the hive (118) and transferred from hive to hive, or from crate to crate as required. (2) The combs built upon worker foundation are composed generally of worker cells,

so that by the employment of this kind of foundation the
rearing of drones can be limited (205), which is always a useful
power in the hands of the beekeeper. (3) All the wax produced;
all old combs, scraps, and cappings removed for extracting
purposes (289) may be given back to the bees in the shape of
foundation, thus effecting a very considerable economy both
of wax and time. For it has been shown that the amount of
honey consumed by bees in the production of wax has a value
far in excess of the wax produced, and this loss may be greatly
reduced by the use of foundation which enables bees to produce
comb at a very considerably reduced cost. The use of full
sheets of foundation at all times and in both sections and
frames is to-day a universally recognised rule of good and
profitable management in all modern apiaries, and every beekeeper who wishes to produce the maximum crops of honey in
the most profitable manner must always make the utmost use
of foundation.

122. **Adulteration.**—It should be stated here that foundation, in common with so many other articles of commerce, has
not escaped the attention of the adulterator, and that it is
very necessary to see that the foundation used in the hive is
pure. That which is adulterated with paraffin wax, or with
ordinary grease or fat, will often be refused by the bees, or if
built upon, will lack the strength to endure the heat of the
hive in summer and will stretch and break down, in either case
imposing much trouble and loss upon the beekeeper. Foundation may be tested for adulteration with tallow, by the smell
when broken; and for adulteration with mineral wax, by
chewing for a few minutes, when if it be pure, it will crumble
in the mouth, and if adulterated with paraffin or ceresin (69),
will adhere in mass, like chewing-gum. This test is, however,
not always reliable, and some more accurate test is necessary to
enable every beekeeper to prove for himself the quality of the
foundation which he buys. If a tumbler, wine glass, or wide-
mouthed bottle be half filled with water, and a small piece of
pure wax, such as may generally be found somewhere in a hive,
be dropped into the water, it will float, because the specific
gravity of the wax (960-970) is less than the specific gravity of
the water (1,000). If now a small quantity of alcohol be slowly
poured into the vessel until the piece of wax no longer floats,
but just sinks to the bottom, and no more alcohol be added than
that which is just sufficient to permit the wax to descend from
the surface, then the water will have been brought to the same
specific gravity as that of pure wax. But wax that is adulterated
with paraffin or ceresin is of lighter specific gravity than that

of pure beeswax, and if dropped into the vessel it will float where pure beeswax will not. This test is inexpensive and sufficiently accurate to serve for practical purposes in the examination of foundation for adulteration with mineral wax. The liquid may be kept in a glass-stoppered bottle for future tests.

123. Change of Colour.—When no longer fresh, foundation may become darker in colour and so brittle that it will break if tested by bending. Warming it slightly before a fire will improve it, and will partially restore its original colour.

124. Quantity Required.—1½ lbs. of medum-weight brood foundation will about fill 11 standard frames (104), 1 lb. of thin super foundation will fill 75, and of extra thin super, 100 sections. Thin brood foundation, though popular on account of one pound filling a 10-frame brood-chamber, is less satisfactory for frames than medium which forms a stronger base for the combs; but for sections the foundation used cannot be too thin, since in the latter case the public consume both wax and honey, and a thick base is a serious detriment to the quality of comb-honey.

125. Fixing Foundation.—Foundation is usually fixed in sections (270) by means of the splits in the tops, or in the tops and sides (109); in frames, the upper edge of the sheet is caught either in a saw-cut in the top bar, or by the groove and wedge already described (104). When full sheets are used in frames, and especially when intended for extracting purposes, the foundation must always be wired to the frames (276). Formerly foundation was fixed with melted wax, but this method, requiring more time and labour, is rapidly falling into disuse. However the fastening may be made, it is generally considered important that the foundation be fixed right side up (Figs. 58, 59, 60). It has been

a   b

Fig. 60. FOUNDATION.

a, RIGHT.   b, WRONG

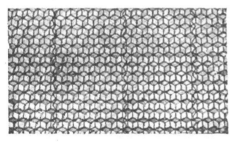

Fig. 60b. DADANT'S WIRED FOUNDATION.

observed by Huber, and Cheshire, and indeed by everyone who has carefully examined a honey comb, that it is customary for bees to build their cells with two of the six sides perpendicular, thus— and in this position foundation should always be used (Fig. 60, *a*). If the sheet be fixed the other way, the impress of the cells will be out of form, thus— and this is not desirable (Fig. 60, *b*). Foundation of various makes, already wired and ready for fixing in frames, is now on the market (Fig. 60b). It saves the beekeeper a great deal of trouble and tends to the production of more perfect, and more economical combs (275) than can be relied upon by the ordinary methods of wiring (126). See also illustration, p. 197, and Fig. 63.

126. Wiring Appliances are used for fastening foundation securely in frames to prevent it from sagging when the heat of the hive softens the wax and the weight of clustering bees tends to bear it down. Combs which may some day find their way to the extractor (143) should always be wired in the frames, lest the centrifugal force employed to throw out the honey should break the comb. The Wiring Board

Fig. 61. WIRING BOARD.

(Fig. 61) is a piece of $\frac{3}{8}''$ wood, cut so as to fit inside the frame. Two projecting pieces are nailed on the back. The illustration shows both sides of the appliance as used (A) for shallow frames (105) and (B) for standard frames (104). Holes are bored in the bars of the frame and No. 30 tinned wire is drawn

Fig. 62. WOIBLET SPUR-EMBEDDER.

through and tightened (275). It is then embedded in the foundation by a heated embedder, which may be a strong bradawl, having a groove cut in its edge. Drawn along the wire it presses it into the foundation, at the same time melting sufficient wax to cover the wire (276). The Woiblet Spur embedder (Fig. 62) has a grooved wheel to act upon the wire. Extensive beekeepers and some others generally use an electric embedder for this purpose. The illustration (Fig. 64) is of that supplied by Messrs. Steele and Brodie. It should be worked from a battery and not from dry cells, and an old motor car battery which has two or three sound cells is as good as any. The embedder is connected up and its prongs are laid on the wire in the following order—1 and 2, 2 and 3, 3 and 4, and the whole wire may be thus embedded in a second of time. Lighting current may be used for this purpose if a small transformer be installed. Other electric embedders may be had that use a higher voltage and embed the whole length of a wire at once.

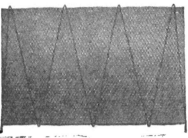

Fig. 63. LEE'S WIRED FOUNDATION

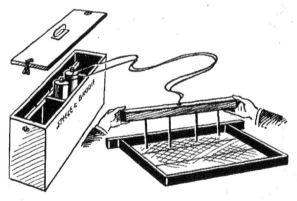

Fig. 64. ELECTRIC EMBEDDER.

CHAPTER XI.

APPLIANCES FOR FEEDING BEES.

127. Feeding.—Bees require to be fed when their stores run short; and at other times, also, it is found to be profitable to supply artificial food (345). For this purpose, it is necessary to have feeders which will supply the food in the proper quantities, and in the proper position, so that the bees may use it for the purpose intended, and may have convenient access to it, without the danger of setting up robbing (341) by attracting stranger bees to the sweets supplied.

Fig. 65.   ECONOMIC FEEDER.

128. The "Economic" Feeder (Fig. 65) is an ordinary syrup tin, with a lever-top lid in which holes are punched. It is inverted upon the frames direct, or upon a single stage of ¼″ wood through which a hole has been cut to give access to the bees. When the feeder is being removed, a corner of the carbolic cloth (136), or a separator (110), may be slipped under it to keep the bees down. Ordinary lever-lid honey tins of 7 lbs. or more capacity make excellent feeders and are very cheap.

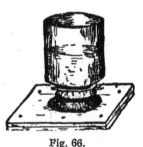

Fig. 66.
BOTTLE AND STAGE FEEDER.

129. The Bottle and Stage Feeder (Fig. 66) can be put together at a trifling expense. It consists of a wide-mouthed bottle, or jar, with a piece of coarse calico tied over the mouth, and two squares of ¼″ wood. In one square a round opening is cut large enough to admit the mouth of the bottle, and in the other square an opening of ¾″, or 1″ smaller in diameter. The squares are then nailed evenly one upon the other. This stage is placed upon the tops of the frames. When the bottle is being removed, a piece of zinc, or cardboard, may be slipped between it and the opening in the stage, to prevent the bees from escaping upwards.

130. The Graduated Bottle and Stage Feeder (Fig. 67) is made upon the same principles with those already described,

but the screw-cap and the stage are so arranged that by turning the bottle round, the supply of syrup can be increased or diminished between 1 and 9 holes, or can be cut off altogether. A pointer attached to the screw-cap, and figures upon the stage indicating the number of holes exposed, enable the supply to be regulated as desired. This feeder can be used for slow or rapid feeding according to the season.

Fig. 67.
GRADUATED FEEDER.

131. Slow and Rapid Feeders (Figs. 68, 69), capable of holding 1 quart or more of syrup, are used chiefly in the autumn when it becomes necessary to feed up the stocks rapidly so that they may be able to store and seal the syrup before the cold weather sets in—wintering bees upon unsealed stores being very likely to lead to dysentery (415). The feeder (Fig. 68) is

Fig. 68. ROUND TIN FEEDER.

Fig. 69. "ALEXANDER" FEEDER.

a round tin box, with a movable lid, and a flange round the bottom to provide the necessary bee space between the frames and the feeder when in use. A round hole in the bottom permits the bees to pass up a funnel into the feeder. A wooden float surrounds the funnel, and outside this is a tin case with a glass top. When the lid is removed and syrup is poured into the box, the wooden float rises. The bees pass out upon the float to reach the syrup, and can be seen through the glass top of the inner case. The "Alexander" Feeder (Fig. 69), described and illustrated in *Gleanings*, is attached to the floor board, and the hive is drawn back to cover it (94). All that is necessary is to lift a block off the projecting end, pour in syrup, and replace the block.

132. The Canadian Feeder (Fig. 70), capable of holding six to ten pounds of syrup, is used when it is desired to give

food rapidly, or to have the winter food for a number of colonies stored and sealed by one stock (349). In the latter case the stock is supplied with drawn out combs, and the feeder is refilled as fast as it is emptied, the combs being removed when sealed and their places supplied

Fig. 70. CANADIAN FEEDER.

by empty combs. By setting apart a stock for this purpose sufficient sealed stores can be provided to supply many colonies with winter food. This feeder has a tin lining, and is fitted with a wooden construction to give the bees foot-hold. This latter can be removed when it is desired to insert honey in comb, either for feeding or for cleaning up purposes. There is a double-hung lid, so that the contents can be seen and the feeder replenished as required.

133. The Miller Feeder (Fig. 71) is much in use in the United States and by some of the most prominent honey-

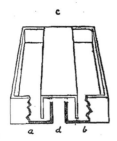

Fig. 71.
THE MILLER FEEDER.

Fig. 72. DIVISION BOARD FEEDER.

producers in Great Britain and Ireland. The late Mr. A. I. Root described it as very excellent, and said: "We use it almost exclusively for feeding up colonies for winter." It holds 25 lbs. of syrup. The illustration shows how the feeder is constructed; *a* and *b* are two reservoirs into which the syrup is poured; *c* is a loose cover of the partition. In the sketch the end is cut to show the construction. The feeder being placed in position on the frames, the bees ascend the passage *d* to reach the syrup, of which up to 25 lbs. may be supplied at one time as required. This feeder may be used as described above (132), if so desired, to provide sealed stores for many colonies by the labours of one.

Fig. 72a. THE BROTHER ADAM FEEDER.

134. The Division Board Feeder (Fig. 72) is a device for giving food in the body of the hive. It is made the same length and depth as an ordinary Division Board or Dummy (100). The top bar is fastened with screws so that it may be removed for cleaning purposes. The food is poured through a hole in the top bar, close to which hole a partition, running from within $\frac{1}{8}''$ of the bottom to the top, shuts the bees off from the hole. A $\frac{1}{4}''$ slit in one side, near the top, admits the bees to the syrup.

134A. "The Adam Type Feeders."—Since the more general use of hives of the single-walled type commonly used in America, Australia, etc. (96, 97, 98), an appropriate kind of feeder has been introduced in more than one form. The basic principle of these feeders is that they cover the entire hive in the same way as does an inner cover or crown board. The Miller feeder (Fig. 71) is so arranged to fit the small eight-frame Langstroth hive used by him, but it can just as easily be made to cover any other size of hive. The " Adam " feeder (Fig. 72a) is on a similar principle, but the access to it is differently arranged, and in its case there is some patented plan of allowing the bees only very limited access in order to produce what is known as slow stimulative feeding. When these feeders are used with a fairly deep flat roof (Fig. 38) they are very satisfactory indeed as they conserve the heat generated by the bees in an effective manner. They are quite easily made at home by any amateur who can use carpenters' tools.

CHAPTER XII.

APPLIANCES FOR SUBDUING AND HANDLING BEES.

135. **The Smoker** (Fig. 73) is employed for subduing bees, and is a most useful appliance in an apiary (180). A puff or two of smoke blown in at the entrance frightens the bees, and causes them to fill themselves with honey, in which condition they are not inclined to give trouble (176). The smoker has a bellows, a fuel box, and a removable nozzle. A roll of dry brown paper, a piece of rag, or a piece of dry, rotten wood, is lighted and placed in the fuel box, lighted end down; the nozzle is put on, and if the smoker be left standing nozzle up it will draw like a chimney and the fuel will keep alight. A still more satisfactory method is to light a small quantity of pine wood shavings and, having by means of the bellows blown them to a blaze in the smoker, place a roll of coarse, soft sacking (burlap) on the burning shavings, blowing the bellows vigorously. To extinguish the fuel the smoker is placed on its side and/or, the nozzle corked with a bunch of twisted up grass. Smoker bellows are easily repaired in a very satisfactory manner by means of a sheet of rubber from an old and rather thin car tyre tube or from the tube of a motor-cycle. The metal parts should be occasionally scraped out to prevent accumulation of scale inside. The type of smoker illustrated (Fig. 73b) is much preferred by many as it has a much more roomy barrel and will burn far longer. Its bent nozzle is found by the larger bee-farmers to be altogether more convenient also. It is usually furnished with a hook on the bellows by means of which it can be hung on the hive side during manipulations.

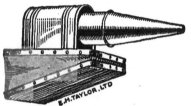

Fig. 73.   Smoker.

136. **The Carbolic Cloth** is also a subduer of bees, and by some is preferred to the smoker. In certain operations it is somewhat easier to work with than is the smoker, and once prepared (185), it requires little or no attention during a long period. Ticking, calico, or muslin, 20″ × 18″, may be used, with (if preferred) a hem on one 18″ edge to take an 18″ lath.

A solution of Calvert's No. 5 Carbolic Acid, one part to ten parts of water, is prepared, and with it the cloth is thoroughly saturated. A reader of this Guide, writing from Manchuria,

points out that Calvert's Carbolic Acid is unknown in distant lands whither the Guide finds its way— the " Practical Bee Guide " has been picked up and purchased in a book-shop in Bagdad, and has been read in Central Africa and in the midst of the Polar pack-ice of Franz Josef Land (see page 215).— The correspondent uses a 2 *per cent*. mixture of a solution containing 1 part water to 10 parts

Fig. 73b. NEW BINGHAM SMOKER.

carbolic and he finds it quite satisfactory. If the cloth, when not in use, be kept in a close-shut tin box, it will retain its objectionable smell for a long time. The solution should be shaken before being used. (Recipe **417**, page 281).

137. Use of Veils.—The veil (Fig. 74) is used to protect the face and neck from stings. Although bees in a hive may

be thoroughly subdued by smoke or carbolic fumes, an occasional bee outside the hive, which has not been within reach of the subduing agent, may develop a warlike spirit sufficiently active to be taken account of (**178**). Many beekeepers, from oft familiarity, hold stings in contempt, no matter where applied, becoming immune to the poison when thoroughly inoculated with it. But others, and especially beginners, are wise in having veils for the protection

Fig. 74. NET VEIL.

of the face and because of the confidence they give during the manipulation of unamiable stocks. The veil may be made of black netting, or of white netting if a piece of black be added for the front, it being easier to see through black netting than through white. A piece of netting 48″ × 24″ will make an ample veil, and 36″ × 18″ will make a veil sufficiently large for most purposes. The ends are sewn together and a hem is run on one edge to carry a piece of elastic arranged to grip tightly round the crown of the hat to be used. If worn as in the illustration (Fig. 74), the free end being carefully tucked in and the coat buttoned, it will be next to impossible for a bee to sting the face. Some veils have a piece of elastic round the lower edge also as an additional protection; it closes round the collar, effectually preventing bees from crawling under.

138. **A Lady's Veil** may be made larger, for wear with a broad-brimmed hat. A strip of broad elastic is sewn in the lower edge so that it will fit over the shoulders and two straps, passing under the arms and buttoning in front, keep the veil in position. Ladies sometimes wear overalls to which the veil is fastened; the overalls are tied or strapped round the waist (178). Mosquito netting makes an excellent lady's veil.

139. **The Wire-Cloth Veil** (Fig. 75) is not so comfortable as a net veil, but it has the advantage that the wind cannot blow it against the tip of the nose, or chin, at the precise moment

when an aggressive bee is seeking a point of attack. On the other hand, it is not easy to carry about, and when midges are worrying one's face it is exasperating to be unable to get at them with the fingers. Net and elastic are used round the crown of the hat, and from the rim down are two pieces of wire cloth 18″ × 7″, joined at the ends by two pieces of netting 4″ × 7″, allowing the veil to fold flat when not in use.

Fig.75.   WIRE-CLOTH VEIL.

The veil is carried down a few inches more with netting which may be either tucked under the coat or caught round the collar by elastic.

140. **Use of Gloves.**—Among experienced beekeepers gloves are held in ill-repute, as clumsy and unnecessary things. Some will almost go so far as to hold that nothing that is accomplished with the aid of gloves can properly be called beekeeping. During many years it was impossible for anyone who covered his hands to qualify as an Expert under the Rules

of the Irish Beekeepers' Association and, quite wisely, under the existing Rules, a candidate for the Association's Expert Certificate is penalised at his examination if he resorts to the use of gloves during manipulations. Nevertheless, gloves, though they be " clumsy things," are in some cases indis-

HANDLING BEES. VEILS, SMOKER, HIVE-TOOL AND GLOVES.

Photo by   *A. S. Rowse*

pensable, and, though they be sneered at by veterans, are often a source of confidence, and, as such, a valuable assistance to beginners (178).

There is another virtue in gloves; they keep the hands more or less free from propolis (80) which is a material of an extremely sticky nature, and very difficult to remove from the hands.

" There are constitutions that cannot endure stings without much pain and inconvenience, and occasionally even positive danger. There are ladies, and strong men also, to whom a 100 *per cent.* hypodermic injection of formic acid, accompanied by the angry buzz of a vicious bee, is always a hateful experience; and there are many who will agree as to the clumsiness of gloves, but who would not dare, without such protection, to engage in the practice of beekeeping at all."—J. G. D. in the *Irish Bee Journal.*

It would be absurd to dissuade such persons from beekeeping for no other reason than that they manipulate with gloves. It must, however, be said that some of the most delicate operations, such as picking a queen off the comb, and wing clipping (222), cannot be carried out as neatly, nor always as successfully, with gloves, and that, generally speaking, the wiser course is to discontinue the use of gloves as soon as possible. There is some authority for the statement that if the hands and wrists be dipped in dilute Izal, bees will be less disposed to sting them. It is now known that bee venom is not formic acid as was at one time supposed, but is akin to snake poison.

141. Various Gloves.—Thick woollen gloves, covered with a pair of white cotton gloves long enough in the wrist to run up on the cuff, are sometimes used; but they are really " clumsy things," and are difficult to work with (178). If soaked in water immediately beforehand, the bees will not be inclined to sting them, and if stung, their thickness prevents the sting from entering the flesh. India rubber gloves are good protectors and are not inconvenient to work with. Ordinary leather gloves may, sometimes, be made to serve the purpose; they are steeped for a minute or two in hot water; are then put upon the hands; and while being held before a fire, have beeswax well rubbed into the leather. It is said that bees commonly respect such gloves, and that if the tips of a finger and thumb be removed from both gloves, and the exposed flesh be anointed with wax, all manipulations can be carried out with safety. Burkitt Bee Gloves (178) are made of soft white leather, having attached a linen gauntlet coming well up the arm and bordered with red braid. Those gloves are quite ornamental when new; the bees do not show any inclination to attack them and operations can be performed without inconvenience.

CHAPTER XIII.

APPLIANCES FOR HONEY AND WAX EXTRACTION.

142. Invention of the Honey Extractor.—When Langstroth, in 1851, had invented the movable-comb hive (85), and Mehring, in 1857, had introduced foundation (119), the next great benefit which discovery was to confer upon the industry was the provision of a means by which honey might be removed from the comb without the destruction of the latter.

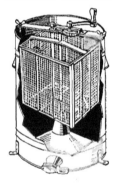

Fig. 76.

MODERN GEARED
EXTRACTOR.

Hitherto honey had been extracted either by crushing the combs or by melting them—an expensive method in every way, as will be gathered from what has already been said upon the subjects of wax secretion and comb building (78). In 1865, von Hruschka, an officer in the Austrian Army then stationed near Venice, observing his son carelessly swinging a piece of honey comb in a basket, noticed that the motion slung some of the honey out of the cells. Taught by what seemed to be a mere accident, he proceeded to apply the principle of centrifugal force to honey extraction, and with a diligence which was crowned with success and has for ever placed beekeepers under a debt of gratitude to the man.

143. The Honey Extractor.—The Honey Extractor is a strong, tinned iron can (Fig. 76) with two or more cages which revolve round a vertical spindle and hold each a frame of comb. The cages are set in motion by the handle on top, and when the honey has been thrown from the outer sides, the combs are reversed and the operation is repeated. The honey is slung out against the sides of the can, is received in the bottom, below the revolving cages, and may be drawn off through the syrup tap (290). If the extracting be properly done, and if the combs have been wired in the frames (289), the combs remain uninjured and may be returned to the hive to be refilled, being used for this purpose year after year, thus effecting a great economy, as already explained (78). Extractors are now usually made with gearing, which lessens the labour and enables a high speed of revolution to be attained. A small form of extractor may be had to extract one comb at a time. This appliance, however, is only suit-able for persons who extract an occasional comb only, and are unlikely ever to become popular. Extractors are also made to carry as many as eight cages and are worked by power, but these have now been largely superseded by the radial type of power extractor which is being more and more generally used on large bee farms. These extractors may carry as many as 50 combs arranged in a radial position as illus-trated (Fig. 76a). This shows a hand-power radial extractor as intro-

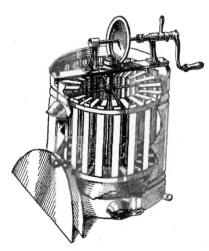

Fig. 76a. "HERROD-HEMPSALL" RADIAL EXTRACTOR.

duced by Mr. W. Herrod-Hempsall some years ago. It is similar to radial American and Continental machines. The radial type is much more suitable for power than for hand work on account of the length of time needed to complete extraction. For the small or medium beekeeper, a machine of the ordinary tangential pattern to take two, three or four combs is probably as good as anything.

144. Uncapping Knife.—Uncapping may be done with a sharp carving knife. But the most useful knife for the

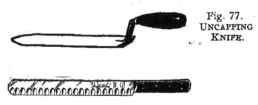

Fig. 77.
UNCAPPING
KNIFE.

Fig. 77a. THE "COLD" UNCAPPING KNIFE.

purpose is the uncapping knife illustrated (Fig 77). It has bevelled edges, and with a little practice it can be used with rapidity and completeness upon the most irregularly built combs (289). These knives must be kept hot by standing them in hot water over a lamp or stove; but there is now on the market a new kind of uncapping knife, known as the " Cold " knife which is specially designed for use unheated. It is quite satisfactory and very suitable for small beekeepers who do not care to go to the expense of a steam-heated knife. This last, however, is undoubtedly the best tool for the man with a large number of combs to uncap. It is a hollow bladed knife through which steam is made to pass from a boiler by means of flexible rubber tubing. The used steam passing away through a second tube. It is not a very expensive appliance and lasts almost indefinitely if taken care of.

Fig. 77b. STEAM KNIFE AND BOILER.

145. The Strainer or Ripener.—After extraction, honey requires to be strained and allowed to stand in a deep tank in order that the particles of wax, air-bubbles and other extraneous matter may rise to the surface. For this purpose the appliance illustrated in Figure 78 and usually termed a " ripener " is used. The strainer is of perforated tin and may have a cheese-cloth tied over it if desired. Usually honey, unless heated, will not pass through anything finer than cheese-cloth; but, if heated, flannel may be used to remove every small particle of dross. Having passed through the strainer into the tank, the honey, after being left a few days to settle, may be drawn off by the syrup tap provided at the bottom.

Fig. 78.
STRAINER AND RIPENER.

146. The Honey Press.—Heather honey, which is too thick to be thrown out by the Honey Extractor (143), and honey which is to be removed from combs that are intended to be rendered into wax, may be pressed by the Honey Press, or, in small quantities, by a potato masher. The Rymer Honey Press (Fig. 79) is made of malleable iron and steel;

it has a square thread screw and all the parts that come in contact with honey are tinned. The honey is forced between the grate and the outer case, and flows into the receptacle underneath (289).

147. Wax Extractors.—These most useful appliances are intended for the rendering into wax of discarded combs, cell cappings (289) and any odd bits of foundation which may be collected from time to time, and—wax being a valuable commodity — may thus be turned to good account (292).

Fig. 79. RYMER HONEY PRESS.

148. The Solar Wax Extractor (Fig. 80) is simple in use, inexpensive, and gives satisfactory results, provided that the

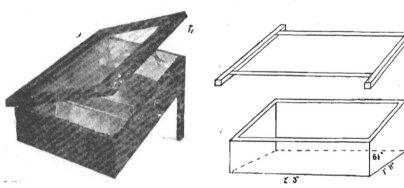

Fig. 80. SOLAR WAX EXTRACTOR.   Fig. 81. READ'S SOLAR WAX EXTRACTOR.

solar element be not wanting. Mr. M. H. Read describes his home-made extractor (Fig. 81) as follows:

" The extractor measures 2′ 3″ long, 1′ 11″ deep, 10″ high at back, and 6½″ high in front, inside measurement. It is made of 1½″ timber, dovetailed. The sides and back of the sash, or cover, are 2″ by 1½″, and the front is 2″ by 1″. The sash is glazed with 24 oz. glass. The inside with (2′ 3″) was fixed upon so as to hold a tray of ordinary corrugated iron, upon which the wax to be purified is laid. The impurities remain on the tray, and the clear wax, as melted, runs down into a trough which runs all along the front.   The trough is cut from a strip of corrugated iron (valley and two corrugations), the two corrugations hammered up, to make one deep trough, the ends of which are hammered up, so that the wax is held in it.   The extractor has a loose-fitting bottom, and is filled up with a sloping bed of cinders, within 4″ of the glass, the trough being set in the ashes in front, and the tray on the bed of ashes and overhanging the edge of the trough. Being fitted with a loose bottom, the extractor can be turned to face the sun, the rays of which should fall perpendicularly on the glass.   A reflector, of a large sheet of tin, could be added."—*Irish Bee Journal.*

149. Steam Wax Extractor. — For extracting by steam, an apparatus (Fig. 82) is supplied which does its work thoroughly, is not difficult to manage, and in our fickle climate which so often denies us the sun, is more generally useful than is the Solar Extractor.   The upper portion has a perforated tin basket into which the pieces of comb are placed, and underneath which is a tray, with an outlet.   When the water in the lower portion boils, the steam ascends to the basket and melts the wax which escapes through the outlet and is caught in a basin of cold water The refuse remains in the basket, and when the wax in the basin cools, it may be lifted out in a cake. **(292).**

Fig. 82. Steam Wax Extractor.

(Other useful and necessary Appliances may be found described in the various chapters of Part III.)

PART III.

MODERN BEEKEEPING

CHAPTER XIV.

PAST AND PRESENT.

150. Past Ignorance.—Previous to the introduction of what are known as "modern methods," beekeeping was carried on under most discouraging conditions. It is true that in very early days something was known of the habits of the honey bee, and that so early as 70 B.C. Virgil, the Latin poet, put forward in verse the results of his study of the habits of bees, with a degree of accuracy sufficient to excite a wondering admiration on the part of twentieth century readers. But to the average beekeeper the hive, until comparatively recent times, was as a sealed book; the marvels that it contains, the excellence of its internal economy, and the unselfish devotion, wisdom, and singular attractiveness of its occupants were, if known at all, known only to the few. Virtues and beauties thus hidden could make but little appeal, as yet, to the respectful admiration of human intelligence. The heroic acts and incomparable works were wrought, like evil deeds, in darkness: and man, loving only the visible, the tangible, sceptic always of the unseen, had not learned that within the secret places of the hive were enshrined mystery upon mystery, and that within the humming insect, flitting in his garden from flower to flower, there beat a heart brave and noble enough to deserve his respect and even to awaken his love.

151. Survival of the Unfit.—Unfamiliar with the instincts of bee-life, man found himself unable to control by gentleness, and thought it necessary to resort to violence for the subjugation of insects armed by nature with stings. The harvest of honey and wax was gathered at the expense of the lives of the colonies. The strongest and fittest—those whose stores were heaviest, were devoted to destruction; the weakest and the sickly were spared; and the sulphur pit—that abominable outrage upon industrious innocence, laid waste the home of vigour and opulence, and secured the survival of the unfit (82).

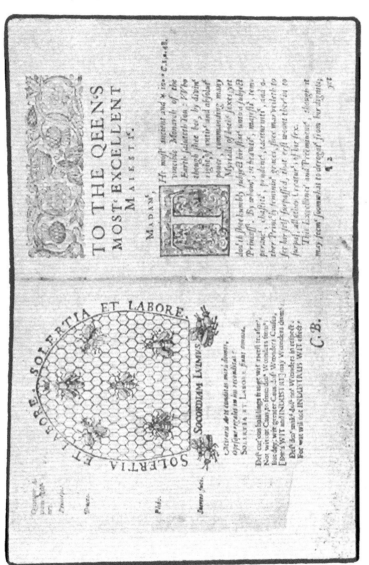

One of the Earliest Bee Books—"[The Histori of Bees," By Chas. Butler, 1634.

It remained for Swammerdam, Reaumur, Huber (85) and other investigators, to dispel the darkness which surrounded the operations of the hive, and to devise means by which the occupants might be controlled, and the industry be worked for increased profit, and upon humane principles. Nor was it the least important result of their researches which put it within our power to correct the errors of the past, and, by careful selection, to effect such improvements in the race of bees as may tend to render them more robust, less liable to disease, gentler, and more prolific and profitable.

152. Modern Beekeeping.—The title " Modern Beekeeping " stands for such skilful management of bees, based upon an intelligent appreciation of their habits, as may secure the maximum results of their labours, and the fullest development of their best characteristics. It represents the desire to minister to their comfort; to assist their industry by thoughtful anticipation of their requirements; and to encourage in them the spirit of amiability by the display of a like spirit on the part of man, and by the avoidance of all roughness and cruelty in dealing with them. Modern beekeeping has so improved upon the older methods that the produce of the bees' labour has been enormously increased, without a corresponding tax upon their strength. It has been made possible for anyone who understands what it means to take pains, to manage bees with a handsome profit to himself. He can now engage in a pursuit which has in itself an enthralling interest, and that, if carefully attended to, will return more than an ample compensation for the time devoted to it. The movable-comb hive permits him to become familiar with the habits, and to explore all the wondrous work of the honey bee (86). He can take out the " waxen palaces," can investigate their beauties, and see with what skill they have been constructed. He can watch the queen as she moves across the combs, depositing her eggs in the vacant cells. He can replace her with a younger queen reared by himself, or imported in a postal packet from foreign lands (313). He can observe the various stages of the egg and larva, and witness the breaking of the capping and the emerging of the new-born bee. By the use of foundation (118) he can supply the material for the building of the combs, and can so regulate the storing of honey that it may be removed in the shape and condition most marketable, and without injury to the gatherers. The extractor (143) enables him to use the same combs again and again, and by increasing the harvest, to make his industry still more profitable. In short, he can so utilize the advantages which modern discovery and invention have supplied, that he can engage in beekeeping as in a delightful occupation and one that is capable of being turned to good practical account.

153. A Profitable Industry.—It is something in favour of modern beekeeping that, if well managed, it can be relied upon to return a good profit. In fact, in proportion to the capital and labour involved, no other agricultural industry can give so good a return. When neither rent nor labour is considered, that is to say, when a man does the necessary work in his spare time and does not enter it as part of his costs of production, bees may sometimes pay cent per cent, or even more. It is also something in its favour that broad acres are not required, since bees range over the land at will. It requires very little space to accommodate a few stocks of bees, and twenty or more may be kept in a garden provided they are so situated as not to annoy neighbours. The amount of labour involved in the management of a small apiary is not great and is usually to be considered in the nature of recreation. The lightness of this labour, however, is relative to the smallness of the undertaking, for when a large number of hives of bees are involved the time factor emerges and things cannot be taken in a leisurely manner. In that case, at times, the labour is very heavy and hours very long. To keep a few bees for pleasure and a small profit, or for the sake of their honey for personal use, is a pleasurable undertaking, consisting of interesting open-air work; but those who wish to secure considerable incomes from bees should clearly understand that it will require considerable capital and a great deal of very hard work. Many men have been able to secure substantial profits from their bees, and it is not at all uncommon for profits of £100 or more to be made through beekeeping as a spare time occupation. If, however, substantial sums are to be realised from keeping bees, modern equipment is necessary. Bees in skeps and boxes cannot produce honey in quantities which are comparable to those possible with well-managed frame hives.

Photo by   *J. G. Digges.*

THE AUTHOR'S HIVES, ON FLAGS, AND COMB STAND (Fig. 96, page 127).

CHAPTER XV.

ARRANGING AN APIARY.

154. Selecting a Position.—Before actually beginning beekeeping, it will be well to select a suitable position for the apiary. Bees in hives are sometimes kept in curious places— on house roofs; in narrow passages; on window sills. A lady in London has several stocks in her drawingroom. A hive may be set up in one's bedroom, the bees having a passage through a hole in the window sash. For an apiary out of doors almost any well-sheltered position will suit. But there ought not to be any serious obstruction to the bees' flight; and there should be room at the back of the hives for the owner, and a reasonable distance between the apiary and the county road or other place of public resort. Many beekeepers have been decreed in the Courts for damages by bees to persons and animals, in consequence of which advantage should be taken of one or other of the Insurance Schemes now available.

155. Bees near Dwellings.—It can hardly be said that bees learn to know their owner as a dog learns to know his master: yet it has been observed that bees located near dwellings become accustomed to persons passing to and fro, and are less likely to make themselves objectionable when one approaches their hives, than if they were situated in a remote, quiet place. Indeed, bees, remarkable at one time for their gentleness, have been known to develop very hasty tempers after having been removed from their old stand near a dwelling to a lonely spot where they were never visited except for the purpose of manipulation. Risk of unpleasantness may be minimised by a wise arrangement of the stocks. If, for example, the hives be placed thirty or forty yards south of a dwelling, and with their backs to the house, the flight will be towards the south, and the bees will give little or no annoyance. Should there be a path or garden in front of them, a high fence, or hedge, will "lift" them over the path, and will serve as a protection for persons passing by. It is desirable to provide against cold storms from the north and west. A hedge of strong privet plants will quickly make an efficient shelter. Although not absolutely necessary, it is advisable to have the hives, or as many of them as possible, facing south-east; because, in that position, they will get the warmth of the early sun about their entrance to entice the occupants out for early labour.

156. Position of the Hives.—The hives ought not to be crowded together. Bees, on taking flight, mark the location of their hives, and with surprising accuracy return from long

distances to the same spot from which they started **(165)**. But, when their hives are close together, and are painted the same colour, with no distinguishing m a r k s

Fig. 83.   SPIRIT LEVEL AND MEASURE

upon them, bees will sometimes enter the wrong hives and meet a warm reception there leading to fighting and general excitement, which should be avoided as far as possible. Bees of a colony quickly detect an intruder. In the case of queens returning from their nuptials, it is of the first importance that they should have every facility for recognizing their own hives **(296)**. The hives may stand four feet from each other, or farther apart if space permit. Those illustrated (p. 106) are six feet apart and are painted (1) white, (2) red, and (3) blue, in succession. They should be perfectly level across the frames in order that the combs may be built plumb. If the frames run at right angles to the entrance, it is well to give the hive a slight tilt towards the front for the escape of moisture. Hives with legs may be

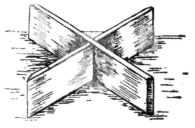

set upon bases of flag, or concrete, upon four bricks, or directly upon the ground. If bases, or bricks, be used, they should be carefully levelled with a spirit level (Fig. 83). A hive without legs may have a simple stand made of two pieces of plank 24″ × 7″ × 1½″, a piece 3½″ × 1½″ being cut out of each, and the

Fig. 84.   "X" STAND.

pieces being nailed together in shape of an X (Fig. 84). The floor board **(90)** being placed in position, should be tested with a level, or with a bowl of water set upon it. When the hive is ready a stout stake may be driven into the ground, at one side of the hive, for use when preparations are being made for winter **(436)**. Grass and weeds must be kept down in the vicinity of the hives. If allowed to grow, they intercept the flight, and should a queen drop off a frame, or a clipped queen (222) fall on the ground at swarming time, she may easily be trodden on, or lost. It will save much trouble if the sod be lifted around and in front

Photo by *A. H. Bowen*
PREPARING FOR THE FIRST EXAMINATION

of the hives, and a good coat of concrete, gravel, or cinders be laid down. The plot selected should be fenced to prevent cattle, pigs, etc., from interfering with the hives.

157. Appliance Press and Apiary House.—It is most inconvenient to have the appliances stored at a distance from the apiary. To leave things about the house means often to have them mislaid; and to run to and fro when engaged manipulating is often to put an undue tax upon one's temper, and to raise a riot among the bees. A press on legs, made of old boxes, painted, with a waterproof roof, and that can be carried from place to place if necessary, will be found to amply repay the trouble of making it. For an apiary of more than five or six hives, an apiary-house should be provided in which all tools and appliances can be kept, frames and sections put together, hives nailed, honey extracted, and all the various jobs have attention. Such a house can be made at a trifling expense, while the assistance it gives and the time it saves are incalculable.

CHAPTER XVI.

COMMENCING BEEKEEPING.

158. Three Words of Advice may be useful to anyone who proposes to try his hand at beekeeping, viz.:—Begin

      (1) Moderately.
      (2) Prudently.
      (3) Intelligently.

159. Begin on a Small Scale.—To begin moderately, begin on a small scale, with one or two stocks. Few things have done more to discourage beginners from persevering with the industry, than has the mistake of starting with more stocks than they could easily manage before they had gained the necessary experience. In due time, when you have learned something of the habits and wants of bees, you will be able to add to the number of your colonies and, perhaps, to attend to twelve or twenty stocks without greater expenditure of time than, at the outset, you will find necessary to devote to two.

160. Purchasing Bees.—To begin prudently, provide yourself with the best hives and appliances that you can get; not necessarily the most expensive, but the best. And if you start by purchasing bees, do not hesitate to give a little more money for a really good stock or swarm. By " Stock " is meant an established colony of bees in a hive. But stocks differ so much in value that if one be worth £3 another may not be worth half-a-crown, and a third may be worth less than nothing. By " Swarm " is meant a queen and attendant bees which have just abandoned a hive (19). These also vary in value from 20s. or 30s. to nothing, according to their numbers, condition of health, the ages of their queens, and the date of their swarming (215). Most important is it to provide against purchasing, or admitting as a free gift to your apiary, bees that are diseased, or that have come from a diseased hive, a diseased apiary, or a diseased neighbourhood (373). It is safest, and often it is necessary, to get someone of experience to inspect bees about to be purchased and the apiary to which they belong, and to report upon their antecedents and condition.

161. Commencing with a Swarm.—Speaking generally,

one may begin at any time of the year in which the " bee fever " takes him. But, if he can arrange it so, it will be best to commence in the spring and, having his apiary and hives in readiness, to purchase the best early swarm that he can procure (215). An ideal swarm will be one that comes off in April, or early in May; that is from a stock which swarmed in the previous year and that contains from 25,000 to 30,000 bees. If it issue early in the spring, it will be able to give some surplus honey and to establish itself well before winter (215): if it be from a stock which swarmed in the previous year, it will have a queen in her prime (20), and if it contain 25,000 or 30,000 bees, it will be strong enough to put heart into its work, and to carry on until the new brood shall be able to fly. The vendor will probably hive the swarm in a skep (82), or box, and will deliver it, or will notify the purchaser that it is ready for removal. The system of obtaining early " swarms " in the shape of " Package Bees," is rapidly coming into favour and is now an important branch of the industry. They are obtained from Southern France and Italy—2 lbs. or 3 lbs. of bees with a queen, in a combless package, arriving from the middle of April to early in May. They are in time for the fruit blossoms and rapidly increase to full-colony size for the main white clover flow. They should be ordered in February or March and should, of course, have young queens. On arrival, the package should be placed in a dark, cool place until evening. Prepare a hive with five or six frames of foundation for a 3 lb. package, or, better still, with four or five of foundation and one of comb containing a little honey, but no brood. Towards evening open the package, remove the queen in her cage and set her—in her cage—on top of the frames; shake the bees into the hive; put on the sheet, a feeder full of syrup (355) and the quilts and roof. After 24 hours, release the queen. Continue feeding until nectar begins to come in plentifully. Such lots, if received in time and properly treated, will usually give a return equal to that of any established stock in the apiary.

162. Moving Swarms.—The transporting of the swarm to the new apiary presents no difficulty. All that is required is to remove it as soon as it has been secured, or, failing that, to wait until the bees have settled down in the evening. The skep should be set down upon a piece of coarse netting, or canvas, which should be firmly tied round the skep, so as to make sure that sufficient air can get in and that no bees can get out. The swarm, thus secure from escape, and asphyxiation, is carried, inverted, to its stand in its new home. If now the skep, or box be weighed, and if it be weighed again when empty, and if 5,000 bees be allowed to the pound, the number of bees in the swarm can be fairly accurately calculated, allowance being made for the weight of honey consumed by a travelled swarm. A lot of 3 lbs. weight, including, say, 15,000 bees, makes a moderate swarm; 5 lbs., or say 25,000 bees, may be regarded with very particular satisfaction.

Fig. 87.
BALANCE FOR WEIGHING
HIVES, UP TO 400 LBS.

163. Sending Out Swarms.—

Swarms and driven bees apart from their combs should always be sent to their destination, if at a distance, by passenger train. Non-returnable travelling boxes may be readily made from light, fairly strong deal boxes, such as groceries are sold in. Such a box should be about 15″ x 10″ x 10″ deep, according to the size of the swarm. The larger the better in reason, so long as it is not rendered weak or unwieldy. The sides may have a number of large holes cut or bored in them and covered with perforated zinc or woven wire nailed on inside the box. The lid of the box may be treated in the same way, but should have a good half of its area composed of ventilating material. The case should be conspicuously labelled, "LIVE BEES REQUIRE AIR." Returnable travelling boxes which can be strongly made of ply-wood are probably to be preferred for use by those who make a regular practice of selling combless bees, while the travelling boxes made to take stocks on combs can as easily be used for sending out swarms. First and last, the really important requirements are plenty of room and ample ventilation.

164. Commencing with a Stock.—

If it be decided to begin by the purchase of an established stock in a skep or frame hive, steps should be taken to ascertain exactly the condition of the colony and of the skep or hive. If the vendor can show a clean bill of health; if the queen be vigorous, the combs even, and well supplied with brood, and not too old, and if the skep or hive be in good condition, a bargain may be made.

165. Moving Stocks.—

The transport of a stock to a new apiary requires some care. Among other considerations, the question of distance must be taken into account. It has already been explained that bees will fly a distance of two miles in search of food, and will return again to the place from which they started (35). But if their hive be moved more than a couple of feet during their absence, or at night, without precautions being taken to cause the bees, in the morning, to take notice of the alteration, a number of them will return to the stand to which they were accustomed and will flutter about it and die there. It follows that if the bees to be purchased are located more than two miles from the purchaser's apiary, they may be transported direct without risk, and that if their old home be less than two miles off, special care must be taken to prevent their return to it. Put briefly, bees may be moved directly two feet and under, or two miles and over; but for intermediate distances due precautions must be observed, viz.—either to move the stock by short stages of two feet, in the evening, after the bees have been flying freely, or to move it from the old stand to a spot more than two miles away, and to let the bees fly there for a few days, then moving them to their new home; provided always that this second journey be not less than two miles. If neither of these precautions can be adopted, a third one may possibly answer the purpose, viz.—the bees can be carried to their new location in the evening, and arrangements can be made to oblige them, when they fly in the morning, to observe that the scene, meanwhile, has changed. This is done by placing about the entrance such impediments to their flight as will demand their attention. A little grass may be pushed into the entrance so that they may have to squeeze their way out; a cloth may be hung down in front of the hive; and boards or branches may be so arranged that the bees, when they leave the hive, will notice at once the alteration that has been made in its position. This will cause them to mark the new situation and to return to it. The impediments may be reduced on the next day, and removed altogether on the day following, provided that the bees have been flying freely meanwhile. When stocks are being moved from one place to another in the same apiary, and more than two feet at a time, similar precautions must be taken, with this addition—that the old sites must be altered as much as possible in appearance, any bees collecting there being carried back in the evening to their hives. Further, it is to be remarked that moving bees two feet per day can be done only on days on which the bees fly, so that they will have marked the position after one move before they be moved again.

166. Moving Stocks in Skeps by Road or Rail.—When moving established stocks by car, cart, rail, or steamer, account

must be taken of the risks which they will have to run over bad roads and indifferent springs, or at the hands of careless railway shunters and porters; and also of the risks which the public and animals in the neighbourhood may be exposed to should any accident release the bees *en route* and give them " cause of action." For stocks in skeps, an old-fashioned and a useful precaution is to push three or four stout wooden skewers through the skep and combs, from side to side, two or three days before the moving. The skewers, fastened by the bees, act as stays to the combs and can be withdrawn after the journey. To further reduce the risk of combs breaking away from their attachments, the skep is travelled bottom up. It is first covered with some ventilating material, as directed above (162), and is then inverted, placed in a large lidless box, and packed underneath and around with straw. A rope handle is attached to the box, and also a label in a prominent position, and bearing the words—" LIVE BEES, AND HONEY COMB: WITH CARE. BEES REQUIRE AIR." An improvement upon these precautions would be—to travel, yourself, with the bees.

167. Moving Stocks in Frame Hives by Road or Rail.— Stocks in frame hives can generally be transported with safety when the following instructions are observed. A hole 4″ × 4″ is cut in the floor board and is covered with perforated zinc. Two lengths of loosely-made straw or hay rope are placed on the floor board at right angles with the frames. Frames with honey and no brood are removed, their places in the hive being filled with frames of old, empty combs, or with empty frames having bands of canvas tacked on from top to bottom, or from end to end, to which the bees may cling. Soft, new combs with brood, if to remain in the hive, are tied in their frames with two broad bands of calico, or canvas, running under the combs and fastened over the top bars. The dummy (100) is moved up and screwed in position. Instead of the sheet and quilts, a piece of coarse canvas, or perforated zinc, is laid on the frames and tacked down. Two strong laths are laid across the frame shoulders, and are securely screwed to the hive. The frames, caught thus between the laths above and the straw ropes below, cannot shake about. In the evening, when all the bees are at home, the doors are removed and the entrance is covered with a piece of perforated zinc securely tacked to the wood. The body box is then screwed to the floor board. The extra frames, roof, doors, etc., travel separately. With large stocks, and in very warm weather, it is advisable to leave in the hive only sufficient bees to cover the brood, and to travel the remainder in a skep as directed for swarms (162), hiving them in the usual way (247) on arrival at the new locality. It is safer to send the bees and combs in a travelling box (Fig. 88), and the hive separately. The illustration shows, in the centre, the bees being subdued in the hive from which the transfer is to be made, the travelling box, to hold eight or ten frames and, leaning against the latter, the lid, which is covered with perforated zinc. At the left, five frames have been transferred. The illustration to the right shows the transfer completed, nothing remaining to be done but to put on the lid

Fig. 88. Transfer to a Travelling box.

and screw it down. The travelling box, which is inexpensive and can be put together without difficulty by any handy person, is made on the principle of the body box (91) and has an entrance. It may be left in the position previously occupied by the hive until all the flying bees shall have returned and entered it; then the entrance should be covered with perforated zinc, and the travelling box, being roped, will be ready for despatch. When sending bees on combs per rail, a wise precaution against damage by the jolting of the train is to place the hive, or box, so that the frames may lie in the direction of the railway lines. An arrow may be chalked on the lid to indicate the proper position, or placing, of the hive in the train.

168. Commencing with Driven Bees.—In districts where skeppists follow the barbarous custom of smothering bees at the close of the season (151), it is generally possible to obtain " condemned lots " at a trifling expense, the owners often being willing to accept a shilling or two for the bees which, otherwise, would be destroyed. When two or more condemned lots can be procured and united on combs of honey, or on frames of comb—if in time to be fed up before cold weather sets in (349) they usually turn out well in the following year,

All that is necessary is to examine the stocks for signs of disease and, if they prove healthy, to get the bees away from their combs (see illus. page 176). This leads on to the operation of " Driving," which, although l o o k e d upon by the uninitiated as a wonderful act of legerdemain, is really one of the simplest operations c o n n e c t e d with modern beekeeping.

Fig. 89. DRIVING BEES.

169. Driving Bees. —A fine day, when bees are fl y i n g freely, is to be preferred. The appliances required are— (a) One or two empty skeps, or a Driving box (Fig. 91); (b) Driving irons (Fig. 90); (c) Smoker (Fig. 73, page 92); (d) Bucket (Fig. 89); and (e) a table or chair. Blow a puff or two of smoke into the skep containing the bees and give them time to run up into the combs and to feed (176). Carry the stock to some sheltered corner, placing on its stand a box, or an empty skep, to decoy any flying bees. Blow some more smoke into the occupied skep, causing the bees to gorge themselves with honey (190). Place the bucket on a table or chair; lift the skep, invert it, and place it, bottom upwards, in the bucket; set a second skep upon it, " like a cockle shell half open," the skeps touching above the ends of two central combs (Fig. 89). At that point push in the skewer (Fig. 90) through the edges of both skeps to hold them together, and stay up the empty skep by the other irons, the points being pushed into the sides of the skeps. These irons are from 15″ to 18″ long. Two laths, with nails driven through the ends, and a skewer of hard wood, may be made to serve the purpose. With the opening between the skeps in front of you, so that you may observe all that occurs, rap the sides of the lower skep—the sides to which the combs are attached—sharply with the palms of your hands, or with two sticks, taking care that while jarring the combs slightly you do not loose or break them down. Carry on the rapping continuously at the rate of about two per second. The bees will speedily run up past the skewer into the upper skep,

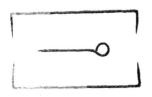

and if a queen be there, careful watching will discover her passing up. "Close Driving," which is necessary in inclement weather, consists in fastening the skeps together edge to edge, tying a cloth round them, and driving as above; but close driving does not permit one to watch the progress of the operation, nor to see the queen

Fig. 90. DRIVING IRONS.

going up. Driving, whether open or close, may usually be completed in about a quarter of an hour. In unfavourable weather, and if there be little honey in the skep, it will be an assistance to sprinkle the combs and bees with warm, thin syrup (Recipe 355) five or ten minutes before driving (190). When all the bees are driven, put them and their skep, or box, back on the old stand in place of the empty skep left there to receive flying bees, which bees should now be shaken out on a board before the entrance to the skep or box containing the driven bees. If two or more driven lots are to be united (261) having queens of different values, only the best queen should be allowed to remain. The bees in each lot may

be thoroughly dusted with flour from a dredging box or sprayed with thin, scented syrup from an asperser to make them unite peaceably. The Asperser (Fig. 92) is sometimes used for the purpose; but spraying with syrup—a messy, troublesome expedient at the best—is not to be recommended. Since the discovery that ordinary flour will serve the purpose as well as scented syrup, the kitchen dredging box has come into favour as a cheaper and less troublesome pacifier. When this has been attended to, the two skeps can be brought with the bottoms together and dumped on the ground, so as to throw those in the upper skep into the lower

Fig. 91.
COLGAN'S DRIVING BOX.

one. The bees, being then shaken together thoroughly, and having the same scent, will unite peaceably. The bees of driven lots may, however, usually be united without either flouring or spraying. If the skep with the first driven lot be placed upon

that of the lot to be driven, as illustrated (Fig. 89), the bees
of the latter move up speedily when driven, and the two lots,

having neither brood nor stores to defend,
unite peaceably. Should fighting by any evil
chance be started, it may be stopped by the
application of a little smoke and by shaking
the bees together vigorously. In the evening,
when they have settled down, they can be
carried off, or forwarded per rail or post, as
described above, and placed upon their new
stand, the canvas or zinc being removed.
Such lots should be fed up liberally and
rapidly (349).

Fig. 92.
ASPERSER.

[See also Illus. p. 176 and " Automatic
transfer from Skep to Modern Hive." (266). It may be mentioned that, of course, bees may be driven from boxes as well
as from skeps, the same procedure being followed *mutatis
mutandis.*]

AN OUTBREAK OF " BEE FEVER."

170. Study the Subject.—To begin intelligently, study the
subject thoroughly. Make yourself familiar with the nature
and habits of bees and with the most improved methods of

management. If you have an experienced beekeeper in your neighbourhood, or among your friends, gather from him all the information that he can supply and ask him to allow you to witness his manipulations from time to time. But, when you have studied a Bee Guide and have seen some of the operations connected with beekeeping, do not suppose that you can afford to proceed with the industry without keeping yourself in touch with the approved literature of apiculture. In order to take advantage of the latest discoveries, and of the experiences of the foremost beekeepers of the day; in order to combine with the interests of the pursuit the profits which it is capable of providing, you should subscribe for a reliable publication and thus acquaint yourself with what is being accomplished elsewhere, with the developments which are constantly taking place, and with the views of the most capable apiculturists upon the innumerable questions which, although outside the purview of a guide book, present themselves in actual experience every day.

Photo by   *A. H. Bowen.*

DRIVING FROM BOX TO SKEP.

CHAPTER XVII.

SUBDUING AND HANDLING BEES.

171. Tranquillizing Influence of Smoke.—When all due homage has been paid to those great scientists whose discoveries and inventions have led up to the present highly developed condition of apiculture, there yet remains a tribute of praise and gratitude to the man (whoever he may have been) who first disclosed a plan by which the bee may be subdued, and reduced to a temper so amiable as to be amenable to handling without showing fight. For, it can hardly be doubted that all the knowledge of bee instincts which has been attained, and all the improvements in bee appliances which have been

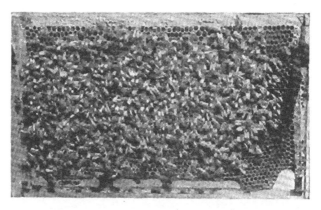

Photo from life   *by J. G. Digges.*
Fig. 93. Subdued Bees on Empty Comb.

effected in modern days, could not avail to bring the industry to its present stage of progress had not some method been devised for breathing a peaceful calm over the occupants of a hive under manipulation. All honour to the man who first discovered the tranquillizing influence of smoke!

172. Unprovoked Stinging Exceptional.—It is an utter fallacy which suggests that the main object, or one of the main objects, of a bee's life, and her greatest happiness, is to drive her sting into human flesh. The sting is her natural protection—a weapon not properly of offence, but of defence. It is the exception, and not the rule, for the sting to be used in a manner unprovoked. Instinct teaches the bee to employ her weapon sparingly, because the fastening of the barbs in the object stung often obliges the bee to retire mutilated from the encounter. (39).

173. Fearless Defence of the Home.—But bees, it must be admitted, sometimes conceive extravagant notions of danger, and, without any cause apparent to us, will attack with fury any other living thing in their neighbourhood. In such circumstances discretion will often prove to be " the better part of valour." Force is no remedy. Attack them with your umbrella, a hay fork, a locomotive, a pom-pom; they will beat you. Bring up the British Army, horse, foot, and dragoons, with tanks and aeroplanes, the bees will win the day. For, behind their assault are their queen, their brood, their home; and in defence of these they are utterly oblivious of danger and indifferent to death. For their fearless anger when aroused, bees have been employed in warfare. There are cases on record in which whole regiments have been routed by the letting loose of bees. In Thuringia (1525) a furious mob, which had stood out against tremendous odds, was instantly put to flight by having hives of bees thrown among them. At Tanga, East Africa (1914) a defeat of British troops was turned almost into a rout by " a sudden outbreak of millions of bees "— *The Star*, Johannesburg, Mch. 17, 1923. To the uninitiated there is something terrifying in the vicious buzzing of bees when they have their abdomens curved for the thrust, and the very air around them seems charged with venom. You cannot oppose your courage to theirs, for they are not amenable to the laws of civilized warfare, and they will fight with irresistible bravery, and will die a thousand deaths, if need be, in defence of their homes.

174. What Constitutes " a Master of Bees."—Therefore, it is necessary, in order to manage bees, whether on the old principles or the new, that one should know how to stay " the beginning of strife," to subdue them to his will, and to bring them completely under control. Firmness, without aggression; gentleness, without fear; and a knowledge of their habits, tastes and fancies, are all that are required to constitute a master of bees. With such qualifications one can do with them as one pleases; can revolutionize their kingdom, depose their queen, regulate their enterprise, intercept their swarms, order the manner of their industry, deprive them of their stores, and, without provoking their anger, turn them again to peaceful labour. It is not a charm that may be worked by a privileged few. It is the application of a knowledge to which all may readily attain.

175. **Swarming Bees Harmless.**—It is well known that bees of a swarm are usually as harmless as butterflies (19). They may be gently lifted in the hand, and dropped, bunch after bunch, without so much as an angry buzz from them. A

Photo from life   *by J. G. Digges.*
Fig. 94. Subdued Bees with Capped Brood.

gentleman carried through the noise and bustle of city streets a swarm that had settled on his head. He walked with them into his office, and secured them in a box. They made no attempt to sting him. There must be some reason for this. Visitors to a Bee Tent (see page 95), look with amazement upon the lecturer driving bees from skep to skep, picking them off the combs, remaining unmoved with bees crawling upon his neck, or hanging to his eyebrows. The onlooker cannot understand it. Yet it is easily explained.

176. **Full of Sweets—Empty of Bitterness.**—Before issuing in a swarm, it is the habit of bees to fill their honey sacs from the stores, instinct teaching them to carry from the home, which they are about to abandon, sufficient food with which to secrete wax for new combs, and to support themselves in the interval (18). In that condition they are most peaceably disposed and will not sting except under violent provocation. If they can, at other times, by any means, be brought into a

similar condition the same results will follow.   It has been
found that any sudden, mysterious alarm communicated to
all the colony in a hive will drive them to the honey cells for
food.   A puff or two of smoke blown in at the entrance (135),
or a carbolic cloth (136) laid on the frames, has the necessary
effect, and a peep under the quilts will then discover the bees
with their heads in the cells, drinking deeply.   A delay of a
minute or two, and the whole colony will be found to be
subdued.   With gentle handling the frames may be taken out;
examined; hung upon a stand (Figs. 93, 94, 96 and 98) and
returned to the hive, not a bee taking wing, nor any attempt
being made to show resentment.   In this manner the fiercest
colony may generally be subdued and handled with safety.
With Maeterlinck this inoffensiveness is the result of happiness;
with Simmins, of homelessness; with Cheshire, of terror; with
Langstroth, of a physiological fact—

" When a bee prepares to sting, she usually curves her abdomen
so that she can drive in her sting perpendicularly.   To withdraw it,
she turns around the wound.   This probably rolls up its barbs, so that
it comes out more readily.   If it had been driven obliquely instead of
perpendicularly, as sometimes happens, she could never have extracted
it by turning around the wound.   When her stomach is empty, a bee
can curve her abdomen easily to sting.   If her honey sac is full, the
rings of the abdomen are distended, and she finds more difficulty in
taking the proper position for stinging."—*Langstroth.*

177. A Firm and Gentle Hand Necessary.—It is known,
also, that bees resent roughness; have a deep-rooted objection to
jarring of their combs; fly into a passion if any of their number
be crushed in the hive; will not tamely submit to being rubbed
the wrong way; are provoked to violence when one sting
has been inflicted, by the mere smell of it; and will often
attack a hand for no other reason than that it has been
suddenly and quickly moved adjacent to them.   Sometimes
bees noted for their peaceable disposition will be found in an
angry humour, some unaccountable influence having disturbed their wonted calm.   Therefore, bees should always be
handled with the utmost deliberation and care.   A firm and
gentle hand is necessary.   There must be no jarring of the
combs, no swiping of the handkerchief at a threatening bee.
Coolness gained by experience, together with the precautions
already, and yet to be, described, will usually render the manipulation of bees as safe as the driving of a flock of geese.
Should bees at any time show marked signs of vindictiveness, it
is better, instead of attempting to fight them, to withdraw in
a manner as quiet and dignified as possible (188).   They will

probably be found, next day, in their normal condition of amiability. To start in and fight them, may render them unmanageable for the remainder of the season, and will certainly lead to a precipitous flight.

" *Effect of Stings.*—A writer in a contemporary wants to persuade us that formic acid is not volatile. He ought to observe its effect on dogs, and even on the slow-footed donkey. A venerable angler, coming too close to a concealed apiary last summer, was seen, inspired with marvellous energy, laying about him with his fishing-rod—when you come to think of it, an absurd weapon for the occasion. After that he took a five-bar gate with the agility of a youngster. The fishing-rod was propping asters in September! We once saw a boy scale a seven-foot glazed wall, and drop into the street on the other side, as it seemed from simple enthusiasm. The gate stood open all the time within a jump of him. He had been trying to scrape honey out of a hive entrance with a three-pronged fork! Formic acid not volatile! Stuff and nonsense! "—*J. G. D.* in the *Irish Bee Journal.*

Fig. 95. A MODERN BEE SUIT.

(N.B. — See par. 140 in reference to the nature of bee-sting venom).

178. Protection for Beginners. — Beginners, and all who have not yet gained confidence from experience, will do well to remember that, until it can safely be dispensed with, a veil will prove a most useful protection for the head and neck against the attacks of the " free lances " of the colony (137-139). Procure a hat with a broad brim (Fig. 74, page 93); draw the veil over it until the elastic grips the lower part of the crown, settle the veil to keep all secure, over the shoulders, button the coat and see that the veil is at least the length of a bee-sting apart from the face, ears, and neck. Next provide against the possibility of a bee crawling up your legs, and fasten your coat-cuffs to protect your arms; for, pressure of the clothes will, certainly, cause a bee there to sting. If you find it necessary to do so, don a pair of bee gloves, to protect your hands and wrists (140). Thick woollen gloves, though safe, are not desirable, because it is difficult to manipulate with them, (141) and, although you may not be hurt, bees will often sting them, mutilating themselves in the operation (39). Apart from the fact that one can never afford needlessly to sacrifice bees, it is not humane, nor in accordance with the principles of modern beekeeping, to provoke them to leave their stings in one's apparel. Burkitt bee gloves offer little hindrance to manipulations, and are seldom attacked (141). It should, however, be the aim of every beginner to dispense with the use of gloves as soon as possible.

179. Treatment of Stings.—If the hand be stung, and the sting be left in the flesh, the sting should be withdrawn immediately, not squeezed, but drawn out with the nail, or a knife-edge; because the reflex action will continue for some time to inject poison into the wound if the sting be not removed

Photo by   *A. H. Bowen*

USING THE SMOKER.

(39). If a drop of ammonia, or of " D.D.D."—an excellent remedy—be at once applied to the wound, the pain and swelling may occasionally be reduced; and if the spot be touched with the carbolic feather (185), the bees will not be excited to further attack by the smell of the sting poison (177). External applications, however, cannot be relied upon to neutralize the injected poison. If, when the sting has been removed, the part stung be not rubbed, but pinched with the finger and thumb until, on loosing it, the pain does not return, little trouble will be experienced. It generally follows that, when one has been frequently stung, one becomes safe from pain and swelling as results of stings. Further, there is much testimony to the fact that such ailments as rheumatism are alleviated and even cured by a sufficient application of the sting of the bee; so that the pain of the sting is not without its compensation.

" I am a firm believer in the efficacy of stings as a cure for rheumatism. Shortly after my recovery from rheumatic fever, a lady presented me with an entire apiary, and in the transfer of the stocks I got a ' murthering ' of stings, and, though I had been subject to rheumatism for years previously, I never, since that stinging, felt a twinge of it."— T. B. O'Bryen, in the *Irish Bee Journal*.

CHAPTER XVIII.

MANIPULATING.

180. Appliances Required.—Before opening a hive for manipulation, be careful to have at hand everything that you may require. A smoker (135), a carbolic cloth (136), a small table that can be carried from hive to hive, a comb stand (181) to hold frames of foundation and frames removed from the hive, a comb box (182), a dinner knife, a wing or soft brush, a pot of vaseline or petroleum jelly (183) are all useful articles.

181. The Comb Stand (Fig. 96) is intended to hold frames when a hive is being manipulated (194).

Fig. 96. COMB STAND.

It is often necessary temporarily to remove one or more frames from a hive when operations are in progress, and it is always useful, when working at hives, to have spare combs at hand in a convenient position. The home-made stand shown holds three frames on each side. It is 2′ 6″ high, and the carriers, fastened on the legs, are 14½″ apart. The stand can be carried about the apiary and set down where required, without danger of breaking the combs or of injuring the bees that may be upon them. Its usefulness may be further observed on referring to the illustration facing page 107; and to figures 93, 94, 98, and 132, page 207.

182. Comb Box.—When combs are being transferred, removed for extraction, or carried about the apiary, it is advisable, in order to minimize the risk of robbing (324), to have a comb box in which they can be placed. The home-made comb box illustrated (Fig. 97), is internally 17½″ long × 9½″ deep × 9″ wide. Two carriers are nailed at the ends inside, 1″ from the top, to take the shoulders of the frames. A handle is fixed on the lid, and a cone escape (286) permits the exit of any bees that may have been shut inside.

183. Vaseline, or Petroleum Jelly, is applied to the shoulders of frames, to the carriers on which they rest, and to the bottoms of supers, etc., to prevent the propolising of them by the bees (279). It is so desirable to have all hive fittings easy of removal, without jarring, the application of vaseline or petroleum jelly should never be omitted by the beekeeper who desires to perform his manipulations without needlessly provoking his bees (177). The material, which is inexpensive, may be applied with a small paste brush.

Fig. 97.   Comb Box.

184. Preparing the Smoker.—The smoker (135) should be in good order, and the fuel prepared beforehand, for it is most disconcerting to have the smoker give out when operations are in progress. Almost any dry fuel that will burn may be used—dry, rotten wood, rag, or brown paper. Put a couple of quarts of hot water into a bowl; dissolve in it, say, one or two ounces of saltpetre; soak a quantity of brown paper in the liquid, and when dry, cut it in strips about four inches wide. Roll one of the strips loosely; light one end, and put it into the smoker, lighted end down. Small rolls of dry brown paper may be added from time to time as the fuel in the smoker becomes exhausted.

185. Preparing the Carbolic Cloth (136).—Procure from any chemist a bottle with an asperser cork. In this make a solution of 1 part Calvert's No. 5 Carbolic Acid to 10 parts water. Take a piece of ticking, calico, or linen, say 24″ × 18″, which, in some operations, may be more conveniently used if prepared like a flag (136). Shake the bottle and thoroughly damp the cloth with the solution. Sprinkle a little also on a feather. Put cloth and feather into a tight-fitting tin box that they may retain the odour.

186. Opening the Hive.—Go, now, to the hive which you want to examine. Blow one or two puffs of smoke through the entrance into the hive, remembering that your object is not to half smother the bees, but just to send them to dinner. Rap smartly with your knuckles on the sides and roof; set down your smoker, nozzle up, so that it may draw like a chimney; take out your carbolic cloth and feather, and wait for a minute before proceeding further. Then place the feather half its length into the entrance to put a stop on the bees there; remove the roof and quilts, leaving only the sheet on the frames, or super. By this time the bees will have gorged themselves into good humour (176). Your position will now depend upon the arrangement of the frames in the hive. If they hang at right angles to the front, stand at the side; if they hang parallel to the front, take your position at the back. Hold the carbolic cloth by the lath, if one has been inserted (136), or by two corners, and let it hang down outside the hive at the side opposite to you. Pick up the corners of the sheet and slowly draw it back upon itself towards you, so bringing the carbolic cloth over the frames as illustrated. Not one bee will get out if you do this carefully. Instantly the bees will begin to make music—a peaceful symphony

DRAWING ON CARBOLIC CLOTH.

which may encourage you. Remove the cloth, or roll it back off two or three frames—you will find the bees with their heads in the cells, or moving about in a bewildered fashion, gentle as lambs, and disposed to treat you with every courtesy if only you reciprocate their gentility.

187. **Manipulating Wicked Stocks.**—In the case of a vicious stock the subduing may require to be of a more thorough-going nature. Give three or four puffs of smoke at the entrance and close the doors; with your shut fists drum on the roof for half a minute; open the doors and give more smoke, and drum again for half a minute. After three or four minutes draw on the carbolic cloth and the bees will probably be found perfectly subdued. Keep the smoker at hand to drive them back if they should show a desire to "boil" over the tops of the frames.

188. **Forcing the Pace.**—In the event of a usually quiet stock proving unruly, as will occasionally occur (177), suspend operations at once, and withdraw. Give them time to calm down and try them again on the next day. Bees, like mortals, sometimes "get their dander up," and probably with better reason. They may have been fighting robber bees (344): they

(D 1052)   F may scent rain in the distance : they may have been provoked by some interfering man or beast—you cannot always tell. But it will be better to let them " sleep upon it " than, by forcing the pace and persevering in your manipulation, to run the risk of turning them into demons for the rest of the season.

189. **Smoking Overdone.**—It must, however, be said that with the general run of bees, elaborate preliminaries to manipulation are unnecessary. When you have gained experience, and have learned how to do it, you will frequently find it possible to open and manipulate a stock without the aid of smoke or carbolic when a heavy flow of honey is proceeding, but these aids to control should always be at hand. In the honey season, thoroughly smoking a colony puts a stop to the gathering of nectar, probably for the rest of the day. The honey that has been gorged has to be disgorged into the cells when you have finished operations. If you stand aside and observe, you will find that nothing like the same energy is displayed at the entrance, and if you weigh the hive next morning, it will be seen that the average increase has been suspended, which shows that a considerable loss of honey has been incurred. Therefore, smoking should never be overdone; for simple operations, such as putting on or taking off a super, it is seldom necessary at all (279), nor, indeed, unless the brood nest is to be disturbed, or the hive manipulated at unsuitable hours.

190. **No Food—No Subjugation.**—It must be added also that the use of smoke for quieting bees presupposes the existence of food in the hive. With the best intentions possible, bees cannot gorge themselves with smoke. If, therefore, there be no food in the hive upon which they can feed liberally, warm syrup may be given. The carbolic cloth can be drawn over the frames as described above, and in a few seconds the syrup may be lightly sprinkled between the combs, the smoker being applied subsequently (355).

191. **Examining the Combs: Finding the Queen.**—Having subdued the bees as described, you may proceed to examine the combs. You must remember that the space between the frame ends and the hive is not more than ⅜″, perhaps only ¼″, perhaps less (88); and that if you draw out a frame carelessly you run the risk of crushing bees, and even of killing the queen if she happen to be on one of the ends of the frame (88). Draw back the dummy (101) as far as it will go. Draw back the frames together from the centre frame, i.e.—if there are nine frames in the hive draw back Nos. 1 to 4 together, and very

slowly, so that the bees on the ends may have time to get out of the way of danger. If you have, up to this, kept the carbolic cloth on the frames, and have kept daylight out of the hive, the queen will probably be found on the centre frame; but if you have flooded the brood-nest with light, she will have made off to the front, or the back, frames. Take the centre frame by the shoulders, in your fingers, and lift it vertically, holding it over the hive. Turn your back to the strongest light, and

Photo from life   *by J. G. Digges.*
Fig. **98.** SUBDUED BEES, WITH CAPPED WORKER AND DRONE BROOD.

examine the side of the frame next to you. If the queen be there you will recognize her by her length, and shape, and colour (4). She is longer than the worker bee, thin for her length, with her abdomen more pointed and somewhat less hairy than the others (Fig. 1, page 2). If young, she will show her activity by " dodging " from one side to the other of the frame. If she be on that frame, it will be well to return it to the hive, lest she take wing and give trouble, in which case you must remain perfectly still and await her return. (See also 195).

192. The Combs Described.—Your frame, upon examination in the summer season, will probably be found to contain honey, capped and uncapped, capped brood, uncapped larvæ, eggs, some empty cells, and perhaps a little pollen (Fig. 26, page 50). Bees store their honey over their brood. The cells, therefore, next the top bar—cells capped with light-coloured wax—contain ripe honey. Next to them will be found unripe honey, not yet capped. Lower down on the comb, cells with a dark capping of wax and pollen contain hatching brood, the wax being mixed with pollen to render the cappings porous. Some of these capped cells stand out from the comb beyond the others (Fig. 98), and have a larger diameter; they contain drone brood (Fig. 26, D). Perhaps one or two cone-shaped cells appear, hanging down; these are queen cells (Fig. 99 and Fig. 26, A, B, C, page 50). Close at hand open cells will show the larvæ, pearly white, in various stages of development (Fig. 99). And others have eggs (199),

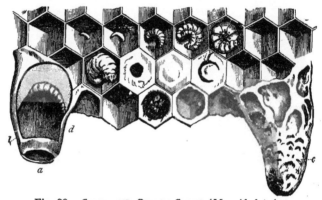

Fig. 99. COMB AND QUEEN CELLS (*Magnified twice*).

a, Queen cell, cut to expose " Royal Jelly " and Grub at upper end ; *b*, Thickness of cell ; *c*, Dimpling outside cell ; *d*, Spot where bowel contents and exuvium are placed.

like little bits of blue-white thread, on the bases of the cells. Some of the eggs stand out at right angles from the comb ; these are one day old : others bend over towards the base ; these are two days old : others lie upon the bases of the cells; these are three days old and are just about to produce larvæ. Other cells, capped and uncapped, contain pollen, or " bee bread," of various hues (79). As bees store pollen near the entrance, brood in the middle, and honey at the back, if your frames run from front to back you may find pollen, brood, and honey in the same comb, while if the frames run from side to side of the hive, pollen will probably be found in the combs next the entrance, honey in those at the back, and brood, with honey higher up, on the other frames.

193. Removing Bees from Combs.—To get bees off a comb, it is sometimes advised that they be jerked off, or brushed off. They may be jerked off if one keeps on jerking long enough, but the second jerk often puts bees on the wing and leads to mischief. They may be brushed off with a goose wing, or a strong feather, but, though bees will often submit meekly to a brush that meets them in the face, if it take them the other way—(as it must take many of them, since they are on the comb '' heads and tails '')—they are apt to rise to

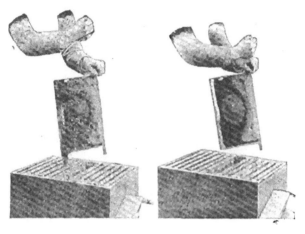

Photo from life *by J. G. Digges.*
Fig. 100. ''THUMPING'' BEES OFF A COMB.

the occasion in a manner that does not always appear to the operator to be quite justified by the circumstances. There is another plan. Hold the frame firmly by one of the shoulders in your left hand, keeping it a few inches over the hive (Fig. 100). Now, with your right fist give a sharp thump on your left hand. To the bees it will be like an earthquake and a thing irresistible. They will drop, to a bee, and scamper down among the other frames as if the end of their world had come. Of course, if you let the frame drop, the '' earthquake '' may possibly astonish yourself. Keep a good grip, and never employ jerking or thumping with a frame that has upon it a queen cell, or much unsealed honey.

194. Turning Combs.—To examine the comb on the other side, you must not turn it up as you would a slate. A comb so used, especially if new, or heavy with honey, may drop from the frame, or sag, and break or may drop honey out of the cells. Therefore, whether the combs to be handled be old or new, wired or not wired (275), make it your rule to turn them in this manner—

Hold the frame by the shoulders (Fig. *101*, 1): raise your left hand, bringing the frame into the position shown (2): give the frame a half turn, like a swinging door, bringing the off side next yourself (3): then lower the left hand into the position shown (4.) Reverse these movements to bring the frame back

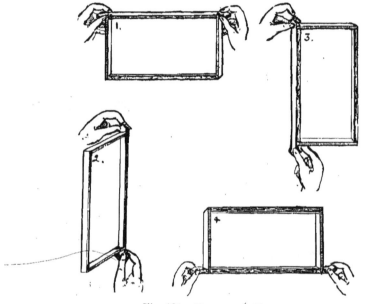

Fig. 101. TURNING A FRAME.

to position 1. If the queen be not upon it, you may now hang it on the comb stand (181) and proceed to examine the other combs. In all these operations, act with deliberation; move your hands slowly; avoid pinching bees with your fingers or crushing them in the hive; and do not jar the frames when putting them back, nor kick the hive legs with your feet. If the bees show signs of getting from under control, draw the carbolic cloth over the frames again, or blow a puff of smoke along the frame tops. When you have finished your inspection, replace the frames, shoulder to shoulder; draw up the dummy; put on the sheet and quilts and roof; and, if the bees have not already thrown it out of the entrance, remove the carbolized feather (186).

195. Searching for the Queen.—In the fascinating game of hide and seek with the queen (191), there are yet other rules to be observed. For example: Every possible effort should be made to avoid frightening the queen. Little smoke should be used, and that only *across* the entrance, for the benefit of the guarding bees there. The removal of the roof, quilts, and sheet should be done with the utmost gentleness. A comb on which the queen may be, when lifted out for inspection, should be held over the hive, so that in the event of her falling off she may drop safely into her home. Combs containing brood should not be hung upon the comb stand (181) for

Photo by   *A. S. Rowse.*

EXAMINING BROOD-COMBS

any length of time in chilly weather lest the brood be chilled. Combs containing much unsealed honey should not have their adhering bees removed by jerking or thumping (193), for this would throw out the honey and do damage to the bees (36). Stand with your back to the sun, and as each frame is withdrawn scan the exposed faces of the combs remaining in the hive, for her majesty may be scampering there towards the darker side. Part any cluster of bees on the frame in your hands, the queen may be hidden there. If still she baffle you, and if it be necessary to find her there and then, either of the following methods may be tried:—Place a hiving board in position (244), a piece of excluder zinc (117) on the hive entrance, and a dummy (100) inside near the hive front. Lift out the frames, one by one, and thump, or brush, every bee on to the hiving board, moving back the dummy and returning the frames in front of it, and in the same order, as they are cleared; when the excluder stops the queen entering you will have her.   Or, procure a super box (116), or any bottomless box about the size of the hive, invert it, and brush every bee into it from frames, hive and floorboard; set up the hive again with the frames in position; place an excluder on the box, set the latter on the frames, with the excluder between, thump on the lid to throw the bees down, then raise the lid and spread a carbolic cloth (136) over the box; the bees will quickly run down to the frames, except the queen and drones, which will be trapped above the excluder.   Some beekeepers mark their queens with a coloured sealing wax dissolved in alcohol or ether, the latter being the better of the two as it dries more rapidly.   Quite recently, however, it has been found that cellulose enamel is both satisfactory and convenient.   It has a smell like pear drops, and experiment shows that until this smell has disappeared, queens so marked require especially careful introduction to stocks to which they are alien.   The method of application is to hold the queen still while a small spot of the marking substance is applied to the back of her thorax.   A record of the queens' ages may be kept in this way, if a different colour be used each year. There is now upon the market a special instrument for the marking of queens by means of which a small disk bearing a number is attached to the thorax.   The queen is thus made easily discernible by the bright colour of the disc and each queen is identifiable by her number.   This is the " Eckhardt " queen marker.

CHAPTER XIX.

BREEDING.

196. Breeding Begins.—Breeding in the hive generally begins towards the end of January (8), perhaps somewhat earlier in a mild season. Moving quite slowly upon the centre combs, the queen, examining the cells and inserting her abdomen, deposits her eggs upon the bases—one egg in each cell, confining herself at first to a small area, and increasing the areas as the season advances; passing from comb to comb, and returning to the cells according as they become vacant through the hatching of the young bees. If, on account of the smallness of the cluster, or the prolificness of the queen, more than one egg be laid in each cell, the workers will generally remove the superfluous eggs.

197. "Congestion" to be Guarded Against.—A comb completely filling a standard frame contains $106\frac{5}{16}$ superficial square inches on each side, or $212\frac{5}{8}$ superficial square inches in all, and in the case of frames having top bars $\frac{1}{2}''$ in depth, $104\frac{5}{8}$ and $209\frac{1}{4}$ square inches respectively. Worker cells measure 27 to 29 to the square inch (71). Taking them as 28 to the square inch, we have 5,953 worker cells in the comb of a standard frame with $\frac{3}{8}''$ top bars, and 5,859 in the case of frames with $\frac{1}{2}''$ top bars (104). Given sufficient room and favourable circumstances, a queen in her prime, laying at the rate of 3,000 eggs per day (45), or 90,000 eggs per month, might occupy with eggs more than half of such a comb per day, and nearly 16 complete combs per month. But the eggs deposited on the first day of the period will hatch out, and the cells become vacant, on the 22nd day (214). Assuming that the queen returns always to the cells as soon as they become vacant, she might, at the rate of 3,000 eggs per day, have filled $11\frac{1}{2}$ complete combs in the twenty-two days before she returns to the former cells. From which calculation it will be seen that, in the height of the season, and with a queen in her prime, the increase of the colony will be very rapid, and that, in a hive containing no more than 10 or 11 standard frames, and with from 30,000 to 50,000 bees depositing honey in the cells, the queen may very quickly find herself hampered for room, and that " congestion " supervene which produces the " swarming fever " (226). It follows that, where the largest possible harvest of honey is desired in preference to an increase in the number of colonies by natural swarming, the beekeeper must so arrange that the queen shall always have more room than she actually requires for the depositing of her eggs, and that the bees shall have, at the same time, sufficient room for the storing of honey. This is what is referred to by the frequent advice to " give room in advance of requirements," so that congestion shall not provoke swarming, and thus disorganize, in the middle of the honey flow, the work of the colony. (226).

198. Drone-breeding Queens.—Until the approach of the swarming season, the queen lays only impregnated, *i.e.*, worker eggs, after which drone cells are prepared and in them she deposits unimpregnated, *i.e.*, drone eggs. A queen in her fourth or fifth year will sometimes, however, become a " drone-breeder " : the supply of fertilizing material in the spermatheca (45) having become exhausted, she is no longer able to fertilize her eggs; and, though she may continue to lay in both worker and drone cells, the produce from both will be drones only—dwarf drones, if reared in the cells intended for worker larvæ. Such a queen should be supplanted at once; in fact, after her second year, a queen ceases to be profitable, and her place should be taken by a young, fertile queen (294-295). A hive which shows too large a proportion of drone brood should be requeened without delay.

199. Age of Larvæ.— From Dr. E. F. Phillips, in *Gleanings*, we have the following data for judging the ages of larvæ. Just hatched, a straight line from head to tail is ⅖th the diameter of the cell; one day old, ⅓rd, the form semi-circular;

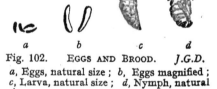

a   b   c   d
Fig. 102.   EGGS AND BROOD.   *J.G.D.*
a, Eggs, natural size ; *b*, Eggs magnified ; *c*, Larva, natural size ; *d*, Nymph, natural size.

two days, head touches tail in a circle nearly ½ the cell diameter; three days, it occupies ⅝ths; four days, it fills the entire diameter of the cell. To be able to tell the age of egg (192) and larva is very desirable, especially when arrangements are being made for queen rearing (306).

200. Worker Brood.—During the first three days the germ feeds upon the substance of the egg and, hatching on the fourth day into a small white grub, it is supplied with a food which is believed to be elaborated for the purpose by the salivary glands of the nurses. After about three or four days more, a mixture of semi-digested honey and pollen is added to the food. On the ninth day from the laying of the egg, in the case of worker

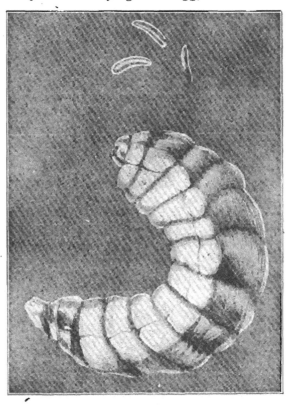

Fig. 103. EGGS AND LARVA (*Magnified*).

brood, the cell, well supplied with food, is sealed with a porous capping consisting of a mixture of wax and pollen; the larva (Figs. 102, *c* and 103) spins a cocoon, casts off one skin after another, and becomes a pupa or nymph (Figs. 102, *d* and 104), gradually becoming transformed into a perfect bee; in which condition, on the twenty-second day, she bites the capping and gains her liberty. The cell is at once cleaned and prepared for the reception of another egg. Twenty-four hours later the young bee begins her life-work by acting as a nurse to the larvæ in their cells; a few more days elapse before she flies from the hive; and, about thirty-six days after the laying of the egg, and fourteen days after her exit from the cell, she begins the work of foraging (214), which work, arduous as it is, will exhaust her energies and bring about her death in five or six weeks of summer.

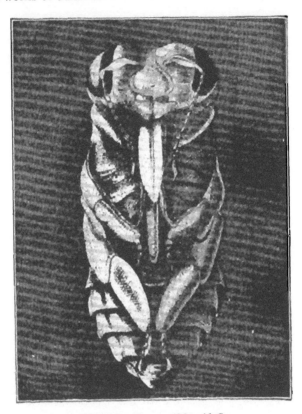

Fig. 104. NYMPH (*Magnified*).

201. New Combs for Breeding.—The adhering to the cell-walls of the cocoons spun by the larvæ (200) tends to reduce the size of the cells, and eventually to render them unsuitable for the rearing of vigorous bees (78). It is said that combs quite twenty years old have been found capable of producing bees as large and as strong as those reared in new combs; but it is not desirable to retain combs so long for breeding purposes; modern beekeeping favours frequent renewal of combs in the brood nest, for the reason indicated, and also upon principles of hygiene. Three or four frames of foundation given to a colony every year, thus renewing the combs every third year, fulfils a rule that is well worthy of general observance.

202. Stimulating in Spring.

—For the rearing of larvæ, pollen (79), liquid food, and a temperature of 80° to 90° are required. As from thirty-five to thirty-six days elapse from the laying of the egg until the resultant worker begins her mission as a forager (200), every effort should be made to induce rapid laying by the queen thirty-five days before the opening of the main honey flow (278). To assist the nurse bees, and to encourage the queen to increase the area of her brood, the bee-keeper begins " stimulative feeding " (347) early in the spring, and also adds fresh, warm wraps to conserve the heat of the hive. A cake of candy is given over the cluster (359). Later on, once or twice a week, the sheet is quietly rolled off the tops of one or two frames, and the cappings of some of the upper honey cells are bruised, to entice the bees, and to cause them to use the honey (347). This can be done without removing the frames or disturbing the bees. If the carbolic feather (185) be passed between the combs the bees will move down before it and, with a flat knife, cappings may be bruised so as to expose the honey, which will stimulate the queen and bees to fresh efforts. A feeder (127) is placed on the frames directly over the brood nest, and each evening, when the bees have ceased flying, a small quantity of thin syrup—no more than the bees will take down during the night—is given warm, the doors of the hive being closed to about half an inch to prevent robbing (344).

Pollen, like honey, is stored by the bees in their combs during the active season for future use; but in a different way. It is a material that will not keep if exposed to the air during the damp winter time, and instinct has taught the bees that pollen must always be stored under honey. Therefore no cell in a hive is ever much more than half filled with pollen, but is first partly filled with that perishable food and then filled to the top with honey and sealed with wax. It follows that, if bees are to breed early in the year before flowers provide a supply of pollen, that there must be present in their combs a supply of pollen stored safely under a layer of honey. Now the modern system of beekeeping provides for the removal as surplus of a large part of the honey which the bees have stored above their brood combs, and, unless some provision is made to obviate the necessity, the bees are compelled to use the honey which is stored over pollen quite early in the autumn or winter instead of utilising that which they had stored above, as they would have done had the beekeeper not removed it. When they do this, the pollen is left exposed and generally becomes mouldy and useless.   The best way, therefore, of ensuring an adequate supply of good pollen for early breeding is to feed heavily in September, so that bees shall have in their combs a plentiful supply of liquid food for use during winter without any need to uncover the pollen so carefully stored away, by being obliged to consume the honey with which it is covered. Bees always store a large amount of pollen towards the close of the honey season, and if they be well fed in the autumn there will almost always be pollen in plenty ready stored in the combs for brood-rearing purposes in the early spring following. Furthermore, if pollen becomes mouldy through neglect of the provision of plenty of liquid food in September, it is not only the loss of the pollen and the potential breeding that is the result, but often of the combs as well; for combs which become a mass of mouldy pollen are usually of little further use.   In fact, the art of wintering and early spring stimulation is largely bound up with liberal autumn feeding.

The provision of flour as " artificial pollen " was at one time recommended; but is now known to be useless as bees are quite unable to assimilate starch, though they will readily carry such flour to their hives.

203. Spreading the Brood.—Spreading the brood consists in enlarging the brood nest by the insertion, in the centre of it, of frames of drawn out comb, or of comb foundation. This is an operation which should not be attempted by inexperienced beekeepers. It must not be recklessly performed, nor without due regard to the strength of the colony; because, if the brood nest be enlarged beyond the covering capacity of the bees, brood may be chilled, and much mischief may ensue (370). But, where wisely and carefully carried out, the effect of spreading the brood is to quickly increase the strength of the colony; for, the queen, finding vacant cells in the centre of the brood nest, will deposit eggs in them at a period of the year when she would not be likely to travel to the colder, outer combs for the purpose. As a general rule brood spreading may be considered safe when, the weather being warm and the nights no longer chilly, the space between the outside comb and the dummy (100) is found to be occupied by bees. In this case, if the outside comb be suitable for brood rearing, i.e., a straight, well-built comb, not overstocked with pollen, and preferably containing some honey, it may be used for the purpose. The carbolic cloth (136) is drawn over the frames and, without exposing the brood nest to cold winds, the dummy and the frames between it and the centre of the brood nest are gently drawn back together a couple of inches; the dummy is then moved back a little farther, and the outside frame is lifted out (191). If it contain capped honey, the cappings are broken, and the frame is placed in the centre of the brood nest; the frames and dummy are closed up, and the sheet, quilts, and roof are placed in position as before. The operation may be repeated from week to week, frames of drawn out comb being used, until the brood chamber is filled with brood. In the absence of drawn out combs, frames of foundation may be used; but it is not advisable in the spring, when every day is of importance, to put upon the bees the necessity for comb build-ing, thus delaying the increase of brood which might otherwise be expedited. Careful beekeepers make it a rule to have always on hand a supply of drawn out combs for this purpose (351). Later in the season, and especially in the summer, frames of comb, or of foundation, should be given in the brood nest as opportunity may offer. (227).

" During summer, whenever a fairly strong stock is opened for any purpose (such as putting on or taking off sections) a frame should be put in the centre. This is a golden rule."—T. B. O'Bryen, in the *Irish Bee Journal*.

204. Drone Brood.—Towards the middle of April, when, in normal seasons, bees are preparing for swarming in May, they construct drone cells (72). These will be readily recognized by their size, being deeper than the worker cells, and $\frac{1}{4}''$ in diameter, whereas worker cells are only   '' in diameter; the cappings of the former standing out beyond the cappings of worker cells (Figs. 26, F, page 50, and 98, page 131). The drone egg, like the worker egg, hatches in three days, and the grub is fed up to the ninth day from the laying of the egg; when the cell is sealed, the spinning of the cocoon takes place, the change from larva to nymph, and on the twenty-fifth day the young drone makes his way out of his cell. About a fortnight later he leaves the hive for flight. (214).

205. Controlling Drone Rearing.—The rearing of drones may be limited by the use of foundation prepared for worker brood, and may be encouraged by the use of drone-brood foundation (121). It will, however, be found that, except in the case of a new swarm, if the former pattern be cut, or broken, or supplied in the frames as " starters " instead of in full sheets, drone cells will be attached to it in large numbers (118). To avoid the extravagant rearing of drones, worker foundation is used in full sheets in all the frames of the brood nest, and the sheets are wired into the frames (125) so that they may not easily become sagged, or broken in the hive or extractor. Drone traps are sometimes recommended for the elimination of superfluous drones from a hive. They are so constructed with queen excluder that the drones are unable to pass out and are guided through spring bee escapes into a compartment in which they must remain. They may be destroyed in this way; but as they have already been reared and the greater part of their honey consumption is already over, it is rather like locking the door of the stable after the horse is stolen, and it is better to endeavour to regulate the production of drones by other means.

206. Queen Cells.—At the approach of the swarming season, if the queen and the rapidly increasing population of the hive become pressed for room; at any time when a colony has been deprived of its queen; or when the bees desire to supplant an old queen whose fertility has ceased, queen cells are started on the combs (76). These are distinguished from all other cells by the material of which they are made, and by their size, shape, and position (Figs. 2, page 9, 26, A, B, C, page 50, and 99, page 132. They are constructed of a mixture of wax and pollen, are about $1''$ long $\times \frac{1}{3}''$ in diameter, are in shape like an acorn, and they hang mouth downwards on the combs. The bees construct queen cells on the face of a comb by breaking down the cells immediately surrounding those containing the eggs from which queens are to be reared. At other times queen cells are made on the sides, or the bottoms, of the combs and, when the queen does not deposit eggs in them, bees have been known to carry eggs to them from other cells; they lengthen the queen cells as the process of feeding the grubs proceeds. The number of queen cells constructed by a colony of native, or black, bees may vary from two to ten or twelve. Other races frequently exceed those figures. Syrian bees (54) will sometimes provide as many as thirty queen cells on one comb, and it is said that more than seventy queen cells have been found in one colony of Syrians. The cells are not all started on the same day, the object being to have the young queens hatch out in succession. In a case of emergency, arising when a colony has been deprived of its queen, if the bees have worker eggs available, or larvæ not more than three days old, i.e., not already weaned (200), they will construct a queen cell around the selected egg or larva. Should they have no worker egg, or larva under four days old, they will, in a desperate effort to retrieve disaster, form queen cells here and there at random, and even around drone larvæ. The latter cells, which may be distinguished from regular queen cells by their smooth walls (Fig. 26, G, page 50) cannot, of course, produce anything but drones—drones which, perhaps, by reason of their too generous nursing, frequently die in their cells.

207. Nursing Queen Larvæ.—There is not any difference between the egg which produces a queen bee and that which produces a worker bee. But the treatment in the process of nursing varies considerably. The larva, in the former case, is given a cell which permits of its growth to the full dimensions of a queen, and is more liberally supplied with food—food of a richer quality, called " Royal Jelly " to distinguish it from the food provided for other larvæ : and, whereas the larva of the worker bee is weaned three days after it has left the egg, and is then supplied with a coarser food (200), the larva in a queen cell continues to receive abundantly the Royal Jelly. Leuckart discovered that the development of the female genital organs begins upon the third day after hatching. This development continues under the liberal treatment referred to and the produce is a mature female, or queen, or ceases with the withdrawal of the stimulating food, when the result is an immature female, or worker. It follows that, for the production of a vigorous queen, the special treatment should begin with the egg, or at least before the larva has passed its third day.

208. Wonderful Effects of Special Nursing.—The effects upon the larva of this continued supply of richer food are among the most wonderful in the history of bee-life. The larva which, in the ordinary course of nature, we should expect to arrive at maturity by slower stages, reaches its full growth in about two-thirds of the time occupied by the worker larva (214). The young queen has her organs fully developed, so that, when inseminated, she can, during the ordinary span of queen-life, produce impregnated eggs to the extent of 100 times her own weight; while the worker can never by any means produce an impregnated egg (210). In colour, shape, and size, she differs materially from the worker, being darker, more delicately formed, and with greater length (4). Her sting is longer, and curved (41). Her hind legs are without corbiculæ (34). Her abdomen is without wax-secreting receptacles (37). Her eyes have only about 10,000 facets, as against the 12,000 facets of the worker (30). Her habits and instincts are, in many respects, the opposite of those of the worker— she confines herself to the duty of egg laying, very seldom, or never, leaving the darkness of the hive after her wedding flight, except when accompanying a swarm : she is not disposed to sting even if molested by the beekeeper : far from sharing the worker's deep-rooted reverence for the person of a queen, she shows a bitter hostility to all others of her own rank, and will fight to the death against a rival queen. She may live for four or five years, whereas the worker's life is limited to about six weeks, except in the case of workers born at the close of autumn and surviving through the winter rest to labour for a few weeks in the spring. So marvellous are the developments brought about by the simple process of feeding.

209. Queen Brood.—The egg from which a queen is to be reared, like the egg which is to produce a worker, hatches in three days; for six days more it continues in its larval state; it then spins its cocoon, is transformed into a nymph, and, on the sixteenth day from the laying of the egg, it emerges a perfect virgin queen. The vacant cell is never employed again for queen rearing, but is cut down, usually within a few hours (76) as shown (Fig. 26, C, H, page 50). Soon the young queen begins her search over the combs for a rival and, if permitted, she will destroy the unhatched virgin queens in their cells. (20). A few days later, if the weather be favourable, she leaves the hive for impregnation. (214. 223).

" Hardly had ten minutes elapsed after the young queen emerged from her cell, when she began to look for sealed queen-cells. She rushed furiously upon the first that she met, and, by dint of hard work, made a small opening in the end. We saw her drawing, with her mandibles, the silk of the cocoon, which covered the inside. But, probably, she did not succeed according to her wishes, for she left the lower end of the cell, and went to work on the upper end, where she finally made a wider opening (Fig. 26, B). As soon as this was sufficiently large she turned about to push her abdomen into it. She made several motions, in different directions, till she succeeded in striking her rival with the deadly sting. Then she left the cell; and the bees, which had remained, so far, perfectly passive, began to enlarge the gap which she had made, and drew out the corpse of a queen just out of her nymphal shell. During this time, the victorious young queen rushed to another queen-cell, and again made a large opening, but she did not introduce her abdomen into it; this second cell containing only a royal-pupa not yet formed. There is some probability that, at this stage of development, the nymphs of queens inspire less anger to their rivals; but they do not escape their doom; for whenever a queen cell has been prematurely opened, the bees throw out its occupant, whether worm, nymph, or queen. Therefore, as soon as the victorious queen had left this second cell, the workers enlarged the opening and drew out the nymph that it contained. The young queen rushed to a third cell; but she was unable to open it. She worked languidly and seemed tired of her first efforts."—*Huber*, A.D 1791.

210. Laying Workers.—Although, as already stated (208), the worker bee is incapable of being impregnated, there are occasionally found, in a queenless hive, one or more workers whose ovaries, partially developed, contain a certain quantity of eggs (Figs. 23, C, page 36, and 104b). Huber supposed

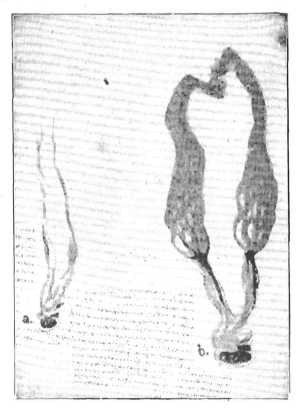

Fig. 104b. OVARIES OF (*a*) WORKER, AND (*b*) LAYING
WORKER (*Magnified*).

that these laying workers were the produce of eggs deposited in cells adjacent to queen cells and that they received a smaller quantity of royal jelly. Possibly they are either workers which, in the early stage of development, were not weaned until after the third day, and whose organs have been partially developed by reason of the excess allowance of the richer food which they have received; or, workers which, in the larval state, were, at an age over three days, selected for special treatment by a queenless colony, and thus, in the earlier stages of their larval growth were deprived of the liberal treatment

necessary for the production of perfect queens (207). It is
very rarely that a laying worker is tolerated in a colony which
has a prolific queen, but, in colonies which are queenless
and have neither eggs nor young larvæ from which to raise
queens, laying workers are occasionally found, and sometimes
in large numbers. Their eggs, being unimpregnated, produce
drones only. Their presence in a hive is indicated by the
irregular manner in which their eggs are deposited, several
eggs being frequently found in one cell, and cells with eggs
appearing side by side with cells containing drone larvæ,
whereas a fertile queen lays her eggs very regularly, as shown
above. (Fig. 98, page 131).

211. Removing Laying Workers.—Laying workers must
be got rid of, or the colony must perish. If a comb containing
eggs from another hive be given to the colony, and if the bees
can be induced to raise a queen, or queens, from those eggs,
the laying workers will be destroyed so soon as a young queen
begins to lay in the hive. But, where a laying worker has
been in possession for some time, the bees of the colony are
often indisposed to rear a queen from eggs supplied to them,
and will refuse to do so while the laying worker remains in
the hive. This difficulty may sometimes be overcome by
altering the position of the hive for a few days; then removing
all the bees, carrying them to a distance of 100 or 200 yards,
and shaking them down there upon a sheet or board; when,
the laying workers, not having been on the wing recently
and, therefore, being unfamiliar with the new position of the
hive, will fail to find it, while the other bees, except the useless
young drones, will return to the hive and will raise a queen
from eggs supplied to them. Beside the fact that a colony
long queenless will be short of, and perhaps destitute of, nurse
bees, this remedy entails a loss of some weeks before the young
queen can begin laying, and of over two months before her
progeny can supply the place of the dwindling workers of
the colony, and it can be adopted (so far as queen rearing
is concerned) only when there are drones flying to inseminate
the young queen. The speediest and the best remedy is to
introduce a young fertile queen (295). But, if a fertile queen
cannot be procured, the colony may be united to another, or
may be broken up and divided among other stocks having
fertile queens.

212. Stimulating in Autumn.—The beekeeper, knowing
that the success of the colony in the ensuing year will depend
largely upon its going into winter quarters with a large supply

of young bees (5), begins to stimulate again by supplying warm syrup, a little each evening, from the termination of the honey flow until about the middle of September (348). In this way queen and bees are induced to keep up the numbers of the colony and the danger of a scarcity of food is lessened.

Photo by   *A. S. Rowse*
SEALED BROOD.

213. Breeding Ceases.—When, with advancing autumn, the flow of nectar diminishes, the drones are destroyed (24); the daily deposit of eggs by the queen lessens (25), occupies fewer combs and smaller circles, as the cluster of bees draws towards the centre of the hive; and finally, in November, or earlier if the season prove very inclement, it ceases altogether. In very mild seasons, and in a hive adequately supplied with stores, the queen will sometimes continue to lay well into December.

214. Metamorphosis of Bees.—The following data are supported by common experience of the metamorphosis, etc., of bees. But it must be understood that the figures and the dates given are only approximate, and are variable according to the strength of the colony, the heat of the hive, and the condition of the weather:

TIME OCCUPIED FROM THE LAYING OF THE EGG.

	Queen	Worker	Drone	Days
Incubation of the egg	3	3	3	,,
Feeding of the larva	5	5	6	,,
Cell sealed on the	9th	9th	9th	,,
Spinning cocoon	1	2	3	,,
Interval of inaction	2	3	3	,,
Change from larva to nymph . .	1	1	1	,,
Change from nymph to exit as perfect insect	3	7	9	,,
Bee evacuates the cell on the . .	16th	22nd	25th	,,
Interval spent chiefly in the hive . .	5	14	14	,,
Bee flies freely from the hive on the .	21st	36th	39th	,,

Interval between issue of top Swarm and issue of 1st Cast . 9 Days.

,,   ,,   1st Cast and 2nd Cast . . . . . 2 Days.

,,   ,,   2nd, 3rd and 4th Casts . . . . . 1 Day.

BEE-METAMORPHOSIS.

In either sex the ovum needs
　　Three days before the chorion breaks,
Five days the female-larva feeds;
　　An extra day the male-grub takes.

A week in prison lies the queen;
　　For thirteen days a worker hides;
A drone develops all unseen
　　A fortnight and a day besides.

The total time is just about
　　A fortnight and a day for mother;
Three weeks will bring a worker out,
　　And three days longer hatch her brother.

CYPRIAN STOCK, in the *Irish Bee Journal*, March, 1922.

CHAPTER XX.

SWARMING.

215. Natural Swarming.—Natural swarming may occur upon any fine day from the middle of spring to the middle of autumn, as the condition of the colony may demand.   As a general rule, swarms may be looked for from the end of May, or in a very favourable season, from the closing days of April, up to the termination of the honey flow.   For profit during the season, early swarms are, of course, most in demand (161), because, if they come off in April or early in May, they have time to build combs and to rear brood before the opening of the honey flow; whereas if they issue late in June or in July, the honey flow, except in heather districts, will have ended before a sufficient number of young bees can be produced to take advantage of it (214); in which case neither the swarm nor the parent stock can store much surplus honey that season, and the former will probably require feeding and careful attention to enable it to survive the autumn and winter.   Hence the well-known adage : —

> A swarm of bees in May
> Is worth a load of hay ;
> A swarm of bees in June
> Is worth a silver spoon ;
> A swarm of bees in July
> Is worth a Butterfly.

216. Signs of Swarming.—With the use of modern hives, the beekeeper is able to calculate, with some degree of accuracy, the date upon which any particular stock is likely to swarm, and, by a little observation, he can avoid being taken completely by surprise.   This is one distinct advantage of modern beekeeping over the old methods; for, if any circumstance of bee-life demands more prompt attention than another it is the issue of a swarm, which must be dealt with at once and may be said, like "time and tide," to wait for no man.   When a colony has increased in numbers to such an extent as to become cramped for room, when nectar is being carried in rapidly, and when drones are on the wing, preparations are made for swarming and, seven or eight days before the event is to take place, queen cells are started upon the combs.   The first of these cells will be sealed over on or about the ninth

day and, when this is observed; when the bees of the colony
are found clustered about the entrance of the hive, or working
in a listless, half-hearted way, while the bees of other stocks

Photo from life   *by J. G. Digges.*
Fig. 105. Congestion (227). Bees Crowded Out.

are actively engaged foraging—the swarm may be expected
to issue. (Fig. 105.)

217. Delay of Swarming.—Should rain and unfavourable
weather generally prevail at the time of the capping of the
earlier queen cells, the swarm will not issue. The mature cells
will be opened, the young queen nymphs will be destroyed,
and swarming will be deferred until the weather improves;
if necessary, fresh queen cells will be prepared, loss of valuable
time ensuing. Should inclement weather be prolonged, swarming may be abandoned altogether for the season.

218. The Swarm.—But, if the weather continue favourable,
the bees will, in the early forenoon, make ready for their
departure. A number will be seen flying in front of the entrance,
gaily sporting themselves, and with their heads towards the
hive. Within, the agitated queen, having ceased ovipositing,
hurries from comb to comb where those of her progeny who
are to accompany her in this reckless abandoning of home,
and stores, and brood, are filling their honey sacs from the
cells, laying in a supply of food sufficient to serve them for
three or four days **(18)**.   Presently wild excitement spreads
through the whole colony; the bees rush hither and thither;
the temperature rises rapidly; and, suddenly, the swarming
bees pour out from the entrance in a steady stream.   The air

seems to be full of them; they fly around in the very abandonment of ecstasy, until the queen mother joining them or alighting upon some neighbouring tree, they settle around her and form the well-known cluster of the swarm. Previous to this scouts have been sent out to find a suitable place in which the swarm may locate itself and lay the foundation of a new home. Usually, until the return of the scouts (which may occur within an hour), the bees will remain in the cluster, and they should be secured at once, because the scouts generally select the new location at a considerable distance (221), and, when the swarm rises from the cluster, it will follow the scouts and may be lost to the owner. (19.) Bees make use of a scent-producing gland, known as the Nassenoff organ, described by a Russian biologist of that name. It is situated on the dorsal side of the end of the abdomen in queens and workers. On discovering a new hive, bees may be seen to elevate their abdomens and expose whitish spots towards the tips, at the same time fanning with their wings. The whitish spot is the opening of the Nassenoff gland, and the scent given off and distributed by the fanning immediately indicates to the rest of the bees that the new home has been found, and these at once join the fanners and take possession of the new dwelling. Similarly, when a swarm is settling, the first bees to alight use this organ of scent and so attract the queen and the remainder of the swarm.

219. Vagaries of Swarms.—Should the queen, from any cause, fail to leave the hive, the bees will return and will endeavour to force her to accompany them; for, they will not venture upon this hazardous enterprise without their mother bee (16). Should the queen leave the hive, and fall to the ground, the bees which discover her will cluster there, and the remainder will return to the hive. Should the swarm, when clustered, disclose a disproportion of young or of old bees, the swarm may go back and may issue again, and this may be repeated several times until the proper proportions are arrived at. Should the scouts fail to find a suitable location before sunset, or should rain suddenly appear, the swarm may remain in the original cluster until the following day. If, on the other hand, the weather be hot, and if the cluster be left unsheltered from the sun, the swarm may decamp at once without awaiting the return of the scouts. Sometimes the queen, a stranger to light and unaccustomed to fly, is unable to reach the selected spot, and will drop, exhausted, on the way, and the new home be started in an unsuitable place. Occasionally two swarms come out at the same time and form one cluster; these should be treated as one swarm and, on being hived, one of the queens may be removed for use elsewhere. If both queens be allowed to enter the new hive, one of them will be destroyed. (See also 195 and 255).

220. **To Encourage Clustering.**—The old-time custom of beating tin cans, in order to cause the swarm to settle quickly may, perhaps, be attributed to the story that the Curetes, wishing to hide the birth of Jupiter from his father Saturn, set up a clashing of cymbals to drown the infant's cries:

> " Cum pueri circúm puerum pernice choreâ
> Armati in numerum pulsarant aribus æra."

The noise attracted a swarm of bees to the cave where the child was, and their honey nourished him; hence the origin of " ringing " to attract swarms. Aristotle (B.C. 384) confessed that he did not know whether the ringing affected the bees through pleasure, or fear, or whether they heard it at all. Milton (*The Honey Bee*, 1851), thought that the noise was intended to prevent the bees from communicating with (hearing) one another, and thus to present an obstacle to their flying away. The custom is possibly due to its having been observed that flying bees hasten home from the fields when thunderstorms threaten in summer; the din one sometimes hears in swarming time is intended to represent the " artillery of the gods." Bees are highly sensitive to the approach of rain, and will seek the shelter of their lives when rain is near. But, it is very probable that it is not the thunder which may precede a summer shower that influences them; and it is not likely that the noise of horns and drummed cans can have much, if any, effect in causing them to cluster rapidly. Water, however, may be used with good effect. If applied through a garden syringe which casts a fine spray, and so that it fall upon the swarming bees from above, like rain, it will hasten their settling, and will cause them to cluster closely, so that they may be the more easily, and the more promptly, secured. It is recorded that truant swarms have been headed off and impelled in the required direction by this means.

221. **Truant Swarms.**—Swarms, when they once rise from the first cluster, seldom remain in the vicinity of their former homes (19). It appears to be their object to settle as far as possible from the hives which they have abandoned, and to leave to their successors not merely the stores there, but also the flowers of the immediate vicinity. This is one of Nature's provisions against the mischief of in-breeding. It is often a

cause of disappointment and loss to the owner, who tries in vain to stay, or to overtake, his truant swarm. The law, as it applies to the ownership of truant swarms, seems to be that if the bees have been seen issuing from their hive, and have been kept in sight by the owner, or by someone on his behalf, while they have been followed and until they have entered the premises where they cluster, they may be legally claimed and removed. Otherwise, they become, in the eyes of the law, *feræ naturæ*, or wild bees, and may be claimed by anyone who takes possession of them.

222. **Clipping Queen's Wings.**—Many devices have been employed to induce swarming bees to cluster in accessible places, and to counteract the instinct which impels them to depart to "fresh woods and pastures new." Decoy hives, furnished with some combs, will sometimes entice swarms to take possession of them. Dry, dark combs, and even black hats and stockings, tied to the lower branches of trees in the apiary, are said, by reason of their resemblance at a distance to clustering bees, to have an attraction for swarms. But, in spite of every such device, swarms will frequently cluster in the high branches of trees, or in other inaccessible places, and they may decamp altogether before they can be secured by the owner. This difficulty may be prevented by the simple

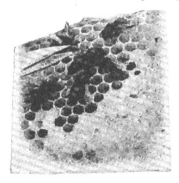

Photo by J. G. Digges.
Fig. 106.
CLIPPING QUEEN'S WING.

expedient of clipping the queen's wings; for, if the queen cannot fly the swarm will not decamp; and if it should settle upon a high branch, it will, when the absence of the queen is discovered, return to the hive. Acordingly, if the queen be picked up, she can be allowed to run in with the bees when the swarm returns to the hive (either the parent hive or a new hive placed on the old stand), and thus the trouble of following and securing the swarm may be obviated. It must, however, be observed that should a swarm with a clipped queen emerge unnoticed, the swarm will return to its hive, but the queen may be lost. To prevent such a disaster, a careful watch should be kept. The queen should be picked up and placed at the entrance of the hive, that she may run in with the swarm.

The proper time for clipping is in the early spring when the population of the hive is small, and when, therefore, the queen can be more readily found. To clip a queen's wings, proceed as follows:—Take out the frame on which the queen is found, drawing the carbolic cloth over the brood nest, and pick off the queen by the wings with the finger and thumb of the right hand, as shown (Fig. 107, A); then gently take her, by the thorax, in the fingers of the left hand, clip the wing (Fig. 107, B), return her to the brood nest, and place the frame in

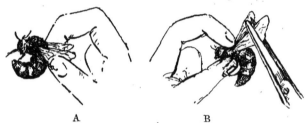

A   B

Fig. 107. CLIPPING QUEEN'S WING.

its former position in the hive. In either case the operation is a delicate one, and should be carefully performed, avoiding all risk of injuring the queen by any pressure upon her abdomen. By this means, also, the ages of queens may be recorded upon their persons, the wings on one side being clipped in their first year, those on the other side, in their second year, and, in their third season, when there are no longer any wings to clip, a young queen should be given to the stock (294). It goes without saying that queens should not have their wings clipped before they have been mated. The risk of losing swarms is minimized also by Artificial Swarming (233).

223. The Parent Stock.—Seven or eight days after the issue of the prime swarm, the first of the virgin queens emerges from her cell and, if the stock decide against further swarming, the young queen, assisted by the bees, destroys the royal nymphs and assumes her position as queen of the colony (209). About five or seven days later, *i.e.*, thirteen to sixteen days after the issue of the prime swarm, she leaves the hive for impregnation and, usually on the twenty-first day after the swarm, her eggs may be found in the cells. Although those dates are only approximate, they are reliable enough to guide the beekeeper in his management. He will know, for example, that, on the twenty-first day after the swarm, all worker brood of the old queen will have emerged from the cells and that the young queen will have only just begun to lay. If, therefore, he desire to transfer bees and combs from skeps to modern hives (265) he will select the twentieth or the twenty-first day after the skep has given a swarm, as offering least risk of injury to brood.

224. Casts.—As stated above (216), swarms usually issue shortly after the sealing of the earliest queen cell, which takes place on the ninth day from the laying of the egg. Seven or eight days later the young queen leaves her cell and attempts to destroy the royal nymphs (209). Early in the morning, or in the afternoon, when the bees are still, her shrill piping may be distinctly heard, and also the muffled, piping answers of the royal nymphs who, still imprisoned in their cells, are conscious of impending danger. If the colony be sufficiently strong to give off a cast, the bees mount guard around the queen cells and refuse to permit the young queen to destroy her rivals. On the following day, which usually is the ninth day after the departure of the prime swarm, the young queen and the second swarm, or cast, issue (20). If, however, the weather be very unfavourable, the exit of the cast may be delayed, and even the queen cells and their occupants may be destroyed (Fig. 26, B, page 50), and further swarming be deferred, or ended for the season. But young, unmated queens are somewhat reckless and impetuous, and will often come out with a cast on a rainy day; they will fly farther than aged queens before alighting; and such casts are more likely than are prime swarms to abscond, even after they have been hived. Second casts usually issue two or three days after the first cast, and third and fourth casts on the next and the following days respectively. Sometimes two or more virgin queens, emerging from their cells on the same day, accompany one cast. The cast being hived, all but one queen will be destroyed. Although, in a favourable season, an early first cast may be made profitable, after-swarms should be discouraged because, weak themselves, they so depopulate the parent stock, neither can be of much use that season.

225. Hunger Swarms.—Occasionally bees will forsake their hives on any day of the year, except in winter, either as a complete colony, or as a swarm, and will locate themselves in any available nook or corner. This may arise from the presence in the hive of something distasteful to the bees (243). But most frequently it is the result of hunger, when, a portion of the bees will abandon the hive, in a spirit of self-denial, leaving such food as remains for the queen and the remainder of the stock; or the whole colony will depart, knowing that starvation is imminent, and in a desperate hope of bettering their condition elsewhere (341). Obviously, the remedy is, in the former case, to introduce them to a clean hive; in the latter case, to provide them with food. Examination of the hive will generally show what has been the cause of the departure of the bees, and, when the cause has been removed, the truants may be returned to their old quarters.

226. Prevention of Swarming.—It is frequently advisable to prevent natural swarming, because of the trouble and risks attending it, and because, when one desires to obtain the largest possible harvest of honey and does not wish to increase his stocks, natural swarming upsets all his arrangements; for, it is not possible, in an average season, to secure both an increase of stocks and a large supply of surplus honey. Even where increase of stocks is chiefly desired, natural swarming may be prevented with advantage and, by artificial swarming, the increase be made by wise selection from the best colonies (233). It must be remembered that it is, generally, quite impossible to prevent swarming when once the bees of a colony have contracted the "swarming fever" (197)—so-called, perhaps, because like any fever that "flesh is heir to," when once it has set in the arrival of the crisis is inevitable. Therefore, the beekeeper, desiring to prevent natural swarming and familiar with the causes which promote it (216), should set himself, in good time, to circumvent them.

227. Giving Room.—One fruitful cause of natural swarming is congestion in the brood chamber, when there is not sufficient room either for ovipositing by the queen, or for honey storing by the bees (197). Therefore, before they are actually needed, frames of comb, or of foundation, should be added to the brood nest and, in the season, new sections or frames to the supers (268). When the honey flow is on, *i.e.*, when nectar is being carried in rapidly, the addition of frames of foundation will not always meet the needs of the case, because, the demand for vacant cells, both for eggs and honey, becomes too urgent and, before the foundation can be drawn out into cells, congestion may set in and preparations for swarming begin. In such circumstances, empty combs should be given. If the hive has already its full complement of frames, one or two combs of honey may be removed, the honey extracted (143) and the combs returned to the hive; and this should be repeated weekly, or more frequently, as required. In a pressing case, one or two combs of brood may be removed and given to another stock, the vacancy being filled with empty combs. Thus, not only is the tendency to swarm checked, but also the storing of honey is largely increased. Afterwards, when supers are put on, the pressure upon the combs in the brood nest is relieved, and if, as each fresh super is added, one or two of the combs in the lower storey have their honey extracted and are returned to the centre of the brood nest, or if a frame of foundation be given there, the queen will have sufficient scope for her energies below, the bees for their energies above, and the inducement to swarm will be minimized, if not entirely removed (203 and illus. page 152).

228. **Ventilation.**—Excessive heat in a crowded hive encourages swarming. Therefore, hives, in warm weather, should be well ventilated; the doors should be opened to full width; the ventilator in the floor board (90) should also be opened. A ventilating dummy (102) may be used at the back of the brood chamber, the body box being moved backwards on the floor board to admit air through the dummy, or an opening in the back of the hive being provided for that purpose, so that it can be closed from the outside, or partially closed as required. The floor board—when constructed so as to admit of this—may be lowered, to admit air from all sides. The body box may be raised half an inch from the floor board by wedges at the corners. The roof may be tilted up in the front, may be shaded from direct sunrays by trees, or by a makeshift shade of one kind or another; in extreme cases, a sack may be soaked in water and placed upon the roof, and be kept damp and cool during the hottest hours of the day. Bees will not for long tolerate an upward draught and, although to meet a sudden emergency an upward draught may be caused by placing a feeding stage (129) upon the sheet and raising the roof, such an expedient must be only temporarily adopted. Hives should never have the floor board permanently fastened to the body box, because of the difficulty, among others, of ventilating, and all ventilators applied to a hive should be of such a nature as to be easily opened, and as easily closed, without the risk of disturbing or crushing bees; for, in our climate, chilly nights frequently follow warm days, when, should the ventilators be left fully open, chilled brood might result (370).

229. **Limiting Drone Rearing.**—A third circumstance incident to swarming lies in the breeding of excessive quantities of drones—fussy, and somewhat pushful insects which raise the temperature of the hive, and by their very presence suggest, continuously, the rearing of young queens. There-

fore, the production of drones should be limited by the use
of only worker-cell foundation, and in full sheets, wired, to
prevent breakage and consequent construction of drone cells
(205), and also by cutting out unnecessary drone comb when
discovered in the hive. The skilful beekeeper makes it a point
to limit drone rearing in all his stocks, except in those that are
headed by his best queens. Thus he secures that the drones
which shall inseminate his young queens shall be of the best
blood in his apiary, and by careful selection he keeps up, and
even improves, the quality of his stocks.

230. Limiting Queen Rearing.—A fourth condition in a
stock which is about to swarm is the presence of queen cells,
and it is sometimes recommended, as a preventive of swarming, to cut out all such cells. The advice is based upon the
theory that it is the mother-queen who causes the swarm by
stirring the bees up to it, and by leading them out; that she
is impelled by her wrath at the rearing of young queens;
and that, if the queen cells be destroyed by the beekeeper,
the old queen will be placated and the swarm be prevented.
But it is evident to careful observers that swarming generally
takes place, not at the instigation of the old queen, but against
her will; that she does not lead the swarm out; and that she
frequently shows a pronounced disinclination to leave her hive
and, sometimes, has to be driven out by the bees. The swarm
becomes necessary by reason of the conditions referred to
above (216); the bees prepare for it in the manner already
described; cutting out the queen cells, while it will delay the
swarm, will not alone prevent it: further queen cells will be
formed; the preparations will be continued; and the bees,
always listless during such periods, will sacrifice much valuable
time and energy in those weeks of the year which, to the beekeeper, are most valuable. Therefore, while cutting out the
queen cells may be adopted in connection with other preventive
measures, it will not, by itself, accomplish the desired object.
Sufficient room and ventilation must be given, and it should
be remembered that, if the various precautions be deferred
until the bees have felt the need of more room, the swarm will
probably issue in spite of all that the beekeeper may do. (226).

231. The "Demaree" System.—This plan of swarm
control is suitable when extracted honey is the object of the
beekeeper. It was first made public by the *American Bee
Journal* in 1892, Mr. Demaree having communicated it to that
periodical. It is much in use in America and has rapidly come
into favour in Great Britain and Ireland. Concerning it,

the Editor of the *American Bee Journal* says: "The only defect of this method is the large amount of work which it entails, but it is probably the best method to prevent swarming altogether." The plan may be described briefly thus: The combs containing brood should have any queen cells on them destroyed and should then be transferred from the brood chamber to an upper storey, above a queen excluder, with the exception of one comb, containing some unsealed brood and eggs, which is left in the brood chamber. The brood chamber is then filled with frames of empty combs or, if empty combs be not available, with frames containing full sheets of foundation. **(118).** The queen has now a new brood nest below the excluder, while the combs of brood—with the one exception mentioned above—are in the super. In twenty-one days all the brood will have hatched out of the combs above and the brood in the lower chamber will have begun to emerge from their cells—a continuous succession of young bees. Usually the combs in the upper storey will have been filled with honey when the brood has hatched. Mr. Demaree says that, if the season be propitious, the yield of honey will be "enormous under proper management." Should the flow of nectar continue, the honey may be extracted from the combs in the upper storey, and that storey may be placed again on the floor board, the queen being transferred to it and the lower storey being placed over the excluder. Thus the queen has always sufficient room for laying; her surroundings are similar to those in which she would find herself after swarming; the desire to swarm is curbed. Under this plan, the population of the hive reaching enormous proportions, the necessity for ample ventilation will arise and ample ventilation must be given. **(228).** A variation of this plan is to use an extra super between the upper storey and the brood chamber. Occasionally the bees will rear a queen above the excluder; in this case an entrance is made in the upper storey, the young queen mates and begins to lay there and, if the old queen be removed, or destroyed, the colony will have been requeened.

232. Prevention of Issue of Swarms and Casts.—When queen cells have been commenced in a stock which is being worked for honey, there is probably no better procedure than the following: On finding queen cells on the combs, remove all queen cells and also the queen. The latter, if not of use elsewhere, may be destroyed, or she may be retained on one comb of brood in a nucleus box. Nine days later again carefully remove all queen cells and introduce a young, fertile queen. If a swarm has actually issued before queen cells have been found, the cells may be destroyed in the same way and the swarm at once returned after the queen has been removed from it.   This is an almost certain preventive of any further attempt to swarm for the rest of the season, and stocks so treated will usually give excellent results.   It is, of course, possible to eliminate all but one queen cell and to allow the virgin which results to mate and become established at the head of the colony; but the risk of loss (which is very considerable in such cases) of the young queen before becoming fertile much more than justifies the expenditure entailed by the purchase of a fertile queen.   Casts may be prevented, when a first swarm has been hived separately, by the removal of all but one queen cell or by the introduction of a fertile queen after all have been removed.   (251-253). If a cast be hived upon a couple of combs of brood, it will quickly increase to a stock sufficiently strong to winter well.

233. Artificial Swarming.—As a substitute for natural swarming, artificial swarming, in the hands of a capable bee-keeper, offers many distinct advantages.   It enables him (1) To arrange, by careful selection, the increase of his stocks, and that always from his best queens: (2) To obtain early swarms, and from stocks which, if left alone, might not swarm naturally: (3) To prevent serious waste of time by stocks in preparation for natural swarming: (4) To avoid excitement and trouble securing and hiving swarms, and the risk of their absconding altogether (221): (5) To provide swarms for sale, as required (238): (6) To introduce strange queens to stocks (311): and (7) To remove bees from infected combs, as in the treatment of foul brood (385).

234. Conditions.—There are certain conditions which require attention in all the following operations, viz. :—(1) The stocks to be operated upon must be strong: (2) There must be drones hatching, or on the wing, to inseminate the young queens: (3) The day must be fine, so that there may be sufficient flying bees to form the swarms: (4) The brood must be carefully protected from cold: (5) The swarms must be fed for a few days, especially if they have no sealed honey in the combs given them.

235. One Swarm from One Colony.—From the stock to be swarmed remove a frame of brood with the queen and adhering bees and place it in a new hive. Add, say, six frames of comb, or of foundation, three on either side of the occupied frame; close up the dummy; put on the quilts and roof; and set the new hive upon the stand of the parent stock, removing the latter to another position at least six feet away. All the flying bees of the parent stock, returning to their old stand, will form the swarm. The parent hive should be given a frame of comb in the place of the frame removed—not a frame of foundation, if comb can be procured, because queenless bees are disposed to build cells suited to the storing of honey rather than to the rearing of workers, and this is to be avoided. If a fertile queen be introduced (308) to the parent stock in the evening, there will be no delay of brood rearing. If a fertile queen cannot be supplied, one or two ripe queen cells may be given. If neither queen nor queen cells be available, the bees will rear a queen for themselves.

236. One Stronger Swarm from Two Colonies.—Prepare a hive (S) with seven or eight frames of wired foundation (126). Remove a strong stock (A) to one side, and place the hive S on A's stand. Set a hiving board with a white cloth upon it (244) and sloping from the ground to the alighting board of hive S. Smoke the bees of hive A, and take out the frames one by one, brushing, shaking, or thumping (193) the bees on to the hiving board until all have been removed from hive A, when they will run into hive S, and will be strengthened by the addition of all the flying bees of A returning to their old stand. The frames of hive A having been returned to their hive, and kept covered to avoid the danger of chilling the brood (370), remove a second strong stock (B) to a new position and place hive A upon B's stand. All the flying bees of hive B, numbering many thousands, will enter hive A to rear the brood and to raise a new queen for themselves. If, in the evening, a fertile queen be introduced to A (308), breeding will proceed without interruption and much valuable time will be saved. By this method a strong swarm is secured without unduly reducing the strength of the two stocks operated upon.

237. Using Three or More Stocks.—When there are more than two stocks available for the purpose, the above method may be varied as follows:—Remove one strong stock to a new position and place an empty hive upon its stand. Take, as required, one, two, or more frames of brood from the other stocks, returning the adhering bees to their hives, and insert the frames in the new hive, supplying their places with frames of comb, or of wired foundation. Thus the first stock supplies the bees, the others the brood, and none of them is appreciably weakened. A new queen, if available, may be given in the evening (295).

238. Making Swarms for Sale.—When swarms are being prepared for sale, they may be made up from one or more stocks, as desired. If from one stock, the frame on which the queen is found is removed, and the bees upon it, with the queen, are brushed, or shaken, into a swarm-box (169), or upturned skep, and as many more bees as are required are also shaken in. If still more bees be required, the box, or skep, may be placed upon the stand of the parent hive until a sufficient number of flying bees have entered it. It may then be prepared for transit (162). Another method is to set the empty skep temporarily upon the stand of the parent hive; a frame is then removed from the parent hive with the queen and some bees; the queen is picked off the frame and placed at the entrance of the skep, and the bees are shaken off the frame so that they may run in with the queen: the operation is continued with other frames until sufficient bees have been transferred to the skep, which is then prepared for transit, the parent hive being returned to its stand. If bees of more than one colony be required, care must be taken to include only one queen in the swarm; and the bees should all be dusted with flour, or aspersed with thin, scented syrup to prevent fighting. (169).

239. One Swarm from a Stock and a Nucleus.—It will be evident that one of the objections to swarming, both natural and artificial, lies in the fact that the stock which has been deprived of its queen, while the older bees are dying off rapidly, must be without a laying queen for at least twenty-one days (223). Careful beekeepers overcome this objection by having a supply of young, fertile queens in nucleus hives (303). Where such queens can be had, artificial swarming may be carried out without any waste of time and, therefore, more successfully. The following procedure may be adopted: Upon a fine day, when nectar is coming in, secure the young laying queen of the nucleus upon one of the frames, by a pipe-cover cage (310) and so that she shall have some honey at her disposal. If the nucleus is in a small hive, transfer the bees and combs to a suitable hive and add sufficient frames of comb, or of foundation. Place the hive containing the nucleus on the stand of a strong stock, removing the latter to the stand formerly occupied by the nucleus. By this method the nucleus receives the flying bees of the stock, both colonies have fertile queens, the risks attached to other methods are avoided, and the bees will work with a will. The caged queen may be released in thirty-six hours.

240. Making Swarms from Stocks in Skeps.—Owing to the inconvenience of feeding and observing bees in skeps, and to the difficulty of supplying swarms in skeps with brood and drawn-out comb, artificial swarming to colonize skeps should be deferred until the stocks are not only strong, but are also near the swarming stage, and until the weather is good and there is an abundance of nectar to be gathered. Drive (169) the stock from which the swarm is to be taken until the queen and about half the bees have gone up. If more than the desired quantity of bees pass up before the queen, pick up the queen and place her in a small box for the moment. Throw the excess bees back among the combs and liberate the queen among the bees in the upper skep. Put back the parent stock upon its old stand, and the driven swarm upon a new stand, or *vice versa* as your object may demand. If the queen has not been found when all the bees have been driven, the stock must be returned to its skep and the operation be repeated later on.

241. A Stronger Swarm from Two Stocks in Skeps.— When a stronger swarm is desired, and when two stocks (A and B) in skeps are available for the purpose, drive the queen and all the bees from stock A; place the driven swarm (S) upon A's stand; place stock A upon the stand of stock B; remove stock B to a new position. Thus A gives all its bees to S, retaining the combs and brood, and securing, on its new stand, all the flying bees of B, while B is not depleted beyond its force of flying bees.

Photo by   *A. H. Bowen.*
A VERY SYMMETRICAL SWARM.

CHAPTER XXI.

HIVING: UNITING: AND TRANSFERRING BEES.

242. Confidence in Protection from Stings.—It has already been stated that bees, when swarming, are most peaceable, and that at other times they may be " subdued to settled quiet " so as to be comparatively harmless (176). But, for the reasons mentioned (178), the beginner will do well to wear a veil and gloves when preparing to hive a swarm; for, until he gains the confidence which follows experience, the confidence arising from the feeling of being, for the occasion, protected from stings, will assist him to carry through the work in hands in a business-like way. (141, 178).

243. Preparing the Hive.—Some days before a swarm is expected, a hive should be prepared to receive it. If the hive has been used before, it should have any necessary repairs and two coats of good paint. The inside, and the dummies, should be scalded, and washed with a solution of 1 part Calvert's No. 5 Carbolic Acid to 2 parts water, or 1 teaspoonful Izal to 1 quart water (418), and the parts should be set out in the air so that the smell of the disinfectant may disappear before the hive may be required; for, any unpleasantness in their new home might cause the bees to forsake it (225). The hive, with eight or nine frames of comb, or of wired foundation, should then be set up in the position which it is to occupy in the apiary, carefully levelled, as previously directed (156), and with the sheet and quilts upon the frames. The sheet, if new, should be soaked in water, and put, while still damp, upon the frames; it will then lie perfectly flat, and will continue to do so when dry.

244. Hiving Swarms Direct.—When a swarm issues, no time should be lost in securing it. If a garden syringe be at hand, spray some water over the bees and, when they cluster, give them some more water to cool them and to cause them to cluster more closely. If they cluster upon a low branch, or shrub, bring the prepared hive as close as possible to the cluster: place a hiving board sloping up to the alighting board of the hive, and raised at the other end so that it may be nearly, but not quite, level: cover the hiving board with a white cloth arranged to lie smoothly right up to the hive entrance, and kept in position by stones at the corners (Fig. 108): draw out the hive doors, and with them wedge up the front of the hive an inch or two from the floor board. If the swarm hang not more than a foot or two above the hiving board, give the branch on which it hangs a smart shake, throwing the bees on to the white cloth. If the branch be too high, cut it off, without disturbing the cluster, and shake the bees on to the white

cloth. They will speedily run into the hive; when, if a sharp look out be kept for the queen, she may be seen passing in. Should the bees delay to enter the hive, take up a handful, and place them at the entrance; or, with a feather move them on (Fig. 108). The "music" which they will make on discovering their new home will act as a "quick march" to the remainder, and the swarm will soon be hived. When the

J. G. D.

Fig. 108.   HIVING BEES.

bees are in, throw the white cloth over the hive, letting it hang down in front, thus sheltering from the sun until the flying bees join the others, when the hive must be carried to its permanent stand for, otherwise, the bees, beginning work, will mark the spot, and will return there after the hive has been moved. Feed for a few days. (247).

245. **Swarms in High Trees.**—If the swarm should settle on a very high branch, the hive need not be removed from its stand. Get a clean skep (83), mouth upwards, under the cluster, and shake the swarm into it (Fig. 109). If you cannot reach high enough, hold up the skep on a pitchfork and get someone to shake the bees in; but take care to have your skep so secured that it will not topple over and drop the swarm upon your head. The job may be more satisfactorily carried through if you provide yourself beforehand with a half sack, arranged on a hoop, and with a long handle, after the fashion of an·

angler's landing net. Get the sack under the swarm; shake the bees in; give the handle a turn, closing the mouth of the bag so that no bees can escape, and carry them to the hive. If the branch must be cut off and removed, with any risk of shaking off the swarm in the process, bore two holes at opposite sides of the skep-mouth and pass two strong cords through the holes: get the skep under the cluster and tie it to the branch: pass a sack up, covering the skep and swarm, and tie it also to the branch: then, no matter what jarring or shaking may ensue, the bees will be secure.

J. G. D.

Fig. 109. Swarm in a High Tree.

246. Swarms in Awkward Places.—Should it be impossible to work any of the above plans: if the swarm has entered a chimney, or has clustered in a thick hedge, or in an old wall; get your skep over it, and drive the bees up with smoke, or with the fumes of a cloth saturated with carbolic solution **(136),** If you can arrange so that the smoke, or the carbolic fumes, will not enter the skep, the bees will march up. If the swarm cluster on a wall, or on the trunk of a tree, get the skep under, and with a brush sweep the bees in. If they alight on the ground, as possibly they may do when the queen's wings have been clipped **(222),** place the skep beside them, and raised an inch or two upon a couple of stones; with a twig, or a feather, or your hand move some of the bees to the entrance: they will pass in, and the remainder will quickly follow.

247. Hiving from a Skep.—Having secured the swarm in your skep, set the skep on a cloth, or on the ground, close to

Fig. 110.

Swarm Taker.

the place where the swarm originally clustered, and raised upon a couple of stones to allow the outside bees to enter: cover with a cloth to shield from hot sunshine until all the bees shall have gone in : then carry it gently to the stand which it is to occupy.   In the afternoon, a couple of hours before sunset, hive the swarm as directed (244). Or, if it be desirable to adopt another and more rapid method, remove the sheet and quilts from the hive which is to receive the swarm; space out the frames as widely as possible; and arrange the hiving board and white cloth as directed above (244). Take the skep; invert it; give it a good " bump " upon the ground to loosen the foothold of the bees; and pour, or shake, some of the swarm on to the frames, and the remainder on to the hiving board.   Then spread the sheet, only, upon the frames; put on a feeder (127) with thin syrup (Recipe 355); and place the roof in position.   In the morning, close up the frames and dummy, first removing any unnecessary frames, and any in which the foundation may have broken down; remove the wedges and lower the hive front to the floor board; put on the coverings and the roof; and continue gentle feeding for about a week.

248. Secure All the Cluster.—If, by any means, you have failed to secure the queen with the swarm, the bees will forsake the hiving skep and will return to the original cluster if the queen be still there, or to the hive from which they swarmed in the event of their being unable to find the queen. Therefore, care should be taken to secure all the bees of the cluster, so that the queen may not be lost.

249. Sweetening the Hiving Skep.—The old-fashioned custom of smearing the skep with treacle, butter, or beer, as an inducement to the bees, is both useless and objectionable; but, a little piece of comb, with honey or brood, fastened by a skewer in the top of the skep, serves as an attraction.

250. Hiving by Caging.—If the beekeeper be on the alert and sees the swarm as it issues, he may often save himself a great deal of trouble if he watches the queen as she comes out on the alighting board, and slips a pipe-cover cage (310) over her.   He then places the prepared hive on the stand of the parent stock; sets the queen, in her cage, on the alighting board of the former; and waits for the swarm to return when the absence of the queen shall have been discovered (219). He then releases the queen, allowing her to go in with the swarm, and either leaves the swarm on the old stand, or removes it to a new position. as his requirements may suggest.   If left upon the old stand, it will receive a large accession of strength from the flying bees of the parent stock, and will work with surprising vigour. (251). For hiving " Package bees," see par. 161.

251. Hiving a Swarm on the Old Stand.—If you are working for honey rather than for an increase of your stocks, place the swarm upon the stand of the parent stock, removing the latter to a new position, and transfer the supers, if any, from the stock to the swarm. Thus, casts will be prevented, the swarm will be strengthened by the flying bees of the stock, and new energy will be thrown into its work. An excluder (117) under the supers will be useful. It should be noted that in this case of hiving a swarm on the old stand and transferring to it the supers from the parent stock—if foundation, only, be given in the frames, the bees will probably carry up pollen to the supers on the first day, having no cells below in which to store it. If even one frame of drawn-out comb be given below, this mischief may be prevented. If, at the close of the honey flow, you unite the two stocks, removing the old queen, in the following year you will have a strong stock with a queen in her prime.

252. The " Heddon " Method.—The Heddon method is to move the parent hive to one side, beside, and at right angles with, its former position, the hive with the swarm being placed on the old stand. Two days later, the parent hive is turned round so that its entrance points in the same direction as the entrance of the hive containing the swarm; and, seven or eight days after the issue of the swarm, i.e., a day or two before a cast might be expected (224), in the middle of the day, when bees are flying freely, the parent hive is changed to a new position, thus giving all its flying bees to the swarm and effectually preventing casts. (232).

253. Returning Swarms.—Another method consists in taking away all brood from the swarmed stock, filling the vacancies with frames of wired foundation, and transferring the brood at once to other hives; after which the swarm is run into the parent hive as directed (244). Thus the swarming impulse is usually satisfied, the bees are kept together, and the foraging propensity receives a new stimulus. It is to be noted that the brood combs, before being given to other stocks, should have their queen cells removed.

254. Retracing Swarms.—Should there be any difficulty

in locating the hive from which a swarm has issued, take from
the cluster a handful of bees : put them into a small box and
dredge them with flour : then carry them to a distance and
shake them out upon a board, or a newspaper If a watch
be kept upon the hives, the bees that have been floured will
be seen returning to the hive from which they issued with
the swarm.

255. Separating Swarms.—Should two swarms unite in
one cluster (219), if it be desired to separate them, preserving
both queens, prepare two hives (243) standing side by side, and
shake the swarms, in about equal portions, on to the cloth-
covered hiving boards (244), as far back from the hive entrances
as convenient; move up a few bees to each entrance and—
having enlisted an assistant to watch one lot while you attend
to the other—secure the first queen that shows herself, placing
a cage, a wineglass, or a tumbler, over her.   If you succeed
in finding the second queen also, admit one queen to each
hive; failing this, watch for signs of queenlessness (297) in one
swarm, and run in the captive queen there.

256. Uniting Bees: Precautions.—Weak stocks can never
be profitable; but, if two or more of such stocks be joined
together they will, in summer, do useful work, and in winter
they will consume less stores, preserve their heat better, and
will survive where, separately, they would perish.   Frequently
it is desirable to unite stock to stock, swarm to stock, or swarm
to swarm, as the case may be.   It must be remembered that
bees of different colonies will not usually unite peaceably,
unless precautions be taken to prevent their fighting.   Such
precautions should aim at—(1) Causing the bees to fill themselves with sweets; and (2) Giving them the same scent.

257.—Uniting Swarms.—Swarms, however, being already
well filled with honey (218) and having neither home nor brood
to defend, may be united at once if they be thrown together
into one skep, or on to a hiving board, and allowed to run into
the hive.   One queen may be removed, or the two queens may
be left to settle their differences in their own way.   (255).

258. Uniting Two Stocks.—Bring the two stocks together
as already directed (165).   Begin the operation of uniting in
the evening when all the bees have returned to their hives from
the fields.   Smoke both stocks a little and remove quilts.   Lay
a sheet of newspaper flat on the frames of one and place the
other at once upon it.   Close all up.   The bees will tear the

paper to shreds and unite without fighting. The weaker of
the two stocks should be placed above the stronger. Combs
may be sorted out a day or two later and the bees relegated to
one brood chamber if desired. An older, but now seldom used
method is to take a third hive, and after opening both colonies
and exposing the combs to the light and after smoking the bees
to some extent, place the combs alternately in the third hive.
This method has the objectionable feature that there are
generally more combs of brood in the two colonies than will
go into one brood chamber and that it requires more labour
and is less satisfactory than the newspaper plan. The old
method of spraying the bees with scented syrup is now discarded; though sprinkling with flour is sometimes used as an
aid in special cases.

259. **Uniting Queenless Bees to a Stock.**—In this case,
protect the queen by caging, as directed (310), and proceed as
before (258). If there be nothing to be gained by transferring
all, or any, of the frames from the queenless colony, the bees
may be shaken into a skep and thrown down upon a hiving
board before the hive of the stock to which they are to be
united. Another usually successful method is to cover the
frames of the queenless stock with a sheet of strong paper,
slightly damped, and having a few small holes pierced in the
centre, then setting the hive with the other stock on top, and
leaving all undisturbed for at least four days. A sheet of
ordinary newspaper, pierced as described above, is frequently
used for the purpose. The bees, above and below, proceed
to cut passages through the paper, acquire the same scent,
gradually become acquainted with each other, and unite
peaceably.

260. **Uniting a Swarm to a Stock.**—Proceed as described
above for uniting queenless bees to a stock; with this addition,
that, if you wish to preserve the queen not of the swarm, but of
the stock, the queen of the swarm should be removed, because,
otherwise, the two queens will fight, and if the queen of the
swarm has not been impregnated, being the queen of an after-
swarm, or cast, the fertile queen will probably be killed. If
you cannot find the queen otherwise, allow only a few bees
to enter the hive, keeping the bulk of the swarm well back
from the entrance: then place a piece of excluder zinc (117)
over the entrance: pick up the queen as she endeavours to pass
through the zinc: remove the zinc, and let the swarm go in.
(See also 191, 195). Sometimes, to further reduce the risk of
fighting, it is preferred to mix the bees more thoroughly by

shaking those of the stock also on to the hiving board, allowing them to run in with the swarm.

261. Uniting Driven Bees.—Driven bees (169) may be united without difficulty. Dust the two lots thoroughly with flour. If they are in skeps, bring the skeps together, mouth to mouth : give them a " bump " on the ground, to throw the upper bees into the lower skep : shake, and mix them well together, and throw them on to the hiving board. The union may, however, be made wihout the use of flour, as already described. (169). If you do not remove one queen, the bees will settle that matter for themselves.

262. Uniting Driven Bees to a Stock.—For this operation, extra precautions against fighting are desirable. Procure a second, temporary hive (T), and to it transfer about half the frames from the stock hive, returning the adhering bees to the latter as you proceed, and, without delay, hive the driven bees by shaking some on to the frames (T) and the remainder on to a hiving board (247). Now bring the two hives close together. After three or four days, unite the two lots as described under the head of " Uniting Two Stocks." (258).

263. Transferring Bees.—When " spring cleaning " (439) is being attended to; when it is desired to change from the old to the modern methods; and at other times, it is found necessary to transfer bees from one hive to another, or from a skep to a modern hive.

264. Transferring from Hive to Hive.—Remove the stock hive to one side and set a clean, empty hive on the vacant stand, with its floor board perfectly level, if the frames are to hang parallel with the entrance (156), and with the frame carriers vaselined (183). Subdue the bees with smoke : remove the quilts and sheet : if there be supers on, set them on two sticks on the ground, or upon a table : draw back the dummy, and space out the frames. Take out the frames, one by one, and insert them, in the same order, in the clean hive : set a hiving board in front, and brush or shake on to it any bees remaining in the old hive : replace the supers (if any) and put on the covering and roof (440).

265. Transferring from Skep to Modern Hive.—The transfer of combs from a skep to the frames of a modern hive, is not often desirable. It is a messy, troublesome job that often leads to chilled brood (368), and the combs are frequently worked out so irregularly in the frames as to render subsequent manipulations very difficult. It is generally preferable to allow the bees to transfer themselves by the automatic method to be described below (266). But, where transfer of the combs is decided upon, the following process may be adopted: Drive all the bees out (169), and set them, in their skep, on their old stand. Take the old skep to a warm kitchen, and with a sharp knife cut it right through between the centre combs. Spread a piece of paper on a board not less than 15″ × 9″, and across it lay, at equal distances, two or three narrow tapes, at least 24″ long. On the tapes place a comb carefully taken from the skep, arranging the tapes so that they may be passed round the comb and tied at the top of the frame. Place a frame over the comb, so that the upper edge of the

comb shall meet the top bar of the frame; and, if the comb be too large for the frame, cut it to fit tightly between the top and bottom bars, or between the side-bars, as the case may be. If the comb be too shallow to fill the frame, put a piece of lath under it and draw one or more tapes under this. Tie the tapes around the frame and comb,

J. G. D.

Fig .111. REPAIRED COMB.

raise the board frame and comb together, and set the frame in the new hive. Transfer the other combs, similarly, excluding drone comb, and being careful to include all the worker brood in the centre combs (223), and to avoid its being chilled. Close up the frames and dummy: put on the covering and roof: set the hive on the old stand: and run in the driven bees as previously described (247). Give a little feeding, or uncap some of the honey cells. In a couple of days, when the bees will have fastened the combs in the frames, remove the tapes. Sometimes wire netting, with a small mesh, is used instead of tapes, and by this means small pieces of comb can be held in position until fastened by the bees. The combs should always hang in the new hive top up, as they were in the skep. The method illustrated here (Fig. 111) may be made to serve the purpose;

several pieces of comb may be held in position in a frame until joined by the bees, or pieces of foundation may be inserted (as in the illustration) either to fill a frame or to substitute worker for drone comb.   The laths have ordinary pins driven through them; these hold the pieces of comb, or foundation, and the pins at the ends are driven into the top bar and bottom bar of the frame.   Or, one may proceed in this way: Cut the lower edge of the comb quite straight; lay the frame over it, with the bottom bar of the frame touching the bottom edge of the comb (Fig. 112); cut a piece of foundation (118) to fill the remaining space and fix this to the top bar of the frame in the usual way (125); bind a piece of thin wire round the frame from side to side and another from top to bottom, as illustrated.   The bees will build a comb completely filling the frame; after which the wires may be removed.—CYPRIAN STOCK, in *Bee Publications*, December, 1914.

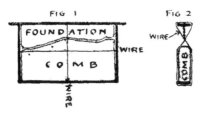

Fig. 112. REPAIRED COMB.

266. Automatic Transfer from Skep, or Box, to Modern Hive.—Stimulate the stock (202, 347, 352) with the object of having the skep crowded with bees in April, or early in May. When this is attained, prepare a modern hive, as directed (243), cutting a central hole of 6″ or 8″ diameter in the sheet.   This hive must now be placed in the position occupied by the skep, and the skep must be set upon the sheet, over the frames. Put on the lift (92), in the summer position (Fig. 172 *b*, p. 290) and pack warmly round the skep so that no bees can get out except through the entrance of the lower hive: put on the roof and open the doors.   The bees will now leave the hive and return through the regular entrance, passing up and down the frames as they come and go; and as they increase in numbers they will occupy the frames.   About ten days after the operation described above, weather permitting, an examination should be made.   When brood is found in more than one frame, make sure that the queen is in the lower hive, and place an excluder (117) on the frames, returning the sheet, skep, and wraps.   Should the queen not be found below, drive all the bees from the skep (169), hive them at the entrance (244), put on an excluder and replace the sheet, skep, and wraps. Twenty-one days later all the worker brood in the skep will have hatched (200, 214). Meanwhile, on suitable days, say once a week, the skep may be raised for a few moments to allow hatching drones to escape. Should the excluder become choked by drones trying to pass through, it must be cleared. The skep, after all the brood in it has hatched, may be left in position to be filled with honey, or it may be removed, the bees being driven from it and returned to the lower hive, the place of the skep being occupied by a crate of sections, or a super box of frames (107, 111, 116). Stocks in boxes may be transferred similarly. This method of transfer is less troublesome and less risky than that described above (265). It sacrifices neither brood nor honey, and gives the best results, but, as stated, the skep, or box, should be crowded with bees in the first instance.

267. The " Heddon " Method of Transfer.—The "Heddon" method, which was published in *Gleanings*, and appears in

MISS W. SEADON (AGED 7 YEARS) DRIVING BEES.

Root's *A. B. C. of Bee Culture*, may be briefly described as follows: Move the skep to one side and in its place set a hive having five or six frames of wired foundation. Drive the bees from the skep (169) until the queen and about two-thirds of the bees have gone up, and throw these on to a hiving board (244) so that they may run into the new hive. Now set the skep about two feet behind the new hive, with the entrance turned at right angles with its original direction.   After twenty-one days, when the worker brood will have hatched out (200, 214), drive all the bees from the skep, put a piece of excluder (117) against the entrance of the hive, cage the queen as before directed (259), thoroughly smoke both lots, and hive the driven bees through the entrance.   Any young queens will be stopped by the excluder.   Should fighting occur, give more smoke and beat upon the hive-sides.   The honey and the broodless combs in the skep can be dealt with as desired.

CHAPTER XXII.

SURPLUS HONEY.

268. Preparing in Time.—The honey flow (278), in these countries, lasts for only a few weeks. To take full advantage of it and to secure a harvest as large as possible, the beekeeper should bring his stocks up to their full strength by stimulating breeding (202), and spreading the brood (203), right up to the opening of the flow, and by uniting all weak stocks (256). He should also have for every hive a supply of crates (111) fitted with sections of foundation, or drawn comb; or a supply of super boxes (116) fitted with frames of wired foundation, or of drawn comb—crates, if he means to work for comb honey; super boxes, if for run, or extracted, honey. The crates, or super boxes, should be prepared, wrapped in paper, and laid aside in a safe place well ahead of the opening of the season. It is an expensive habit to defer the preparation of such appliances until they are actually required.

269. Extracted Honey more Profitable than Comb Honey.—Whether he shall work for comb honey, for extracted honey, or for both, each beekeeper must decide for himself, and his decision should be made sufficiently early to enable him to make his arrangements accordingly. As between the two— section and extracted honey—the question of profit can be answered only in favour of the latter. The output of extracted honey, where strong stocks are employed, is greater by from 50% to 100% than that of comb honey: the expenses are less, the same combs serving for many years: the marketing is simpler and cheaper, freights being lower, and breakages infrequent: "depreciation" and risks are reduced to a minimum: and the management of the stocks is simplified, there being fewer swarms (279), and, accordingly, less upsetting of the bee-man's arrangements. If there be any extra trouble in dealing with extracted honey, there is less trouble in dealing with the bees. If it be an objection that extracted honey fetches a lower price, there is the compensation that one has about double the quantity to sell, and at a lower cost of production. If the initial cost of an extracting outfit (143-145) be a discouragement, the yearly saving in the cost of sections and foundation is a far more than sufficient set off. Suppose the extracting outfit to cost £3 (which is a liberal allowance for a small apiary), the annual charge, at 5%, upon that outlay, with allowance of 15% for depreciation, may be set down at 12s. But the sections and foundation required for four hives (124) may cost £2 9s. 4d. per annum; for six hives, £3 14s.; for ten hives, £6 3s. 4d., which shows a very substantial economy in favour of working for extracted honey, where more than three strong stocks are employed.

270. **Preparing Crates and Sections.**—If the crate has been used before, let it be well scalded, washed, and scraped clean from propolis and wax. Fasten a section folding block (which is a piece of wood 4″ × 4″ × 1½″ or 2″) to a bench, or table, by a screw through the centre of the block: take a section and carefully fold it upon the four sides of the block, fastening the ends together: proceed until you have folded

twenty-one sections, which will be sufficient for one ordinary crate. If the sections be very dry, and inclined to break at the corners, damp them at the V cuts on both sides some time before folding. The " Woodman " Combined Section Press and Foundation Fixer (Fig. 113) is highly spoken of. The appliance aids in folding the sections and will fasten a full sheet of foundation to the top, or both top and bottom starters, thus saving both time and labour. Though not used in these countries, except by a few producers, the plain sections without saw-cuts, grooves or splits is the standard section in America and Canada and elsewhere, and these necessitate the use of a form of mechanical fixer such as the one illustrated.

Fig. 113.
"Woodman" Section Press and Foundation Fixer.

271. **Three-Split Sections.**—If you are using three-split sections (109), foundation can be fixed in three sections at one time. Place three sections in the crate, as shown (Fig. 114), and with the unsplit sides down: between the further side of one of the end sections and the side of the crate, push in a wedge, to hold the sections tightly: draw out the nearer halves of the sections, and drop in a 12¾″ × 4″ or 4¼″ sheet of super foundation, right side up (125): remove the wedge, and, with the follower (114) press the sections together, so that the foundation may be gripped. Remove the follower: put in one long, or three short separators (110): add three more sections; and proceed as before until the crate has its full quantity. When the last row of sections is in press the rows together

tightly by the follower, and wedge the latter, either by clips, or wooden wedges, to keep all secure. Scrape off the foundation appearing above the sections, and put it aside for

the wax extractor (292). By this means sections and crates can be filled rapidly; but it is essential that the sections be arranged perfectly square and the sides flush with one another. If tin, or zinc bars be used to carry the sections (111), the sheets of foundation must be cut, to permit them to drop nearly to the bottom of the sections. Separators between the sections must never be omitted; for, otherwise, the bees may

Fig. 114.   *J.G.D.*

FIXING FOUNDATION IN THREE-SPLIT SECTIONS

draw out the comb beyond the wood of the sections, making it impossible to pack the latter safely for transit; or, they may build comb to comb and work ruin in the crate.

272. **Split-Top Sections.**—These sections (109) have a bevelled split in one side, to grip the foundation and, in folding, should have only one half of the split fastened at the dovetail, and that, what may be called the under-lap half. Place several sheets of super foundation, one upon the other, and flush at the ends and sides: on these set the folding block, flush with one end of the parcel, and with a sharp knife cut through the foundation; proceeding until you have a sufficient number of squares cut, and taking care that the squares will fit properly in the sections. Place an end of one square on the bevel of the section top, right side up (125), and shut down and fasten the other half, fixing the sheet of foundation so that it will hang vertically in the section, and allowing just a little space at the bottom to provide for possible stretching of the square. Place each section, as it is finished, in the crate with separators between the rows, and the follower and wedges at the back.

273.—**Unsplit Sections.**—Fixing foundation in unsplit sections (109) is somewhat more troublesome. The plan frequently recommended is, to prepare a folding block nearly half as thick as the section is wide; the square of foundation is laid upon the block, right side up (125), and the section is placed in position; melted wax is then poured in at the upper edge of the foundation to fasten it to the wood. There are simpler methods which work sufficiently well:—In a saucepan of hot water place a teaspoon, handle down: bend the edge of the foundation at right angles, and place it on the wood so that the square, when fastened, will hang in the centre of the section: with the hot end of the spoon, press the bent edge to the wood: the wax will melt and adhere. In a warm room, the foundation can be readily fixed by pressure. Place the section top-side down, and lay the square of foundation on the inside of the top, projecting about $\frac{1}{4}''$ beyond the centre, and held at the centre by a guide, which may be made from a quarter section cut to the right width. Pressure with any smooth instrument, such as the handle of a dinner knife, will cause the foundation to adhere to the wood. Reverse the section, and arrange the foundation to hang plumb.

274. Preparing Frames.—Frames (104) are generally supplied in the flat, the pieces being made to fit into and grip each other. Assemble your frames so that the angles at the corners shall be true right angles, because the frame will not hang properly in the hive, or super box, if it has been put together out of square. Fasten the frame at the corners with small tacks, or wire nails.

275. Wiring Frames.—All frames should be wired so that the foundation may be well supported, and the resultant combs rendered strong and safe from breakage and sagging with the consequent evils. (126).

" Of course there are some who never wire their frames at all. Happy-go-lucky in their methods, they trust much to the ' lucky '; happy, indeed, until the combs lie broken in the extractor, and then it is not any longer safe for a cat to laugh in the house! "—J. G. D. in the *Irish Bee Journal*.

The frame having been nailed together, with a fine bradawl, bore three or four holes through each of its sides at about equal distances, thread the wire (tinned or rustless metal wire supplied by appliance firms for the purpose) from the top hole on one side to the top hole on the other, then back through the second hole and across the frame again to the second on the other side, and so on. The ends may be fastened either by means of twisting them round tacks partly driven into the wood and finally driven home after the wire has been secured, or by twisting around the frame ends. The wire should be stretched across tightly before being secured. It will always pay to give thorough attention to this matter of wiring frames for, no matter for what purpose the comb is to be used, wiring is necessary. While four wires, or at least three, should be inserted in a British standard frame, shallow frames require two only. Deep frames, such as the Modified Dadant, may be better to have five wires. The crossing of wires was at one time recommended, but straight wires are preferable, indeed they are essential when electric embedding is to be done.

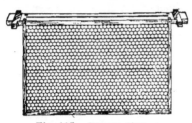

Fig. 115.   WIRED FRAME.

Fig. 116.   WIRED FRAME.

276. Fixing Foundation in Frames.—The frames, commonly used in these countries, have two long grooves cut in the under sides of the top bars; and long, wedge-shaped slips are supplied with the frames. Brood foundation (120) is used in frames, and is supplied in sheets of the proper size. To fix the foundation, introduce an edge of the sheet into the groove in the centre of the top bar: place the wedge in the other groove, and press it home, thus gripping the foundation. Place the frame on your wiring board (126), wires uppermost and with a sheet of paper on the board: and, with a heated embedder (126), press the wires into the foundation so that they will grip it, and that the wax melted by the embedder may cover the wire. Some follow Miss Emma Wilson's method, as described in *Bee Publications*, September, 1918, as follows:

"Take your wired frame, holding it flat, and lay your foundation upon the wires; move the frame slowly over the heat of a lamp or stove, following the direction of the wire, letting the tips of the fingers of one hand press lightly upon the part of the foundation over the heat. A little practice will teach you how fast to move, and how much pressure to make."

When many frames have to be dealt with, the electric embedder (126), or wired foundation (125), is generally used.

Put the frames, when completed, in vacant hives, or super boxes; and cover up, safe from damp and dust, mice and moths.

277. Three "Dont's."—Do not allow the wood of the sections to become soiled : dirty sections fetch low prices. Do not fall into the absurd error of using only slips of foundation, or "starters" : true economy calls for full sheets in sections and frames (121). Do not put in the foundation wrong side up : bees build their cells with vertical sides, and with angles at top and bottom. (125).

278. The Honey Flow opens at the latter end of May, or in June, according to the district, when nectar is secreted freely in the flowers. When the flow opens, the bees begin to draw out with new, white wax, the cells next the top bars of the frames in the body box. The custom is to watch for this infallible sign and, immediately on perceiving it, to give the stock a crate, or super box : but in practice it is found that if supers be not on the hives before the lengthening of the cells referred to, they are late so far as the purpose of preventing swarms is concerned. Dr. C. C. Miller—probably in his day the world's champion producer of comb honey, who depended almost exclusively upon white clover for the purpose—did not wait for " the little bits of pure, white wax " to appear under the top bars of the frames : he watched for "the very first white clover blossoms " and, ten days later, he put on supers. When a regular drinking place is provided in the apiary, the commencement of a honey flow may be known by the fact that the bees cease to visit the water at such times for they secure all the water required with the nectar; but if the beekeeper is to be successful, he should endeavour always to have at least one super in position and occupied by the bees *before* the honey flow begins.

279. Putting on Supers.—If you are working for comb honey, bring out the prepared section super or crate (111) to the hive, and see that the foundation hangs vertically in the sections, and that separators have not been forgotten. Remove the roof, quilts, and packing, leaving the sheet still on the frames. Take off the riser (92), transferring the porch from it to the body box, if not already done; and set the riser on the ground beside the hive. Give a good coat of vaseline, or petroleum jelly (183) to the bottom of the crate, and of the laths on which the sections rest, so that they may not be tightly propolised to the frames by the bees; and set the crate on the edges of the riser. Give a puff or two of smoke to the bees, if you think it necessary—it ought not to be necessary with this operation, and if unnecessary, it should be avoided (189). Roll

off the sheet, and draw on the carbolic cloth, as directed (186), to drive the bees down and to avoid the risk of crushing with the crate any that may be on the frame tops. With a piece of glass, or other scraper, clean off any wax or propolis from the frame tops. If ten or more frames be in the body box, the crate will fit properly across the frames; if less than ten frames be in, the crate must be put on with its sides running with the frames; or, either a piece of wood $17''$ long × $\frac{1}{2}''$ thick, or extra frames covered with canvas or ticking on the top bars, must be added behind the dummy to prevent the

J. G. D.

Fig. 117. PUTTING ON A CRATE.

escape of bees from under the crate. Take the crate in one hand and hold it just above the carbolic cloth (without touching the latter, lest the vaseline be rubbed off), and in the position which it is to occupy, as illustrated (Fig. 117): with the other hand draw out the carbolic cloth, quickly setting the crate upon the frames, and arrange the crate to fit so that no bees may escape outside it. Put on the sheet and the riser: pack all round the crate with warm stuff, or newspapers: spread a couple of newspapers on the sheet: and add the quilts and roof. If crates be not kept warm, the bees will be slow to take to them, and their work in the sections will be indifferently performed. For the proper filling of sections, it is necessary that the bees be well crowded into the crates; and this points the difficulty of working for perfect sections and at the same time restraining swarming; for, crowding, as we know, is an incitement to swarming (216), and without a certain amount of crowding the sections are likely to be built with pop holes at the corners, and to be imperfectly drawn and fastened next the wood. Bees are sometimes slow to take to the first crates at the beginning of the season. They may be encouraged to start work above if some sections with drawn out comb, or with comb contain-

ing a little honey, be given them. For this purpose it is useful
to keep over, in a warm, clean place, some unfinished sections
from the previous year (291). The Section Frame (115) may be
used to get sections started in the brood chamber, and these,
with the adhering bees, may be inserted in the first crates;
when, if the latter be kept warm, work will be commenced
there. In the absence of such " bait sections," a plan that is
frequently quite successful is to dip some pieces of thin lath,
or stick, in honey and slip them down here and there between
the sections; the bees suck the honey and remain in the supers;
then the sticks are removed.

280. **Putting on Extracting Supers.**—Frame supers or
super boxes, commonly known as extracting supers (275), may
with advantage be vaselined, and set on the hives in the same
way as are comb honey supers, with these variations: —
(1), excluders are generally used (117) in order that the queen
shall not be able to breed in the combs that are intended to
be passed through the centrifugal extractor, and (2), as these
extracting supers with frames are heavier than crates of
sections, the manner of removing the carbolic cloth and putting
the super box in position, so as not to allow the bees to fly
up during the operation, must be modified. If you have an
assistant, get him to pull off the carbolic cloth while you hold
the extracting super in position just above the cloth, ready
to be set in its place on the frames. If you are alone, stand
behind the hive: hold the super box down to the cloth, which
you will catch with your right hand and, giving a quick jerk
with your arms to the right, pulling off the cloth; and
immediately place the super box in position on the hive.
With a little practice, this can be done so rapidly that, the
bees having been driven down by the carbolic, not one will
have time to escape before you have the super in its place and
covered. Another simple method is to stand at the side and
slide the super box along the frames, pushing the carbolic
cloth before it. The objections to this method are, that a little
propolis or wax, on the top bars of the frames, may cause a
difficulty in sliding on the super box; and, unless your hive
be so constructed that the ends of the top bars are held by the
outer hive walls, as they always ought to be (91), the friction
of the super box in sliding on may cause the ends of the frames
to come into contact with the inner walls of the hive and thus
crush many of the bees, perhaps even killing the queen, should
she happen to be in the way. Many beekeepers, however,
always place their supers, whether for comb or extracted honey,
on their hives without having recourse to any carbolic cloth

at all, simply driving the bees down by means of a smoker and setting the super in its place immediately after.

281. Use of Excluders.—Frames in the brood chamber should hang one and a half inches from centre to centre. But in the super box, spaces of two inches from centre to centre give better results, because they enable the bees to build longer cells, which, of course, hold more honey and are easier to uncap for extracting (289). When frames are used in this way, the spaces between the shoulders must be filled, to prevent the escape of bees. It is also claimed for the two-inch spacing, that the queen will not deposit eggs in combs so spaced because of the depth of the cells, and that, therefore, excluders under the frames are unnecessary. Many experienced bee-keepers work their supers in this way, and avoid what certainly is an objection to the excluder, namely, the impediment it offers to bees loaded with honey (117). But, it is better to use an excluder than to have the combs, intended for honey, occupied by brood; when frames in supers are spaced one and a half inch from centre to centre, as in the brood chamber, excluders should always be used. With respect to the use of excluders under crates of sections, opinions differ widely. In some districts, and with some stocks, excluders are found to be necessary; in other cases, not. In cold, wet seasons, queens will often go up to the warmer part of the hive and take possession of the crates; and bees have been known, in exceptionally unfavourable seasons, to rear queens in the sections, and even to swarm, leaving frames of foundation in the brood chamber untouched and combs unoccupied. But, making due allowance for the vagaries both of the climate and the bees, crates may be generally used without excluders underneath if sufficient room be given to the queen in the brood chamber (203). When excluder zinc is used, it should lie flat upon the frames, leaving no space at the edges for the queen to ascend. It may be laid upon the carbolic cloth, and held while the cloth is drawn from under it; then, if the cloth be spread for a moment upon the excluder, the super box, or crate, can be put on as directed above.

282. Tiering Crates.—In a good season, a strong stock may require a second crate within a week. If honey be coming in rapidly and the days be fine, the second crate may be given when it is seen that the bees have drawn out the foundation in their sections and are storing honey there. In the height of the honey flow, swarming may be provoked by a day's delay in giving more super room when it is required. Give the second crate underneath the first one. Prepare it as before (270); and set it on the riser beside the hive. Subdue the bees with smoke. If the first crate has been well vaselined, it will come off easily; if not, prise it up at the corners and insert bits of broken sections there. If the laths on which the sections rest be too thick or too thin, or if they have sagged, the bees will, probably, have fastened them and the sections to the frames (111); and the loosening may exasperate both the bees and their owner. Grasp the crate with both hands and twist it gently to right and left until it is loose for removing; then twist it back to its original position for a moment. If it be too tightly fastened to be loosened by twisting, draw a piece of thin wire under it to cut the connections and prise it up, taking care not to allow bees to escape. If you have an assistant, stand at the back of the hive. Raise the crate just free from the frames, and take it off along, and not across, the frames; your helper following it closely with the carbolic cloth, as illustrated (Fig. 125). If you are alone, stand at the side of the hive. Take the carbolic cloth at two corners between the fingers, with both hands, and let it hang down outside the hive as shown (Fig. 119)—at the side, if your

J. G. D.

Fig. 119. REMOVING A CRATE.

frames hang parallel with the entrance: at the front if the frames run from front to back — in which case your position will be at the back. Grasp the crate, ease it, and take it along, and not across, the frames, letting the carbolic cloth cover the frames as you remove the crate. Hold the crate for a moment over the cloth, to cause the bees to run up into the sections; then, set it upon the second crate, and lift both back on to the frames, drawing away the cloth as directed above (280), and settling the crates evenly upon the frames. The sheet and quilts not having been taken off the first crate, the operation may be carried out without allowing any bees to give trouble. This tiering up of crates (Fig. 120) may be continued while the honey flow lasts, the empty crate being placed underneath. The upper crates may be removed when finished, and before the faces of the combs become soiled by the constant coming and going of the bees: but, if the crates be tiered up until the close of the honey flow, the honey will keep its flavour best on the hive; the bees, hav-ing so much room, will be less inclined to swarm, and, not being deprived of their stores, will be less inclined to give trouble. In a good season, as many as five crates may be re-quired for a strong stock; in which case, if tiering be prac-tised, an extra make-shift riser (92) will be required, and assist-ance in lifting the crates toge-ther will be necessary. It is a good plan to use a Divisional Crate (112) for the last addition to the tier, and at the close of the season where tiering is not practised; because, seven or fourteen sections may be given when the season has advanced too far to admit of twenty-one sections being added with any prospect of their being filled and sealed and, because the parts may be removed as the sections in each are completed, the last unfinished sections being placed over the centre of the cluster. The Section Frame (115) may be used to get sections com-pleted in the brood chamber. Towards the close of the season, when a crate is put on—not because actually needed, but on the chance that it may be needed—that crate is put on top of the others rather than underneath. If not required by the bees, it will, at least, act as a " safety valve."

J. G. D.

Fig. 120. CRATES TIERED.

283. Doubling and Storifying.—When extracted honey is being worked for, " Doubling " may be practised with excel-lent results, both as regards the harvest that may be obtained from it and the restraint it exercises upon the swarming impulse. About three weeks before the opening of the honey flow (278), take, from a strong stock, all the frames containing brood, except one on which the queen must be left: return the adhering bees to their hive; fill the vacancies with frames of comb, or of foundation. Place the frames of brood in another body box, or in a super box, and set them on top of a second strong stock, with an excluder **(117)** underneath, thus doubling the hive (Fig. 121). The stock, increasing daily by the emerging brood in both stories, will become very strong, and will be capable of storing honey very rapidly in the upper frames as the brood there hatches out. The combs of honey may be removed from above to have their contents extracted, and to be returned at once to the hive for re-filling, drones being removed; or, the two storeys may be used as brood chambers, and a third and a fourth storey may be placed on top for honey only, the excluder zinc being placed above the brood chambers to safeguard the upper storeys from the queen's attentions. When the combs in the uppermost storey have been filled, they can have their honey extracted, and may be returned over the excluder, the unfinished storeys being placed above them. (Ills. p. 199).

J. G. D.

Fig. 121. HIVE DOUBLED.

284. Supering Skeps.—Skeps with flat tops **(83)** may be supplied with crates. A "riser," or case (Fig. 122), 9″ deep, and large enough to hold a crate, is fitted with a false bottom $4\frac{1}{2}''$ from the top. A hole in the false bottom, corresponding with the hole in the top of the skep, is covered with excluder zinc **(117)**. The riser is fastened to the skep by four nails; and a deep roof permits the use of two tiered crates. (Fig. 123).

Fig. 122. SKEP WITH SUPER CASE AND ROOF.

285. Removing Supers.—When the honey flow is over, and the nights grow chill, the bees will begin to take down honey from the supers to the brood frames. Therefore, supers should be removed in good time, and it is better to remove them a little too soon than a little too late. This is an operation which requires some care, in order to avoid the risk of setting up robbing (341), and of exasperating the bees. The point to be aimed at is to take away the supers so skilfully as neither to expose honey to the bees outside, nor to put too severe a strain upon the patience of the bees within.

Fig. 123. SUPERING A SKEP.

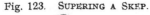

a   *b*   *J.G.D.*
Fig. 124. (*a*) CONE ESCAPE.
(*b*) DANGER! QUEEN ON THE CONE.

286. Use of Cone Escapes.—On fine, warm days, the cone escapes (Fig. 124) in the hive roof may be used, with moderate success, to clear the supers of bees. Through a round hole 1½″ in diameter, in the front gable of the roof, a cone escape is passed from the inside, and tacked; and a second cone is fitted on the outside. (93). Early in the day, having lifted the crates or super boxes, as directed above, draw, or get an assistant to draw, a towel over the frames, covering them completely. Set the supers back upon the towel; remove the sheet and other coverings, and put on the roof. If there be no hole in the towel, the bees in the supers will be unable to get down to the frames: they will come to the top of the supers, and, seeing the light through the cones, they will pass out that way, returning to the hive through the usual entrance; and in the evening the supers should be free from bees. If there be a ventilator in any other part of the roof, it should be closed, so that the bees may see light only through the cones. •There are, how-

ever, some objections to the use of cone escapes for this purpose; for, if the day be cold or wet, the bees will not leave the hive roof; and if there should be, in the crates, young bees that have not yet been on the wing, they may be lost on emerging from the cones. Moreover, the bees, being shut off from the brood combs, are very likely to tear the cappings of the sections; thus reduc-ing their value for

J.G.D.

[Fig. 125. Removing a Frame Super.

marketing purposes. Another objection is that wasps (429) may, and often do, find their way, even through double cones, and ruin the sections. A queen has been known to emerge through the cones—a most undesirable occurrence. The use of cone escapes for clearing bees from supers is described here, but is not recommended. There is a much better and an inexpensive method. (287).

287. The Super Clearer (Fig. 126) has simplified the once laborious and trying operation of removing surplus honey from

bees. It is useful, also, when extracted combs require to be cleaned up by the bees before being stored away (291). It consists of a $2'' \times 2''$ frame of wood, $17''$ long $\times$ $15\frac{3}{4}''$ wide, in which is a panel $\frac{3}{4}''$ thick, bee space being thus provided on both sides of the panel

Fig. 126. Super Clearer.

when the clearer is in position in the hive. In the centre of the panel is inserted a bee escape, and at one side, near the frame, is a 1½″ hole, which may be opened or closed by a shutter worked from the edge of the frame. When the clearer is placed on a hive and supers are set upon it, the bees pass down from the supers through the escape, and cannot return. The side hole is opened only when it is desired to admit the bees to the combs for cleaning up

Fig. 127. PORTER ESCAPE.

purposes. The combs are placed upon the clearer and, the side hole being open, the bees quickly take down every particle of honey and leave the combs perfectly dry. The shutter is then closed, and the bees clear through the escape. The super clearer has this advantage over the cone escape (286) that whereas the cone escape operates only during daylight, and upon genial days, and has besides other objectionable features, the super clearer can be worked by day and night, and no matter what the weather outside may be. The " Porter " Bee

Fig. 128.
" FEDERATION " ESCAPE.

Escape (Fig. 127), for super clearers, is a metal box, with an arrangement of delicate springs which permit bees to pass out. Sometimes, however, an " awkward drone," getting stuck in the passage, bars the way against all others, and thus renders the escape inoperative. In use, the round hole is on top. The "Federation" Bee Escape (Fig. 128), for super clearers, is not so liable to get blocked as is the Porter escape. The bees pass through

a tube which is large enough to admit drones freely; they then drop upon a tin platform, and get down through a hole in the centre, under the tube. In the illustration, the perforated zinc has been cut, in order to disclose the tube. In use, the perforated zinc is on top. The escape is made of timber 16½″ × 14½″ × ¾″. On this a frame of 1½″ × ½″ stuff is nailed above and below, projecting ½″ all round. Thus the escape measures 17½″ × 15½″ out to out. The hole in the panel is 2″ in diameter; the tube is 2″ long and ¼″ in diameter; and the hole in the piece of tin underneath is ¼″. A groove is cut in the panel to admit the tube. A piece is cut from the upper side of the tube, where it extends outside the perforated zinc, to give free access to the bees. At one side of the panel, and ½″ from the inside edge of the frame, a hole 1½″ × ¼″ is cut through. When not required, this hole is closed by a tin slide 3¼″ × 2″, which is slipped under the frame, and turned up outside; a slit is made in the slide, and a nail driven through the frame and slit permits the slide to move in and out, i.e., to cover the hole when supers are being cleared, or to leave it free to the bees when the object is to return combs for cleaning up purposes. (291).

288. Use of the Super Clearer.—Super clearers permit the bees to pass down from the supers without having to leave the warmth of the hive, and, therefore, they may be used by day or night, and in all kinds of weather. Examine the clearer, and see that the escape is in working order, and that the side hole (287) is closed. Set the clearer beside the hive, right side up: lift the supers without removing the sheet and quilts; set them on the clearer; and put all back on the frames. The bees will pass down to the body box, and, next day, the supers will, probably, be found emptied of bees, and may be removed, little disturbance of the colony having been caused by the operation (330). This " little disturbance " is a great gain and of much importance; for, as the bees are really unaware of the fact that they are being robbed of their stores, they have no inclination to break the cappings of the combs (176), and are much less likely to show resentment. It goes without saying that there should be very little, or no use of smoke, or carbolic, during the operation, lest the bees should be excited to tamper with the combs and honey.

CHAPTER XXIII.

EXTRACTING HONEY.

289. Extracting.—This should always be done indoors and the room should be made bee-tight, so that all bees are effectually excluded. Otherwise large numbers will enter and prove an unmitigated nuisance, besides which, if the extracting place be near the apiary, robbing (341) may be set up. Though it may be just possible, at the height of a very heavy honey flow, to perform a little extracting out of doors, this should never on any account be attempted. When there are many combs to be extracted, time will be saved if two uncapping knives be used (144). See that the edges are as sharp as they can be made, and heat the blades in a vessel of hot water while in use. Lay a strong lath across a crock, or other similar vessel. Take up one of the frames; hold it with one end resting on the lath; and, with your uncapping knife, working from the bottom upwards, as illustrated, page 195, pare off the cappings, inclining the frame towards the knife so that the cappings, as they are pared off, may fall into the vessel underneath. Having uncapped both sides, proceed in the same way with a second frame. Put the frames, ends up, in the extractor (143), one in each cage, and so that, in revolving, the bottom bars of the frames may travel first, because in that position—the cells having an upward slope (75) —the honey may be more easily extracted. Turn the handle, slowly at first, and increasing in speed by degrees, being careful not to revolve the cages so furiously as to break the combs. The centrifugal force will throw the honey out of the cells. When one side of each comb is finished, or nearly so, reverse the frames in the cages, and extract from the other sides. With new, soft comb, it is better to extract only about half from one side, then reversing, and returning to the first side to finish. Honey, being more fluid when warm than when cold, may be extracted more easily if it has just been taken off the hive, and if the extractor be warmed with boiling water immediately before use, and be kept near a good fire during the operation. With extractors which are not geared, the turning of the handle is often a laborious job when a number of combs have to be done. The work may be simplified by arranging what may be called a " cord gearing " by means of a strong cord, about four feet long, with a loop on one end, which is slipped over the handle. The operator then stands out from the extractor (as illustrated); gets the cord at right angles with the handle-crank; gives a slight pull at the cord with one

EXTRACTING HONEY, WITH "CORD GEARING."

Photo by: J. G. Digges.

finger, thus revolving the cages, and assisting each revolution by another slight pull. After a few minutes' practice one can extract honey in this way with little exertion. This economical and excellent substitute for expensive gearing was suggested by the ingenious boy who is shown in the illustration, is now a man and a father, and is still an enthusiastic beekeeper. His device may be used for other purposes also, for example, such as working a box churn. Sections that are not completely filled, or that are otherwise unfit for the market, may have their honey extracted in the same way, six sections being placed in each cage. The extractor for sections only (Fig. 129) consists of a vessel 12″ in diameter and 7″ in depth, one-third of the cover being a hinged lid. and inside the vessel a frame containing four cages to take four sections. The frame is revolved by means of a leather strap which, passing over two self-adjusting guide pulleys, engages on a 9″ driving wheel. All the movements are on ball bearings and all the parts with which honey comes in contact are tinned. The extractor is made to stand on a table, was designed by Mr. Ryan, Dunmanway, and described in the *Irish Bee Journal*, April, 1910, page 36. All cappings may have the adhering honey pressed out, and may then be rendered into wax (292). Heather honey requires special treatment, and can be thoroughly separated from the comb only by means of a honey press (146). A piece of clean cheese cloth, large enough to fold down to the bottom, is placed over the top of the press. The combs are placed in the press vertically, as they hung in the hive; the cheese cloth is folded over them; the plunger is then brought over, and the screw is revolved. The honey falls to the drawer beneath, and the wax is lifted out in the cloth. (See also 333-335). A potato masher may be used for small quantities.

Fig. 129.

EXTRACTOR FOR SECTIONS.

290. Straining and Ripening.—Extracted honey may be strained from the extractor into a ripener (145), and should be left, for a few days, covered, in some place with a high temperature, after which the honey may be bottled for market (325), the thin honey on the top being used for bee food only.

291. Cleaning Extracted Combs.—Frames and sections having had their honey extracted, may be given to the bees to clean up before being stored away for use in the next season. Place a super clearer (287) on the frames of a strong stock; and, in the evening, when the bees have ceased flying, draw open the side trap; set the frames and sections on the clearer;

and cover up, safe from marauding bees. The bees of the colony will come up through the side trap and will carry down all the honey, leaving the combs clean and dry. The side trap may then be closed; the bees above the clearer will then pass down through the trap in the centre, and will not be able to return. The same object can be attained by giving the combs behind the dummy (100), leaving a bee space between the dummy and the floor board; or behind the " Federation " dummy (102), with excluder zinc attachment. Frames and sections, when cleaned, should be removed, wrapped carefully in clean paper, and stored away in some dry place, safe from mice, flies, and other adventurers. (427). It is a good plan to keep over, for the following season, a few unfinished sections, having a little honey in them, for use as " bait sections " in the first crates; thus coaxing the bees to take to those crates, and to begin work at once. (279).

CHAPTER XXIV.

EXTRACTING WAX.

292. Use of Wax Extractors.—Wax is so valuable, no careful beekeeper will permit the smallest piece of it to be wasted. Clippings of foundation, cappings removed from combs, and old or broken combs, should be collected and rendered, either for sale, or for manufacture into foundation. The light coloured and the dark coloured wax should be rendered separately, as the former fetches the higher price. As already described, both the Solar Wax Extractor **(148)** and the Steam Wax Extractor **(149)** give good results. The combs should be soaked for twenty-four hours in cold water before being rendered. The best-coloured wax is obtained by means of extractors; but a large amount of wax remains in the debris, and it is only by subjecting it to considerable pressure while hot, that the mass can be made to yield nearly all its wax. This is especially the case when old combs are being dealt with. Wax presses of various makes may be procured for this purpose. Sometimes rendered wax shows an appearance like oatmeal, which is supposed to be pollen, and is, therefore, discarded. It is not pollen; it is wax—granulated wax, and should be treated quite slowly with dry heat. (See also **337**).

293. Extracting by Boiling.—A third method of rendering wax may be adopted as follows:—Soak the wax in rain-water for twenty-four hours, as directed **(292)**. Into a canvas bag, or a clean, closely-made sack, put a large stone: throw in also all the wax that is to be melted: and tie the bag tightly. Place the bag in a farm boiler, or a large pot, of rain-water, with a piece of wood under the bag to prevent burning. When the water has boiled for a couple of hours (or less in the case of clean, fresh combs), let it cool: and, when cold, remove the cake of wax from the top. Scrape the dirty wax from the bottom of the cake into the bag, and boil it again for two or three hours, when, on cooling, a cake of inferior wax may be taken off. The first cake should be broken up, and put into an enamelled vessel of hot water, and the vessel set in a pot of boiling water near the fire until the wax melts, after which it can be poured into shapes, and cooled slowly, as before. The colour of the inferior wax may be improved by adding a little vitriol to the water in which it is boiled, in the proportion

of three tablespoonsful (1½ oz.) of vitriol to one gallon of
water. Smaller quantities may be wrapped in a piece of cheese
cloth and suspended over a vessel of water in the oven. When
melted, cooling must be very gradual to avoid cracks. The
wax cake may be removed from the vessel of water when cold
(337). Only rain-water or other soft water must be used for
wax rendering if it can be obtained; otherwise acid must be
added or the wax will be largely spoiled.

Photo by   R. B. Manley.

MR. MANLEY'S STORIED HIVES: Supers set back to admit of egress and
ventilation above the lowest super.

CHAPTER XXV.

QUEEN REARING AND INTRODUCTION.

294. Old Queens.—Attention has already been called to the necessity for supplying young, prolific queens to all stocks requiring them (222). Too much emphasis cannot be laid upon the fact that queens past their second year are usually past their prime (198). The beekeeper who desires to work his stocks to the best advantage will not fail to supplant all such queens. He will not be content to leave this most important part of his work to take care of itself. Either he will purchase good queens from other queen-raisers and thus introduce new blood into his apiary, or he will do his own queen rearing. It is quite certain that the supplanting of old queens is not attended to as it should be. This may be due to the supposed difficulty of rearing queens. There are so many capable keepers of bees who are satisfied with average harvests, satisfied with the second best, and deterred from attempting to rear their own queens because of the trouble or the difficulty which they think that that part of a bee-man's work involves. Beekeeping can never be raised to the level to which it ought to attain until queen rearing is practised, not by the few, but by the many.

295. Defective Queens.—Sometimes queens are found to be defective, and their places must be supplied by fertile queens if the colony is to be preserved. Queens that have not been impregnated within three weeks after leaving the cell usually become drone breeders (198). Queens that have been chilled, or half starved, or that have been " balled " (309), or injured in the hive, may lose their fertility and become useless. The bees will generally supplant such queens, but they cannot do so unless the conditions are favourable (206), nor without loss of valuable time.

296. Queenlessness.—Beside the necessity for supplanting aged and defective queens, there often arises a necessity for supplying fertile queens to stocks whose queens have been lost, or killed, or that have died natural deaths. This is an urgent need which, whether it be observed or not, presents itself more frequently than many suppose. At the time of swarming, queens are sometimes lost if they alight apart from the swarm, undiscovered by the bees or the owner. Unskilful, or careless manipulations of frames are accountable for the crushing and death of many queens (191). When they leave the hive to meet the drones, some queens, either through some defect of their wings hindering their return, or through the assaults of birds, or of strong winds, fail to reach their homes again. By far the largest number of lost queens become lost through their inability to recognize their own hives when returning from their wedding flight (156). This disaster is frequently due to the habit of using hives so close together, and so similar in their make, colour, and situation, that, although the virgin queen takes all due precautions to mark the position of her own hive before her flight (21), it is next to impossible for her to distinguish it from the others when she returns, and, entering a strange hive by mistake, she is immediately killed. This is a fact of sufficient importance to point the necessity for keeping careful watch over all casts and swarmed stocks until one is satisfied of the mating and laying of the queens; and also to lead to the re-arrangement of any apiary (447) in which the conditions are such as favour the loss of newly-mated queens. And it should be noted that, although a colony deprived of its queen can, in certain circumstances, supply the loss (17); if the loss occur when there are neither eggs nor larvæ under three days old in the combs (as in the case of a swarmed stock, or a cast), a new queen cannot be raised, and the colony, if left to itself, must dwindle and perish.

297. **Signs of Queenlessness.**—When a colony has become queenless, the fact may soon be discovered by observing the conduct of the bees. They hurry about the hive, in and out, and over the porch, sides, and roof, as if in search of their lost mother.

> The commons, like an angry hive of bees,
> That want their leader, scatter up and down,
> And care not who they sting in his revenge.
> —*Shakespeare.* Henry VI, ii. Act 3, Scene 2.

This may continue for two or three days; after which work is resumed, but in a listless, half-hearted way: the bees returning from the fields loiter about the alighting board with little apparent anxiety to enter the hive, and a general air of indifference prevails in the colony. In spring, they carry in little or no pollen, there being no brood to feed. In late autumn and winter, they permit the drones to remain in the hive. Such signs as these will indicate to the owner that something is wrong with the colony; and, if on examining the

frames he finds no queen, and neither eggs nor brood, at a
time when they ought to be present, or only the eggs or brood
of a drone-breeder (198, 210), he will know that he can save
the colony only by taking measures for re-queening it, or by
uniting it to another stock.

298. **Nucleus Hives.**—The proper time to begin preparations
for queen rearing is in the winter, when a supply of nucleus
hives sufficient to meet the needs of the apiary should be prepared.   Hive; which are not required for other purposes, can
be temporarily transformed into nucleus hives, so that they
may be turned to use again for swarms and stocks at a
moment's notice.   Divide the hive into three parts by inserting
two close-fitting dummies (100).   Make an opening, $\frac{3}{8}''$ deep
(427) in the back, and another midway in one side, level with
the floor board, to form two additional entrances.   Part of a
broken section, tacked to a piece of inch wood nailed or screwed

Fig. 130.
MAKESHIFT NUCLEUS HIVE.

below the augur hole, will serve
as an alighting board, and a
porch, or rain shoot, may be
similarly constructed.   When
the hive is required again for a
stock or swarm, all that will be
necessary will be to remove one
or both dummies, and to stop
the augur holes with corks.
Nucleus hives may be inexpen-
sively made up from grocers'
boxes (Fig. 130), provided that
the timber be sweet and clean.
They should be made to take
three, four, or five frames, and
should measure internally $14\frac{3}{4}''$

long × $9''$ deep. If the sides be made $17''$ long, and if the end
pieces be $8\frac{1}{2}''$ deep and be nailed $14\frac{3}{4}''$ apart, two pieces can be
fastened to enclose the frame shoulders, and the bottom board
can be also $17''$ long to provide an alighting place for the bees.
The sides may be made of $11''$ timber, which will leave a space
of $2''$ above the frames for quilts, etc.; but a shallow riser (92),
which would admit of the use of a feeder, would be preferable.
A piece of board, two or three inches longer and wider than the
hive, may be set on for a roof, and if a brick or a heavy stone
be laid on top it will keep all secure.   Legs may be added, or
the hive may be set upon a couple of bricks, with a tilt to the
front, or back, to throw off rain.

299. **Queen Rearing.**—Early in the spring, the scene of

operations will be transferred to the stocks which are to be used. It should be borne in mind that, to secure the best results, the young queens should be reared when the stocks are strong, when nectar is coming in rapidly, when drones are on the wing, and when the condition of the stocks is such as prevails in the swarming season; and, also, that the queen rearing should be from the eggs of those queens which are in their prime, *i.e.*, in their second year, and have distinguished themselves as the best in the apiary by reason of the excellence of their laying powers and the vigour and diligence of their progeny. It is desirable, further, that the mating of the young queens should be with the best drones, the temperament of the progeny being largely influenced by the male element. If you have a sufficient number of stocks to permit of two being set apart for the purpose, select two of the most desirable (A and B), and keep up regular stimulative feeding (202), and the other methods already described (203) to bring the two stocks rapidly to full strength. When the hive B (which is to rear the drones), is sufficiently strong, insert two drone combs, or two frames of drone foundation, in the centre of the brood nest, and do not permit the feeding to flag, so that drones may be flying from that hive in time to inseminate the young queens. To carry the preparations further, drone breeding may be limited, or prevented, in the other stocks, by cutting out or removing all drone comb, and by supplying only worker comb or worker foundation. (205).

300. Using a Swarmed Stock.—Suppose that the good stock (A) sends off a prime swarm. The swarm may be hived, and placed upon the stand previously occupied by the parent stock, and may receive from the latter the supers, and the flying bees returning to their old stand (251). That swarm should give a good account of itself. The parent stock is removed to another part of the apiary and examined. It will be found to have a number of queen cells, and a good supply of young bees upon, let us suppose, nine or ten frames. Now, a prepared hive with three compartments, or three nucleus hives, being at hand, the combs with the bees from the parent stock are inserted so as to form three nuclei, each having one or two queen cells. When a queen has been hatched and impregnated, she can be introduced to a stock which requires requeening, and the nucleus from which she has been taken may be used to rear more queens. Eventually the two dummies may be removed, and the bees may be united into one stock (258), or, the bees and frames may be given to other stocks. This operation, it will be seen, has the recommendation of extreme simplicity.

301. The Returned Swarm Method.—A plan which is sometimes adopted is, to let the best stock swarm, and from this, the prime or first swarm, to remove the old queen, allowing the swarm to return to the hive. Nine days later the swarm, increased in size, will re-issue, headed by a virgin queen. The swarm is then hived on the stand of the parent stock, which latter is moved to a new stand, or is divided into four or five nuclei, each provided with a ripe queen cell of its own rearing.

302. Using an Unswarmed Stock.—When the desired drones begin to hatch out in hive B (299) insert a frame of worker comb, or of worker foundation, in the centre of the brood nest of hive A. On the third or fourth day, if eggs have been deposited in that comb, transfer the queen and three frames—one of brood and two of honey—with the adhering bees, to a nucleus hive, pushing a little grass into the entrance to prevent the bees from returning at once to their old home. Supply syrup if necessary. Remove also from hive A all combs having unsealed larvæ, returning the adhering bees, and give the combs to other stocks. Now take out the frame which you inserted in the centre of the brood nest, and in which the queen has deposited eggs, and with a penknife cut " scollops," or V-cuts, from the bottom of the comb up to where the eggs are found and, with a pencil or match, enlarge the cells at the apex of each scollop to encourage the bees to build a queen cell there: or, cut holes through the comb immediately under the eggs, returning the frame as quickly as possible, and covering up the brood nest warmly (370). Another successful method may be described as follows : Take the comb in which eggs have been deposited ; with a sharp knife (144) shave down the cells to half their depth ; crush down two rows of cells, skip a row and• crush down two more rows, continuing to crush and to skip until the comb—or as much of it as you require—has been so treated ; in the rows of uncrushed cells, crush the eggs, or larvæ, in two adjoining cells, skip one cell and crush the eggs, or larvæ, in two cells, and so on. Place this prepared comb horizontally, with the side that has been treated downwards, over the frames of a strong, queenless colony, so arranged in a shallow make-shift frame, $2\frac{1}{2}''$ deep, that there shall be a full bee-way under it. A large number of queen cells may be obtained in this way. If honey and pollen be not coming in plentifully, you must supply them artificially (202) during the next few days. Nine or ten days after the scolloping of the comb, there should be a quantity of queen cells upon it, and you must then prepare nucleus colonies to receive them.

303. Forming Nuclei.—Take from a strong stock, one frame of honey and two frames of brood, with the adhering bees, supplying their places with frames of comb, or of foundation, and insert the removed frames and bees in a nucleus hive (298), taking care to leave the queen in the parent hive. Stop the entrance of the nucleus hive with grass : arrange obstacles about it as directed elsewhere (165) to cause the bees, when they fly, to mark the new situation : supply food : and, should the colony become reduced too much by bees returning to the old hive, shake some more, and preferably young bees, into it from the parent stock, or from other stocks, using, in the latter case, the precautions described under the head of " Uniting Bees " (256). Place the nucleus at some distance from the other stocks, and continue the operation until a sufficient number of nuclei have been formed.

304. Inserting Queen Cells.—Having, on the ninth or tenth day, formed your nuclei, supply them with ripe queen cells on the following day, by which time they will have realized their · queenless condition and will be prepared to receive assistance. When queen cells are ripe, that is, within two or three days of hatching, the bees remove some of the wax from the points of the cells, thus roughening them and facilitating the egress of the young queens, and enabling the beekeeper to recognize the cells as ripe and ready for use. You must remember that frames with queen cells will not admit of being cleared (193) by shaking or thumping, and that on no account must the royal brood be suffered to become chilled during the operation of transfer. Gently drive the bees off one of the ripe cells with a carbolic feather : cut out the cell with a piece of the comb above it (Fig. 131) : return the frame to its hive, and insert the queen cell between two combs of a nucleus, fastening it by thinning the attached piece of comb and turning it down upon the frame-top, pressing it flat. If the queen cell has been built upon the face of a comb, cut round the queen cell, right through the comb, and from the brood comb of the nucleus cut out a piece the same size, and insert in its place the piece with the queen cell. The cell must not be pressed in the least by the fingers. A couple of days later, examine to see whether the cell has been accepted ; if it be found to have been destroyed and other cells to have been built, remove the latter and give another ripe queen cell. The risk of chilling the queen brood may be avoided by heating in the fire a 4-oz.

Fig. 131.
QUEEN CELL, CUT OUT FOR INSERTION.

weight, or other piece of metal, until it is as hot as you can bear in the hand : place this in a small box and cover it with three or four thicknesses of felt : lay the queen cells upon the felt, close the box and put it in your pocket. This will keep the cells and their brood warm while you are preparing to insert them in their new positions.

305. **Management of Nuclei.**—When all the nuclei have been supplied with queen cells, they must be warmly covered up, and gently fed with syrup. There is a danger of the bees of a nucleus leaving the hive with the young queen when the latter takes her mating flight. If a frame of young brood be given to them, they will not be likely to forsake it. The original queen of hive A (302), with her attendant bees, may then be returned to her old home; or she may be used elsewhere, in which case the parent stock should have one or two of the queen cells left to it. If, however, more queens be required, the parent stock may have another frame of eggs from the same queen given to it, and that stock may be kept at queen rearing all the season. When the young queens of the nuclei have been impregnated, and have begun to lay, they may be introduced (308) to the stocks which need them, or may be utilized otherwise as desired.

306. **Using Two Stocks.**—When two stocks can be spared, one to produce the eggs and another to rear the queens, the following plan may be adopted with good results : Select the best stock (A), and the second best (C). Into the centre of the brood nest of A put a frame of foundation. From C remove the queen and three frames, one of brood and two of honey, with the adhering bees, and place them in a third hive taking the precautions suggested above (302). Three or four days later, open hive C and rub off all queen cells that have been formed upon the combs. Take from A the frame given it, which should have a quantity of eggs of the right age in its cells; " scollop," or otherwise prepare it as directed above (302); put it in the middle of the brood nest of C, and leave it for ten days, when you should find upon it a quantity of queen cells within two days of hatching. Now form nuclei, as described above (303), and give to each one or two queen cells, and one or two queen cells to the nucleus in which is the queen of stock C, which queen you may return to C by the " direct method " to be described below (312). By this means you have queens raised from eggs laid by your best queen, and nursed by the bees of another good stock, which is always desirable. The illustration above (Fig. 132) shows a modi-

fication of the former plan, which has some distinct advantages. Cut two pieces of wood, $3'' \times \frac{7}{8}''$, and long enough to fit into a frame. Make two saw-cuts in an edge of each, $2\frac{1}{2}''$ and $5''$ respectively from one end: tack them into the ends of the

Photo from life by   *J. G. Digges.*

Fig. 132. QUEEN REARING—ONE QUEEN CELL LEFT ON PREPARED FRAME (306)

frame, with the saw-cuts to the centre: cut two thin $\frac{7}{8}''$ laths to slide in and out of the saw-cuts, thus making three miniature frames. If longer laths be desired, they may be cut the full length of the inside of the frame and may be supported on small blocks fastened to the inner sides of the frame-ends. Remove the queen from stock C. Three days later cut a $4''$ piece of comb with eggs from your best stock A. Make strips of this piece by running a knife through alternate rows of cells: with a sharp, hot knife cut down the cells on one side to half their depth: destroy every alternate egg on that side with a match: fasten the strips (prepared cells downwards) to the top bar and laths with melted wax: and give the frame to stock C, after rubbing off all queen cells started there. Nine days afterwards you should have a number of queen cells built on the top bar and movable laths, and these cells you can distribute as required. Give more strips of comb with eggs to stock C. You can keep that stock rearing queens all the season. The illustration above, which is from a photograph, shows the prepared frame with all the queen cells removed, save one left to the bees to enable them to re-queen themselves. (*For " Queen Rearing on a Large Scale," see below, pars.* 314-319.)

307. Distributing the Nuclei.—When the nuclei are no longer required for queen rearing, the bees and frames may be distributed among the stocks in the apiary, or they may be formed into one stock, headed by a young queen.

308. Queen Introduction.—Most of the methods of safe introduction at present in use are based upon the belief, gathered from experience, that, if a colony be really queenless, and if a new queen can be introduced, and protected from assault until she has acquired the peculiar scent of the colony, and until the bees have become accustomed to her, she will be accepted. The operation requires care on the part of the bee-keeper, because there is always some danger, and often much danger, that the queen may be roughly treated and even killed.

309. Balling the Queen.—When the bees of a colony are intent upon regicide, they usually surround the queen, enclosing her in a living ball, so firm and close that it is not always easy to break it up. This is known among beekeepers as "balling the queen." A strange queen, carelessly introduced, or liberated in a colony that is being attacked by robber bees, so that the queen may be mistaken for an enemy; and even the queen of the colony, when manipulations are carried on at unseasonable times, may be balled and hugged to death, before the owner can discover the mischief and remedy it. The poetic fancy of Maeterlinck who, while he admits that "bees are not sentimental," will not allow the possibility of individual disloyalty in the hive, attributes the balling of the queen to a law which "invests her person, whoever she be, with a sort of inviolability," and prohibits the direct assault of any one bee:

"No bee, it would seem, dare take on itself the horror of direct and bloody regicide. Whenever, therefore, the good order and prosperity of the republic appear to demand that a queen shall die, they endeavour to give her death some semblance of natural disease, and by infinite subdivision of the crime, to render it almost anonymous. They will, therefore, to use the picturesque expression of the apiarist, 'ball' the queenly intruder; in other words, they will entirely surround her with their innumerable, interlaced bodies. They will thus form a sort of living prison, wherein the captive is unable to move; and in this prison they will keep her for twenty-four hours, if need be, till the victim die of suffocation or hunger."—*Maeterlinck.*

Huber thus describes the balling of the queen:

"If another queen is introduced into the hive within twelve hours after the removal of the reigning one, they surround, seize, and keep her a very long time captive, in an impenetrable cluster, and she commonly dies either from hunger or want of air. If eighteen hours elapse before the substitution of a stranger-queen, she is treated, at first, in the same way, but the bees leave her sooner, nor is the surrounding cluster so close; they gradually disperse, and the queen is at last liberated; she moves languidly, and sometimes expires in a few minutes. Some, however, escape in good health, and afterwards reign in the hive."—*Huber.* 1791.

When a valuable queen has been balled, prompt measures should be taken for her release. If one endeavours to break up the ball with his fingers, or with the aid of a smoker, it frequently happens that, when the outside bees disperse, one or more of those in immediate contact with the queen will sting and kill her. But if the ball be dropped into a small basin of water, it will fall to pieces; the alarm will be so great that the murderous design will be abandoned and the queen may be rescued unhurt.

Fig. 133.
PIPE-COVER CAGE.

310. Use of Queen Cages.—In order to give the strange queen time to acquire the scent of the colony, and to permit the bees to become accustomed to her before her release, she should be caged on one of the centre combs containing brood and uncapped honey. The pipe cover cage (Fig. 133) is the least complicated and a most useful cage for the purpose. Pick up the queen and let her run into the cage, sliding a card underneath. Take out the centre comb: uncap a few honey cells next to capped brood: put down the cage so that it will cover some brood and uncapped honey: withdraw the card; and

Fig. 134.
ABBOTT QUEEN CAGE.

press, or screw, the rim into the comb as far as the mid-rib, or the bases of the cells, carefully avoiding injury to the queen in any way. Do not disturb the bees again for at least three days, or for twice that time if they have been long queenless. Releasing is safer if done in the evening, when the bees have quieted down. If, on releasing her, the bees on the comb show any inclination to crowd or molest the queen, cage her again until the next day. Sometimes the bees will release the queen themselves by eating through the comb; and, if a circular piece of the comb be cut from the opposite side, under the cage, and be put back again, the bees will be encouraged to release and welcome the queen in that way. Of course, there must not be another queen in the hive, and if there be any queen cells on the combs, they should be removed. The Abbott Queen Cage (Fig. 134) is a device by which a queen may be imprisoned in the midst of the cluster, and released without exciting the bees or uncovering the combs. The cage is slipped between two of the frames; the queen is admitted at the top; and, when the wire is drawn up, an exit at the bottom opens and allows her to pass out. When a cage (Fig. 136), or a cage on similar lines, is used, introduction may usually be effected with safety to the queen. It has been discovered that bees of a colony do not hurt the new queen if allowed access to her, one at a time, in a cage after she has been in the hive for two days. Accordingly, a small piece of queen excluder (117), containing one slot, is fixed over the candy hole of the cage. The bees eat the candy, which occupies them for about two days: they then pass through the excluder into the cage and become familiar with the queen, and after a couple of days the queen may be released. Mr. Thomas Chantry, who made the discovery, completes the appliance by arranging a second plug of candy filling a tunnel in the cage and ending in an exit having no excluder. The bees which enter the cage proceed to eat their way through the tunnel to the unguarded exit and the queen escapes quietly with them into the hive and is almost always accepted, having been already virtually introduced. Mr. C. P. Dadant—*American Bee Journal*—describes a simple plan of which he declares: "It succeeds when all other methods fail." The old queen is caged for from two to four hours between two combs in the centre, near the brood; she is then removed and the new queen is put into the same cage in the same position, after which the hive is not opened for at least two days. "This gives the bees the suggestion that it is their own queen that is in the hive."

311. Introduction by Artificial Swarming.—As it is found that bees of a swarm will generally accept a new queen readily, queens are sometimes introduced by making an artificial swarm of the stock (233), removing the old queen, and shaking the bees off the frames before an empty skep placed on their stand. The hive is then replaced on the stand and the bees are shaken on to a hiving board, the new queen being dropped among them as they run in. This plan is not only troublesome, but is attended with extra risks, and there is danger of having the brood chilled during the operation.

312. Direct Introduction.—It is found that a new queen can generally be introduced safely if run into the hive from above, at night, without disturbance of the stock, and when the queen is in a hungry condition and, therefore, ready to accept food from the bees and to show neither fear nor fight. Remove the old queen a few hours before nightfall. When darkness is setting in take out the young queen and put her into a matchbox, keeping her in your pocket and without food for not less than half an hour. When it is quite dark, take a lantern to the stock : quietly raise a corner of the quilt, and let the young queen run out of the match-box down among the frames : cover up : and do not open that hive again until at least 48 hours afterwards. The same match-box must not be used for another queen. This is the " direct method " introduced by Mr. Simmins many years ago, and one of the simplest and most successful methods that can be adopted.

313. Sending Queens per Post.—Queens, being sent per post, or upon any long journey, require to have some attendant bees, and a supply of suitable food *en route*. The simplest travelling box (Fig. 135), one that can be made without expense and that has been used with satisfactory results, consists of a piece of soft wood $3'' \times 1'' \times \frac{3}{4}''$. With a $\frac{3}{4}''$ centre

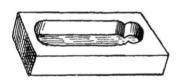

Fig. 135.

QUEEN TRAVELLING BOX.

bit, two holes, $1''$ from centre to centre, are bored nearly through the wood, and one hole with a $\frac{3}{8}''$ centre bit. The wood between the holes is cut away, as shown; and, for ventilation, three or four holes in each side are bored with a fine bradawl. The food, consisting of honey and fine, powdered sugar, as a tough dough, goes into the small hole, and the queen and her attendants occupy the remainder of the space. A piece of broken section, $3'' \times 1''$, makes a lid. The box is wrapped in flannel and brown paper (ventilation being provided for), has a tie-on label, and is dropped into the post like an ordinary letter. More elaborate travelling boxes are made to serve as introducing cages also (Fig. 136), so that the box can be introduced at once to the hive and the queen be liberated in due course, as described above (310).

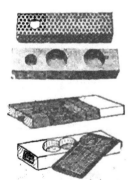

Fig. 136. QUEEN] CAGES

314. Queen Rearing on a Large Scale.—For commercial

purposes, none of the methods already described (299-306) will suffice. The Queen Breeder, whose business it is to raise and sell queens, and, indeed, the owners of large apiaries, cannot afford to depend upon any plan that will not provide queens in quantities and at the right moment. In such cases, recourse must be had to cell-cups, or to artificial cells, and to the transfer of " Royal jelly " and larvæ (207).

315. Artificial Queen Cells.—For the preparation of artificial cells, a mandril (Fig. 137, *a*) will be required. This may be formed from a piece of rounded wood, cut to the size of the interior of a queen cell, and smoothed with glass paper; or one may be purchased for a few pence. The mandril should be marked at a distance of 9/16 inch from the end. We now require a bowl of cold water, and a vessel containing melted

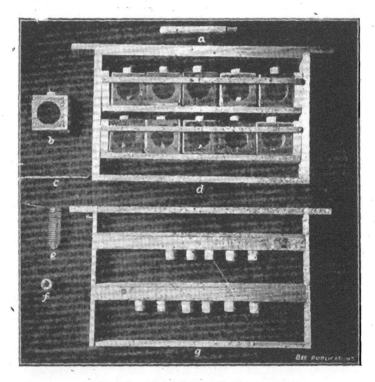

Fig. 137.   QUEEN REARING APPLIANCES.

a, Mandril. *b*, Nursery cage   *c*, Transferring tool. *d*, Nursery cages in Standard frame. *e*, Cell protector. *f*, Wooden cell-cup. *g*, Cell-cups on laths in Standard frame.

wax, placed in a tin dish containing water and set over a spirit lamp, or any other suitable contrivance which will keep the wax at melting point, but not much beyond that. The mandril is dipped into the bowl, the water is shaken off it, and it is inserted for an instant in the wax up to the 9/16 inch mark, withdrawn at once and spun rapidly in the fingers with the object of getting an even distribution of the wax on the mandril. The mandril is then dipped a second time, but to a less depth, say to ½ inch, withdrawn and spun as before, in such a manner that the lower end shall receive most of the wax. As the wax sets, the process is continued five or six times, the mandril being immersed a shade less on each occasion so that the thickness of the covering of wax shall be mainly at the point of the cell.   When cold, the cell may be twisted off the mandril. The operation may be expedited by the use of two or three mandrils, one being dipped and spun while the others are cooling : with this object, a block of wood, with grooves to hold the mandrils, will be useful.   The cells are then fastened, by melted wax, to one side of a lath cut to fit into a frame from side to side (306 and Fig. 132), or they may be inserted in the commonly-used wooden cups, which are fixed by small spikes to the lath (Fig. 137, g) or, if flanged at one end, are passed through holes cut for the purpose in the lath.   We take the mandril—with the wax-cell still attached to it—and with the mandril, push the cell into the cup and gently withdraw the mandril, leaving the cup fitted with its artificial cell.   It is an improvement to support the laths (Fig. 137, g) on small blocks fastened to the inner sides of the frame-ends (306), or as illustrated (Fig. 138), so that the laths may be removable.   The method may be much simplified, and the making of artificial cells obviated, by the use of wooden cell-cups prepared and sold for the purpose.   These are lined with wax and may be had either with nail points for fixing them to the laths, or with flanges as described above.   The bees build queen cells in these cups.   If the frame (Fig. 137, g) be left empty between the top bar and the upper cell-cups bar, as shown in the illustration, the bees will probably build drone comb there; to prevent which the space should be filled with worker-cell comb, or worker-cell foundation, as in Fig. 138.

316. Supplying " Royal Jelly."—The cells having been prepared either artificially or by the bees, take from a stock a queen cell which is nearly ready to be sealed, remove the larva and stir up the jelly in the cell.   Then, with the spoon end of the transferring tool (Fig. 137, c) remove a very small quantity of the jelly and insert it at the bottom of one of the new queen

cells, or cell-cups, proceeding until all have been supplied. Doolittle, to whom so much credit is due for his discoveries, gave jelly the size of a B.B. shot, or 1/8th inch in thickness, to each cell.

317. **Inserting the Larvæ.**—Now go to a stock occupied by a " best tested queen " (299), remove a comb containing young worker larvæ, brush off the bees, wrap the comb in flannel, or place it in a heated box (304) and carry it to a warm room. The cell-cups, supplied with jelly, are arranged, mouth uppermost. With the curved point of the transferring tool, lift from the cells larvæ 24 hours, or not more than 36 hours, old (296), and place one on the jelly in each cell-cup. The lifting of the larvæ may be simplified and expedited if the cells be first cut down with a warm, sharp knife. To judge the age of larvæ requires some observation, but is not difficult. All that is necessary is to observe eggs hatching into larvæ and to examine these 36 hours later. One soon becomes familiar with the appearance, and selects his larvæ before, or immediately upon their reaching, the 36 hours' stage (199).

318. **Management of the Queen Cells.**—The cells, or cups, with their larvæ and jelly, are now attached to the laths alternately in double lines, thus— :······: —cells being fastened with hot wax, and cell-cups similarly or by means of their nail points, or flanges (315), and one of the laths is inserted in the

Fig. 138. QUEEN CELLS FROM ARTIFICIAL CELLS.

centre of a frame of comb, the lower half of the comb having been cut out to admit it; or, two or three laths may be set into one frame (Fig. 137, *g*), with a strip of foundation above the uppermost lath (Fig. 138). The cells should be given to the nursing stock, without delay, and it is most important that they be kept warm during all the operations. To obtain the best results, the nursing stock should be one that is very strong in bees—twenty standard frames of bees will not be too many— from which the queen and one frame of brood and two of honey, with the adhering bees, have been removed to a nucleus hive (298) three days earlier; for, after three days' queenlessness the bees will be ready to receive the queen cells, which should be given in the centre of the brood nest. Liquid food should

Photo by   *A. S. Rowse*

QUEEN-CELL BUILDING. ARTIFICIAL CELLS ON A GRAFT DUMMY.

be supplied regularly if honey be not coming in freely. The extra-strong nursing stock may be used for the purpose until the cells given to it have been sealed, after which the cells may be distributed among other stocks to continue the hatching of the young queens. The queens should hatch out in about 11 or 12 days from the transfer of the larvæ. If the date of transfer of the larvæ be marked upon the frame-top, one will know when to expect the queens. This stock may be kept nursing relays of queen larvæ if hatching brood be supplied to it from time to time; otherwise, after one or two lots had been reared, there would be no young nurse bees in the hive, and nursing by older bees is never satisfactory in its results. When the stock is no longer required for nursing, its queen, and the bees and frames with her in the nucleus hive, may be returned to it. An objection to the above plan is that the nurs-ing colony must be kept queenless, and is of little use for any other purpose while so engaged. If better, or even equal results could be obtained by using full colonies for queen nursing and honey production at the same time, the advantage would be great. Doolittle discovered that this can be accomplished. Select a strong stock, remove two frames of hatching brood to an upper storey, supplying their places with two frames of foundation; set a queen excluder upon the lower frames and the upper storey on it, adding frames of hatching brood from other colonies, or frames of foundation, or of drawn comb, on either side of the two frames of brood, and the frame of cell-cups between the latter. The bees coming up through the excluder, having no queen in the upper storey, will raise, and will con-tinue to raise, queens there in the cell-cups throughout the season, without any loss in honey production and brood rear-ing, while fresh frames of cell-cups may be given above at intervals of three or four days, and with the best results if a frame of sealed brood be given in the upper storey every ten days.

319. Protecting the Young Queens.—It must be noted that if one queen be allowed to emerge from her cell and to have access to the other cells, the young queens in those cells will be destroyed (209, 223). When they are ready to hatch out, the young queens, in their cells, should be distributed among the nuclei (303-304), or in mating boxes, or divided hives (298), or to full colonies which it is desired to requeen, such colonies having been previously rendered queenless for twenty-four hours, and the cells being given in wire cell-protectors (Fig. 137, e). If distribution cannot be made in any of these direc-tions, and if the cells are to remain in the nursing colony until the queens emerge, they may be protected in nursing cages (Fig. 137, b). Ten of these cages fit into a standard frame (Fig. 137, d). Their sides are protected by wire cloth, and they have two holes, one to admit a queen cell and cup, the other for food. Candy made as directed (313), is packed into the latter hole; a queen cell is taken from the hive, its point is dipped in honey, and the cell is inserted in the nursery cage. When the frame of cages is complete, it is given to the stock in the upper storey. The hatched queens, safe in their nurseries and with food provided for them, may be utilized as required. It must, however, be observed that virgin queens, immediately upon emerging from their cells, require a large supply of natural pollen and honey to build up their constitu-tions, and these cannot be conveniently provided in nursery cages. The need may be met by caging them on combs containing pollen and honey easy of access by the queens (310). These combs may be quite small, arranged in mating boxes, of which a large number should be available. In all these operations, bees must not be shaken from frames which have queen cells, but must be brushed off, nor should the cells be inverted at any time after having been sealed; for, any shaking or rough usage of queen cells will most probably injure the occupants.

A ROADSIDE APIARY AND HONEY STALL.

CHAPTER XXVI.

MARKETING HONEY.

320. Home Honey.—The honey produced in these Islands, as to quality, can hold its own with any produced elsewhere; we beekeepers, close as we are to the best market in the world, should find little difficulty in disposing of our produce to advantage. But, while the home market is to a considerable extent supplied from our own hives, very large quantities are annually imported from the dominions, colonies and foreign countries. To compete successfuly in such a market, it is necessary, not only that the quality of the article be excellent, but also that the manner of presenting it for sale should place it on a level with, if not superior to, that of any other honey offered to the public. As to the quality, that may be left to the bees and to the flowers of our unrivalled hills and valleys. As to the presentation of the article, that is a matter to which insufficient attention has hitherto been given, and which must be more carefully attended to in the future if our honey is to attain to that position in the markets to which its quality entitles it. To the beekeeper it is no less important than the harvesting of a large quantity of honey, that the honey should be so presented to the buyer in the best possible condition as to quality and "make-up," that the customer may desire more, and be willing to pay a fair price for it.

321. Storing Honey.—Sections, when removed from the hive, should be stored, preferably in close tin boxes, and in a dry, warm place, safe from dust, flies, mice, etc. If left in a cold, damp place, the distinctive flavour and aroma due to the essential oils of the flowers will be sacrificed, and the honey, a supersaturated liquid, will absorb moisture from the atmosphere; will become thin; will increase in bulk; will ferment; and will exude through the cappings in minute drops: from which we have the too familiar "weeping section," with its whiteness and beauty gone, and its value also gone to no small extent. Or, cold may cause the honey to crystallize in the cells, which spoils it for the market, and causes many a large buyer to say: "I never purchase sections after September." Extracted honey, stored in a cold place, will granulate. It keeps best in bulk, and should be so stored until it is required for marketing (333).

322. Preparing Comb Honey for Market.—Before despatching comb honey to the market, the whole stock should be gone over carefully and graded into first, second, and third classes. This is a detail which should never be neglected; because, a few indifferent sections in an otherwise prime lot may pull down the price of the whole consignment to second, or third quality rates, thus imposing a serious loss upon the producer. First quality sections must be well sealed and free from pop-holes. They should be well filled out and built securely to the wood. The National Mark Honey Grading Scheme of the Ministry of Agriculture in London has laid it down as a rule for packers that first grade, or select comb honey shall have a minimum net weight of 15 ozs. per section. They must otherwise be of good quality. Second grade sections are those which are lighter, but otherwise presentable and well sealed, and third grade are those which may be partly unsealed or otherwise inferior. In Ireland, wholesale buyers have been accustomed to demand heavier weights, partly on account of the use of the 2-inch section commonly used in that country. It should be remembered that the comb honey section is a nominal 1-lb. retail pack, and that this includes both wood and wax, but that any wrapping, glass or carton used for packing it cannot be included in the net weight. The chief requisite in the case of comb honey for the high-class market is a perfectly clean, bright comb surface, well built to the wood. Dirty or travel-stained cappings are a more serious defect than any extra weight can rectify. The wood should be scraped quite clean, great care being taken not to injure the comb in the process; but a slight accident of that kind may sometimes be repaired with a small piece of clean cappings or a piece of clean, white wax spread upon the breakage with the flat of a warm knife. All repaired combs, however, should be relegated to the second grade, no matter how good they otherwise may be. If the sections are to be sold unglazed, each section should be wrapped in cellophane or other cellulose transparent paper, or in waxed paper, the fold being made on the top of the section, the ends being turned in securely, the flap and ends being lightly touched with a paste brush to fasten them down. Cellulose paper is much superior to waxed paper as it is transparent and light in weight. It is also virtually leak-proof and forms an attractive display for the shop counter. It may be procured of suitable thickness and should be in sheets of $13'' \times 7\frac{1}{2}''$. Thus prepared, should a leakage occur during transport in any one section, the other sections will be protected from soiling. (See also 330-331).

323. Glazing Sections.—Sections that are glazed (Fig. 139), and neatly finished with embossed lace, or plain, paper, present an exceedingly attractive appearance and, being safe from flies

Fig. 139. GLAZED SECTION.

and dust, are preferred by many retailers, who are generally willing to pay an increased price for them. The slips of paper should be exactly 17″ long, and ¾″ wider than the section; glass should measure exactly 4¼″ × 4¼″, and should be cut without irregular corners. Photographers often have quantities of useless negatives which can be purchased cheaply, and cut to the correct size. Give the paper a coat of good paste: set the section, top side up, upon it, exactly in the middle from side to side, and projecting about ¼″ beyond one end of the slip.   Place a square of glass against each side and turn all

Fig. 140. GLAZED SECTION BOX

over on the slip, pressing the edges of the paper on the glass as each side is turned, and fastening the corners neatly with a little paste.   The fold will be on the bottom; and a neat label describing the contents, and with the producer's name and address, may be pasted on the top (325).   The glass should be polished clean, and the section should then be wrapped in paper. Glazed boxes for sections are much used (Fig. 140).   They are inexpensive, entail little or no trouble, and are convenient packages on a merchant's counter.   (See also 331).

324. Packing Sections for Transport.—Honey-comb sent per post or rail requires careful packing to avoid breakage *en route*.   The travelling crate illustrated (Fig. 141) takes one dozen sections, and has an arrangement of light springs underneath, to minimise jolting of the contents, while the glass sides disclose the fragile nature of the goods within, and appeal to the compassion of railway porters and other transport agents. The Home-made Travelling Crate (Fig. 142) consists of two squares of wood, 5½″ × 5½″ × ½″, and 12 pieces of plaster lath, 14″ × 1″ × ¼″.   The laths are tacked on three sides of the squares; two pieces of corrugated cardboard, 5½″ × 5½″, are slipped in at each end; and the crate is well lined with straw. Six sections, carefully wrapped in cellophane (322), are inserted; straw is laid on top; and the remaining laths are tacked on. If this crate be corded, and a tie-on label attached, it may be sent per post with confidence. The cost of such a crate is trivial. When larger quantities are being dealt with, say, 6 dozen, it is advisable to pack each dozen sections in a cardboard box 13″ × 9″ × 4½″, to hold them close enough to prevent their moving. When filled, the box should be wrapped in paper and tied with stout cord. Such boxes,

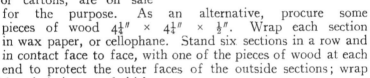

Fig. 141. TRAVELLING CRATE.

or cartons, are on sale for the purpose. As an alternative, procure some pieces of wood 4¼″ × 4¼″ × ½″. Wrap each section in wax paper, or cellophane. Stand six sections in a row and in contact face to face, with one of the pieces of wood at each end to protect the outer faces of the outside sections; wrap the whole in several thicknesses of paper, folding well down over the ends, and tie with strong string around the package from end to end. These boxes, or packages, should travel in a strong case, 33″ × 17″ × 14″, with sides ½″ full and ends ¾″ full, 2 battens on each end, outside, and 2 battens, 2″ × ½″, on the top and bottom, outside. The

Fig. 142.
HOME-MADE TRAVELLING CRATE.

case should have a rope handle, or a wooden hand grip at each end to facilitate railway porters, who might otherwise throw it about instead of handling it carefully. It is important to see that the bottom of the case is firmly nailed on before the packages, or cartons, are inserted. The packing should be composed, not of hay, but of straw. Put a layer of six inches of straw on the bottom of the case, well pressed down and level; on this set some of the boxes, side by side, and with a couple of inches of straw packing between them and the case on all four sides: on top of the boxes put another layer of two inches of straw: set on more boxes: pack all round: cover with at least two or three inches of straw: add, on top, a note specifying the nature and quantity of the contents: screw on the lid: tie with strong rope: and, on the lid, affix a large card with the following, in distinct characters:—

This Side Up.   Fragile.   Honey Comb.   With Care.

For————   From————   Date————

An additional precaution will be to so arrange the case in the train that the combs may be parallel with the railway rails. **(167).** When honey has been despatched, an invoice should be

sent to the consignee specifying the date, quantity, number of packages, net weight, and how sent, *i.e.*, per post, or per rail, goods train, or passenger train. Books of duplicating invoice forms are very cheap and may be obtained at any stationery shop; such forms pass through the post with a ½d. stamp.

Fig. 143.   Glass Honey Jars.

325. Preparing Extracted Honey for Market.—For the sale of extracted honey in bulk, tins with a capacity of 28-lbs. or 56-lbs. are generally used, the former being the more popular and handy of the two. Such tins should be lacquered inside and out. This is a recent development for the prevention of rust on the outside of the tin and blackening inside. The extra cost of lacquered tins is trifling. Smaller tins for retail trade may be had either plain lacquered or lithographed in attractive colours (Fig. 147) in 2½-lbs. to 10-lbs. sizes. For extracted honey, the retail packs which are used almost universally in shops, are glass jars having metal screw caps or similar caps with intermittent grips which are secured in place by a half turn, as is the case with the jars approved by the National Mark Committee. (Fig. 143). Tie-over jars are used, to-day, only for private sales or in very exceptional cases, and the use of corks is now a thing of the past. The squat-shaped jars are rapidly coming into favour: the producer prefers them because they are easily washed, and the consumer, because the contents are so easily extracted. While cork wads are still frequently fitted to the caps to effect the air-tight sealing which is necessary, it is far better to use the waxed white card wad. The latter is cleaner in appearance and does not tend to form a black deposit at the point of contact as composite cork wads so often do. Also the white wad reflects light down into the honey which tends to brighten its appearance.

Extracted honey may be bottled soon after extraction, but, if so, it will granulate or set solid in the jars. This will be quite in order when sales in that form are expected; but if it is required to sell the honey in its clear form, it must be so treated that it will not, after being bottled, tend to granulate for a considerable time. If honey has once granulated in jars it must be so sold because, if melted in hot water, a scum of froth will be certain to rise to the top and spoil its appearance completely. Therefore to bottle clear honey, proceed as follows: Store the honey in large tins, and when required to bottle, set a tin or tins in a vessel of water and heat the whole slowly until all honey has liquified, then pour through a fine strainer into the tank or ripener (145) and allow to stand until the next day, when the jars may be filled. In order to make sure that granulation shall not take place in the jars, these may, after being filled and sealed with the caps, be stood in a vessel of water and heated up to about 150° F. with the caps screwed down. Honey should never be heated to a temperature higher than 160° F.; 144° F. will usually be sufficient and, as that is the point at which beeswax melts (67), if a small piece of wax be put into the honey it will indicate when the temperature of the honey has been raised sufficiently.

Fig. 144. DECORATED PULP CARTONS.

The jars should be perfectly clean, and an attractive label should be pasted on, as advised above (323). There is a great deal more in the label, and general get up of the article than many bee-men suppose. The label illustrated (Fig. 145) was procured from Messrs. E. H. Taylor, Ltd.; it is the well-known old label in several colours, designed many years ago by Tom Sell, and is one of the most attractive of general labels. It can be had for " English," " Scotch," " Welsh," " Irish " or " Heather " Honey, as required. The name and address of the producer, or the society marketing the honey,

can be printed on the label, so that the purchaser or his friends, if pleased with the article, may have no difficulty in repeating orders. Thus the label serves, not only as an ornament, but also as a useful advertisement. As dealers frequently object to granulated honey, supposing it to be necessarily impure or deteriorated, it is wise to add a notice to the following effect in cases where honey is not properly understood by the buyer: " NOTICE— *Honey that is pure will candy, becoming hard or crystallised. If it be wished to render it liquid, set the jar in hot water until the contents melt and become clear.*"

Fig. 145. HONEY LABEL.

When labelled, each jar should be wrapped in paper to protect the label and exclude dirt. Travelling boxes to hold twelve or twenty-four jars are made. They are lined with corrugated paper and have divisions of the same material which

form separate compartments for the bottles (Fig. 146). When large quantities are being dealt with, the wrapped bottles should be packed in a strong box, with a liberal allowance of straw or "woodwool," underneath, around the sides, between the jars, and on top, it being very important to pack the jars tightly. The box should be strongly corded; only non-returnable boxes should be used, customers objecting strongly—and naturally—to the trouble and expense of returning boxes.

Fig. 146. TRAVELLING BOX FOR HONEY JARS

Cartons made of waxed wood-pulp (Figs. 144 and 148) are

inexpensive, and very light. They make attractive retail packages. They are used chiefly for direct sales to consumers, and when they are not likely to be stored for very long after being filled, are very useful. They are now made with screwtops as well as with friction discs and, like glass jars, may be had in several sizes, from 2-lbs. down to 4-ozs. They are not

Fig. 147. LITHOGRAPHED HONEY TINS.

very popular with shop-keepers for they do not show their contents as do glass jars and, if stored for long in damp weather, are apt to absorb moisture which may cause fermentation or leakage. They may be procured plain, to take

Fig. 148. " MONO " |HONEY CONTAINER.

the producer's own label attached, not with paste, but with gum. For retail trade the most popular sizes are 1-lb. and ½-lb., the former being the most in demand. Smaller sizes are also largely used ; but, though to some extent in use, larger sizes, such as 2-lbs., are little in demand.

325A. Marketing Organization.—In marketing organization the beekeepers of Great Britain and Ireland are extremely weak, and too much stress can hardly be laid upon the desirability of combination through associations for the purpose of improving our marketing methods. During the last few years the Ministry of Agriculture in London has set up the National Mark Scheme for the Marketing of English and Welsh honey. Under this scheme, large individual producers or associations of small beekeepers are allowed to enrol as licensed National Mark packers and to use a special label. It cannot be amiss to emphasise that all over these Islands, local associations could do a great deal to assist individual producers by combination for marketing purposes. In England many associations, quite independently of the Government scheme, arrange to supply members with special labels guaranteeing the purity of their produce, and also assist members to dispose of their crops to advantage. In Scotland, also, this is the case; but Ireland suffers from the fact that her market is an export market, and in the case of Irish producers, combination and organization is doubly needed—and would be much easier than on the other side of the Channel. Producers in the Green Isle are generally isolated and a prey to dealers who make very low cash offers which are generally accepted. Fine Irish sections have often been sold by the producer at 5s. per dozen, which have finally reached the consumer at 2s. 6d. each, and it would seem that a combination of Irish beekeepers who could send a salesman to London, should make a good thing of it. In Great Britain central packing organizations by producers are a far more difficult problem, because the small producer is so close to the market, and is so often tempted to accept prices which do not cover costs of production and a fair profit. Still, much may be done by careful work, and the beekeepers' slogan should be, " Unity is Strength."

CHAPTER XXVII.

EXHIBITING AND JUDGING BEE PRODUCTS.

326. Points to be Aimed at.—The chief features of excellence which are looked for by judges of Bee Products at the leading shows may be summarized as follows, the marks attached to each being those approved and recommended by the Irish Beekeepers' Association.

SECTIONS.—*Completeness of filling*, including weight and freedom from popholes and unsealed cells, 25; *condition*, including uniformity of cappings, flatness of surface, and freedom from " travel stain," propolis, " weeping," bruising, and other disfigurements, 20; *flavour and aroma*, 20; *colour* of cappings, 10; *general appearance* of the exhibit, including squareness and cleanness of the wood and glass, glazing, suitability of paper decorations—if any (the overlap of paper not to exceed ⅜″), method of staging—if any, and general attractiveness, 25. Total marks, 100.

EXTRACTED HONEY (Liquid).—*Colour*, which, in classes for " Light " Honey, may range from clear to a pale straw tint, " Medium " Honey from light to dark, Heather Honey to dark brown, 10; *density, or thickness*, 30; *flavour and aroma*, 25; *condition*, including clearness and freedom from froth, air bubbles, suspended matter, and granulation, 20; *general appearance* of the exhibit, including quality and make of bottle, or jar, safety from leakage, neatness of label, and general attractiveness, 15. Total marks, 100.

EXTRACTED HONEY (Granulated).—*Colour*, which may range from white to amber, and, in the case of Heather Honey, to dark brown, 10; *condition*, including regularity and completeness of granulation and fineness of grain, 35; *flavour and aroma*, 25; *general appearance* of the exhibit, including quality and make of bottle, or jar, neatness of label, and general attractiveness, 15. Total marks, 85.

SUPERS OF HONEY, exhibited as removed from the hive, without re-arrangement or cleaning.—*Preliminary preparation, and condition as exhibited*, including squareness of sections, suitability of separators, follower, and spring, evenness of comb, and freedom from " travel stain," propolis, and other disfigurements of super, sections, or frames, and comb, 20; *weight of contents*, 20; *uniformity and colour* of cappings, 10. Total marks, 50.

BEESWAX.—*Colour*, ranging from lemon to pale amber, 20; *freshness, cleanness and purity*, including absence of dross, 20; *aroma*, 10; *texture*, including freedom from brittleness, 10. Total marks, 60.

MEAD.—*Flavour*, 10; *clearness and brilliancy*, 10; *attractiveness* of bottle and label, 10.   Total marks, 30.

VINEGAR.—*Flavour*, 10; *clearness and brilliancy*, 10; *attractiveness* of bottle and label, 10.   Total marks, 30.

327. Early Exhibition Sections.—As it is necessary to have the cappings of exhibition sections uniform in colour and perfectly free from " travel stain," the sections must be finished as quickly as possible, and must be removed from the hive as soon as they have been finished. If an exhibit of the current season be needed for an early show, select more than the required number of good, clean sections well filled with comb from the previous season, and, with the opening of the first honey flow, place these, over an excluder, on the strongest stock that gives the whitest cappings (46-48, 50), and wrap them up as warmly as possible at the sides, ends, and on top of the crate.   Defer as long as you safely can the addition of an extra crate, and if the exhibition lot is not fit for removal when a second crate must be given in order to prevent swarming, leave the first crate undisturbed, and give the second crate on top.   But, assuming that the first crate was set upon nine frames only—which is common enough in the early season— the addition of a second crate may be postponed by giving an extra frame, or frames, as required, in the brood nest, and this will help to prevent a slackening of work in the crate. Should a swarm issue, hive it on the old stand in a new hive fitted with only six or seven frames of foundation; add a half inch board (279) behind the dummy to prevent the escape of bees there; place the excluder, and the exhibition crate with its bees, on top to be finished by the swarm.   When completed, remove the crate by means of a super clearer (287-288), and in no other way, or you will probably have broken cappings to destroy your exhibit (330).   Be careful that no cappings become bruised when the sections are being taken from the crate; proceed in this way—remove the spring, or wedge, from behind the follower (114, and Figs. 51 and 53, pp. 78, 79), place a tray, or a clean, flat board upon the crate, carefully turn all over on a table, then loose the crate and lift it off the sections, when the latter may be separated without risk of being damaged.

328. Mid-Season Exhibition Sections.—Sections intended for the Clover, or " Light " Honey exhibition classes, should be worked from the foundation in the current season. Before the flow from clover opens, select a stock that is already doing good work, through an excluder, in its first crate, and that can be relied upon for white cappings (46-48, 50), and when clover begins to yield, give that stock, under its first crate, a crate of clean, new sections, carefully folded, and furnished with full sheets of worker-comb foundation stopping an eighth of an inch from the bottom of each section. Do not disturb the stock again for a week. If then the first crate proves to be ready for removal, remove it with the aid of a super clearer (287-288), without in any way disturbing the exhibition crate, and give a new crate on top. On the question of giving the bees more room before the completion of the exhibition crate, careful judgment must be exercised. If more frames should be required, or another crate, or should the stock swarm, and for the removal of the exhibition crate and the separation of the sections, the instructions given in the preceding paragraph (327) should be followed.

329. Heather Sections for Exhibition.—If it be intended to enter competition in the classes for Heather, or " Dark," Honey Sections, select more than the required number of incomplete, but well-built sections from the earlier season's crates; extract the honey, and give the sections, wet from the extractor and over an excluder, to your best stock, placing the choicest specimens in the central positions in the crate. Not more than one or two crates should be given to that stock, and such exhibition crate, or crates, should be wrapped as warmly as possible round the sides and ends, and on the top. Should the bees appear to be unable to use to advantage all their available space before the exhibition sections are completed, do not hesitate to reduce the space, either by removing sections or by withdrawing frames, so that the required sections may receive from the bees all the attention necessary. For the subsequent details, as to removing the sections from the hive and from the crate, the preceding instructions should be followed (327).

330. Selecting Exhibition Sections.—The most unselfish and unbiased skill, care and judgment must now be brought to bear upon the delicate task of selecting the sections for exhibition, for it is at this point that so many exhibitors come to grief. Assume that the sections belong to your bitterest enemy—if you have such—and that you are the appointed judge, bound in honour to give them the most critical examination and to discover the slightest defect. During the selection keep in mind the following essential considerations: Sections for exhibition should be filled to the wood on all sides and completely sealed. The weight should be not less than 16 ozs., and in fine sections may be considerably more, especially if the 2″ section is used; but weight much in excess of 1-lb. should not merit points, since the section is to be regarded as a 1-lb. retail package. Bulging, or any unevenness, of the comb is a fault which must be excluded from the show bench; the surface of the comb should be quite flat corresponding with the cut-away sides of bee-way sections, or in the case of no bee-way sections, about $\frac{1}{8}$″ short of the edges of the wood on both sides. "Travel stain," which is the result of leaving sections too long in the hive, detracts from the appearance and sacrifices marks in competition. Propolis on the wood must be removed. Punctured cappings (327) are to be avoided; they are generally the result of a defective method of clearing the bees from supers—much smoke, or excessive use of carbolic or other intimidating medium, having the effect of driving the bees to gorge at the cells, and thus the appearance of the contents is injured and their value reduced: this defect may be obviated by the proper use of super clearers (287-288, 327). "Weeping" describes the condition of a comb that has been stored in a cold, damp place, the honey, with its absorbed moisture, exuding through the cappings in minute drops (321): to state the cause is to describe the necessary precautions to be taken; no weeping sections have any chance with a moderately competent judge (322).

331. Preparing Exhibition Sections.—Having made your selection, prepare the sections for display on the show bench (322). With a cabinetmaker's scraper, a piece of glass, or a blunt penknife, scrape the wood of the sections thoroughly, avoiding any injury to the comb, and finish off with fine sandpaper. No matter what covering or ornamentation it is intended to subsequently employ, this cleaning of the wood should invariably be attended to because it is right and seemly in itself, and because any experienced judge will look for it. The sections may then be glazed, as described (323), neatness, taste, and the most scrupulous cleanliness being essential here : the overlap of paper, or of lace paper, should not exceed $\frac{3}{8}''$, and all tinsel and gaudy colours should be rigorously excluded. Sections may be shown in special boxes made and sold for the purpose (323, and Fig.

140, page 220), or in exhibition cases (Fig. 149), or failing any of the foregoing, they may be wrapped in wax paper, or cellophane (322), and tied with narrow ribbon. All extravagant and fantastic designs of decoration should be avoided.

Fig. 149.   GLAZED EXHIBITION CASE.

The exhibit should be carefully packed ready for despatch, and should be kept in a warm place, meanwhile, to avoid "weeping." Where it is possible to do so, exhibitors should stage their own exhibits, leaving them in the best order and condition for the judge.

332. Extracted Clover, or "Light," Honey for Exhibition.—To secure suitable specimens of Clover, or "Light," Honey, for extraction, it is desirable to have on hands a supply of frames of good, clean combs, absolutely free from honey and pollen; they should have had their honey extracted, and have been given back to the bees, over a super clearer, to be cleaned (287), and should then have been carefully wrapped up and stored until required. Immediately upon the clover coming into bloom, the frames should be given, in a super box and over an excluder, to a strong stock, and should be removed, whether finished or not, so soon as the flow from clover ceases.

333. Extracting and Preparing Clover, or "Light," Honey for Exhibition.—Extracting may be carried out according to the instructions already given (289-291). The extractor (143), strainer (145), and ripener (145) must be as clean as it is possible to make them, and nothing must be permitted to add either flavour or colour to the honey after its removal from the hive. Density, which is an essential qualification, cannot be secured to the full extent in honey extracted from unsealed cells, because such honey has not been thoroughly ripened, and for show purposes it will not do to ripen it artificially. If, therefore, the combs to be dealt with contain the least quantity of unsealed honey, that honey must

first be extracted and stored away, and then the remainder of
the combs may be uncapped and their contents may be extracted
for exhibition; or, as an alternative, such combs may be
uncapped, and revolved in the extractor at a speed only
sufficient to throw out the unripe honey, which must be drawn
off, the combs being then revolved at the speed necessary to
extract the ripe honey required.   One week after extraction
(289) and straining (290), the ripe honey may be run off from
the bottom of the ripener, and should be kept in bulk, in an air-
tight tin and in a warm place.   Three or four days from the
date of the show at which the exhibit is to be made, the tin of
honey should be set in a vessel of hot water until the honey
reaches 80° Fahr., when it may be run into the selected jars.
The jars must be left in a warm place, covered from dust, until
all air bubbles, or scum, in the honey shall have risen to the
top, when the bubbles, or scum, must be carefully skimmed off
and, if necessary, an addition of ripened and skimmed honey
should be added to bring the contents of each jar up to 16 oz.
Uniformity being necessary, with respect to flavour, colour,
and density, if there be any difference in the exhibits, the
quantity required for the jars should be mixed in one vessel
beforehand.   Care must be taken to exclude any honey that
may have been tainted with honey dew (66), because such an
admixture would utterly spoil the colour and flavour of the
exhibit.   The jars for exhibition purposes must be carefully
selected, of clear, flawless glass, and, preferably, with screw
caps fitted with cork wads (325).   For each jar, cut a circular
piece of wax paper the same size as the cork wad; put this on
the mouth of the jar, set the cork wad upon it, and screw the
cap tightly home.   A neat label should be added (325).

334. **Extracted Heather, or " Dark," Honey for Exhibi-**
tion.—As in the case of Heather sections (329), built out combs,
wet from the extractor, should be used over an excluder.
Owing to the difficulty of removing heather honey from the
combs in an ordinary extractor, if the extractor is to be used
the combs to be employed should be tough and strong, and
preferably drone combs.   If the honey is to be extracted by
means of the Honey Press (146), or by melting (335), fresh,
virgin combs will serve best.

335. **Extracting and Preparing Heather, or " Dark,"**
Honey for Exhibition.—If it be intended to remove the
heather honey by means of an extractor, everything required
should be in readiness, in a warm room, to extract the honey
hot from the hives, for if it be allowed to cool, extraction will

be exceedingly difficult. It will be found more practicable to crush the comb in a Honey Press (146, 289), or to melt the wax. In the former case, the combs should be heated up to 120° Fahr., being placed in the Press as directed (289). If the melting process is to be adopted, the sealed combs should be cut out and placed in a tin vessel, which should then be set in a pot of warm water, with a wire mat, or other suitable device, underneath, to keep the tin about $\frac{1}{2}''$ up from the bottom of the pot; the water must then be heated gradually, and the contents of the tin must be stirred frequently until the wax begins to melt, at which point the temperature must be maintained until all the wax has melted, for if the melting point of wax (144°, 67) be exceeded, the flavour of the honey may be spoiled (325). When all the wax has melted, the contents of the tin must be allowed to cool until the wax can be lifted off the top in a cake, after which, without further cooling, the honey may be strained into the selected jars and treated as described above (333).

336. Supers of Honey for Exhibition.—The object of this class is to encourage careful handling of the sections, frames, foundation, crates, and super boxes, and to judge of the capability of the exhibitor through the perfection, or otherwise, of his entire exhibit, his aim being to produce the maximum of good comb and honey with the minimum of propolis, travel stain, popholes, and other detractions. If the crate, or super box, is to be exhibited exactly as taken from the hive, none of the contents may be handled subsequently, nor may any marks or stains be removed. Accordingly, all the more care must be taken with the preliminary details, viz.: The choice of a stock that may be relied upon to give good work and to finish with white cappings (46-48, 50); the selection of the crate, or super box, only such as are absolutely accurate in all their measurements (111, 116) being employed; the folding of sections and the putting together of frames; the insertion of foundation, separators, follower, and spring or wedge; the application of vaseline, or petroleum jelly (183), to minimise propolising; the accurate fitting and evenness of sheet and quilts; the careful wrapping of the crate, or super box, with warm materials, to conserve heat and expedite the work. If these details be properly attended to, the results should be satisfactory, but if any of these details should be neglected, failure will probably follow.

337. Beeswax for Exhibition.—The best results are obtained from cappings and virgin comb. When preparing combs for the extractor, the whitest cappings should be taken off with as little as possible adhering comb, and be set apart for exhibition purposes, and when the honey from them has drained off, they should be left in a vessel of clean rain water for a few days. Hard water, or water containing lime, should never be used in any of the processes adopted for wax-rendering, for it injures the quality of the wax. Upon removal from the water the wax should be dried, kneaded into small balls, and inserted, preferably in a steam wax extractor (149), or, if such an extractor be not available, the wax may be put into a perfectly clean earthenware jar in a moderately hot oven, or in a pot of boiling water on the range. When the wax has melted it should be strained through fine muslin into a bowl of warm water, and allowed to cool slowly, for rapid cooling produces cracks in the wax. When cool, and before it is perfectly cold, the cake of wax should be lifted off the water, and should have all dross and dirt scraped away; it may then be broken up, re-melted, and poured through muslin into a suitable mould, or moulds, previously wet with clean cold water, and should be allowed to cool as slowly as possible. The processes of melting, straining, and scraping may be repeated so long as there remain any impurities to be removed, but they should not be carried to the point of injuring the texture of the wax and making it brittle. As elsewhere stated (293), dark wax may have its colour improved by the addition of sulphuric acid (vitriol) to the water in which it is to be melted. When old combs are being dealt with for exhibition purposes, the following method may be adopted with advantage: Set two vessels of hot water side by side on the range; into one crush as many combs as it will hold, leaving some inches to spare for the swelling of the wax when it boils. As the wax melts, skim it off, as free as possible from dirt, into the second vessel, and discontinue this process when the wax becomes too dirty for the purpose; the first vessel is then to be emptied and cleaned, its wax contents being reserved for further treatment. Now put some boiling water into the empty vessel, and also a large, clean jam crock containing some boiling water; strain the wax from the second vessel, through fine muslin, into the crock; then stir it with a thin piece of wood, and as you stir, drop a little sulphuric acid, drop by drop, on to the wax; this will improve the colour and will help to remove any impurities that may have escaped the strainer. Now remove the vessel containing the crock and wax to the side of the range, cover it with a lid, and let the cooling be very gradual. When the cake of wax is cool scrape, or cut, from it all impurities. From a number of cakes so prepared select the best specimens, weighing in all a little more than is required, and re-melt these in the crock after having thoroughly cleaned the latter. Damp the inside of your mould with clean cold water, pour in the melted wax, and set the mould in a pot of hot water where the wax may cool as slowly as possible to avoid cracks. This method, even when applied to combs black with age, has resulted in first prizes at leading shows, where competition was exceptionally keen, the careful skimming of the wax before it had time to become discoloured, and the subsequent processes, having produced cakes of wax of exceptional merit. As an alternative to the former methods —although not one which can be as strongly recommended— the boiling process (293) previously described may be adopted, the wax being ladelled off as it rises, to be treated as advised above.

338. Mead for Exhibition.—Mead for the show bench should be well flavoured, full bodied, clear, and, if possible, sparkling. The honey used in its manufacture should be light and well ripened, and throughout the whole process the utmost cleanliness must be secured, not only in the ingredients, but also in every vessel employed. Use 4 lbs. honey to each gallon of water, and allow the honey to dissolve, then put it into a copper, or large boiler, add 1 oz. hops and $\frac{1}{2}$ oz. ginger per gallon, and boil it for one hour, skimming off the scum as it rises. When sufficiently boiled, pour it into a wooden vessel, and when its temperature has reduced to 120° add 1 oz. of brewer's yeast per gallon, mix this well with the liquor, which must then be covered and allowed to stand in the vessel for about eight hours. Next it must be poured into a perfectly clean barrel, and as the contents ferment, the barrel must be filled up with more of the liquor, an extra half-gallon having been prepared for the purpose beyond what the barrel is constructed to hold. When fermentation has ceased, dissolve $\frac{1}{4}$ oz. of isinglass in a cupful of water, pour it into the barrel, and stir well; this is to clear the liquid. After about six days draw off the liquor into a second perfectly clean barrel, filling the barrel completely, and drive in the bung as tightly as possible. It must stand for at least six months, after which it may be bottled. The bottles must, of course, be perfectly clean, the corks should be new, and they should be fastened with wire and covered with tinfoil, a neat label being pasted on the side of each bottle.

339. Vinegar for Exhibition.—For the production of a superior exhibit of vinegar, all that is necessary is to use the right ingredients, to study cleanliness in all the processes, and to regulate the temperature with a certain degree of accuracy. Take 1 lb. of good extracted honey, add it to 7 lbs. of fresh clean water in a wooden vessel (or 1 lb. of honey to 5½ pints of water), and stir the mixture thoroughly. Cover the vessel with two thicknesses of fine muslin, and keep it at a temperature of about 80° Fahr. It may be exposed to the sunshine in summer, being brought into a warm kitchen for the night. After about six weeks, if the vinegar prove right to the taste, strain it into another wooden vessel, stir in ¼ oz. of isinglass dissolved in a few ounces of water, and allow it to stand for a fortnight; then bottle it in clear glass bottles, using new corks, which may be covered with tinfoil; put on an attractive label.

340. Judging Bee Products.—No one who accepts appointment as a judge of Bee Products hopes to please and satisfy all the exhibitors; but if he desires to do absolute justice, and to carry out his mission creditably, he will be wise to adopt a fixed scale of marks for the various points, and to rigidly adhere to those marks. By no other method can judging be conducted satisfactorily. In a previous paragraph (326) the points have been described, and attached to each is the scale of marks adopted and recommended by the Irish Beekeepers' Association. No judge can go far astray who follows the lead thus given. He will require a glass taster—which can be procured for a few pence—a magnifying glass, and a scales with the necessary weights up to 20 oz., which should be supplied by the Show Committee. He should also be provided by the Show Committee with a supply of judge's cards, which should contain, in parallel columns, spaces for the exhibitors' numbers, for the marks to be awarded under each point, for the total marks obtained by each exhibitor, for the maximum marks possible, and for the award, with a space in which the judge's remarks upon any exhibit may be entered opposite the number and marks of that exhibit. As the judge proceeds to examine the sections, he will first enter the maximum marks possible at the head of the columns for points (if this has not been already done), and then he will enter the numbers attached to the exhibits, in vertical order, in the first column on his card; next he will test each exhibit for "completeness of filling, including weight and freedom from popholes and unsealed cells." The exhibits will be weighed, and each exhibit that turns the scale at 17 oz. will be entitled to full marks for weight (say 15), nor will any competent judge award extra marks for weight over 17 oz., no more than he would to 1¼ lbs. of butter exhibited as a 1 lb. roll; if the sections are free from popholes and unsealed cells they will be entitled to full marks (say 10), thus securing the maximum of 25 marks under the first point, and the marks

THE COMMITTEE AND GUESTS
8th National Honey Show. Crystal Palace, London, Sept. 10, 1930.

will be entered, under their proper heading, in the second column of the card. The exhibit will next be examined for the other points set forth in paragraph 326, the marks being extended in their proper columns accordingly. Any sections that come short of the requirements will lose marks proportionally. The judge will then proceed with the remaining exhibits, and mark them as they deserve. The points of excellence required in extracted honey, beeswax, mead, and vinegar have already been described (326), with the marks to be assigned. When judging extracted honey for density, or thickness, the jars should be inverted, and the rising of the air bubbles should be accurately timed, the highest marks being awarded to the exhibit in which the air bubbles rise slowest, having regard to the air space in each jar. Weight should be judged by the scales; 1 lb. bottles should contain 16 oz. of honey, short weights being penalised and extra weights deriving no advantage. " Granulated honey " should be granulated, and not merely thickened. For the judging of wax the magnifying glass will be useful. Supers of frames and crates of sections should be carefully scrutinized for signs of cleaning and of substitution of frames from other supers or of sections from other crates, and, assuming that the conditions laid down (326) apply, any exhibit which shows signs of having been improperly manipulated for the show bench, should be disqualified. Mead should be well flavoured and clear, and should be securely corked in glass bottles, bearing suitable labels. Vinegar should show similar qualities, and should be put up in clear glass bottles, well corked and labelled. When all the exhibits in any class shall have been marked for their various points, the judge should tot the marks for each exhibitor in that class, and enter the totals in the column provided for that purpose; above these will appear the total maximum marks obtainable, and the last column will announce

Photo by   *W. H. Coldwells*

A CORNER OF THE NATIONAL HONEY SHOW AT THE CRYSTAL PALACE
IN 1935.

the awards—1st, 2nd, 3rd, V.H.C., H.C., C.,* according to the rules of the particular show. Thus the exhibitor will receive an award according to the total of his marks, and the judge himself will not know the results until he has made his tots; in the margin he will enter any special remarks upon any exhibit, as he may think desirable. When such cards have been completed, signed by the judge, and placed in position on, or over, the exhibits, the competitors and the general public can see in what respects the several exhibits have been successful, or the reverse, and the show becomes not only a means of awarding or gaining prizes, but also an object lesson in the science and practice of Beekeeping, with educational advantages of great use and importance.

*V.H.C—Very highly commended.   H.C.—Highly commended.
C.—Commended.

CHAPTER XXVIII.

ROBBING AND FIGHTING.

341. Robbing.—It must be admitted that bees, notwithstanding their many excellent qualities, sometimes become very capable and persistent robbers, and that, when once this sordid vice has taken hold of them, it is exceedingly difficult to induce them to shake it off. In spring and autumn, when nectar is scarce out of doors, a careless bee-man may turn all his virtuous pets into thieving rascals, by dropping honey or syrup anywhere near the hives, or by unduly exposing it during manipulations. Then, the strong stocks destroy the weak stocks, carry off their stores, and leave them to perish of hunger. Sometimes the robbed colony, when further resistance becomes hopeless, join the robbers and, having helped to empty their own combs, sally forth to do unto others as they, themselves, have been done by; and the owner, paying a belated visit to his colonies, is surprised to find one or more hives empty of bees and honey (225), and, upon the ground, in front, the carcasses of the slain. Even when no sweets have been carelessly exposed about the apiary, weak stocks, acting as a temptation to the strong, encourage robbing and often fall victims to it. They will, indeed, maintain a strenuous resistance against the aggressors for a time (12); but this is a case in which there is safety only in numbers, and a weak colony, in such circumstances, if left without assistance, must eventually submit to defeat.

342. Precautions against Robbing.—Obviously the precautions necessary to prevent robbing are: To avoid exposing sweets when nectar is scarce in the fields: to do all feeding in the evenings, when bees have ceased flying: and to keep all stocks strong, by uniting the weak, and by helping the well-to-do.

343. Signs of Robbing.—The signs which denote that robbing is in progress are unmistakable. Wild excitement manifests itself about the entrance of the hive attacked: robbers hunt about the hive corners, and at all openings, seeking an entrance where there are no guards: returning bees hurry indoors, as if in haste to escape the turmoil without; a loud buzzing is kept up without intermission: and, on the

alighting board, an angry fight is carried on between the
robbers and the defenders of the hive; bees will be seen
struggling together and rolling in couples to the ground, where
one or both of them will show signs of having been injured,
and where, if the fight has been fast and furious, many dead
will have already fallen.

344. Treatment.—When robbing has commenced, it must be
dealt with at once, or the whole apiary may be thrown into
confusion. The first thing to do is to close, to one bee-space,
the entrance of the hive that is being attacked; thus giving
the defenders an advantage by making the enemy advance in
single file. If the attack continue, one or more of the following remedies should be applied : Dredge with flour the bees
as they leave the attacked hive and watch floured robbers
entering their own hive, or hives; then place a handful of wet
grass, or hay, at the entrance of each hive from which the
robbers come, to baffle them there. Place a handful of wet
grass, or hay, at the entrance of the robbed hive, so that
while the bees of the hive will force their way through, the
process may be too slow for robbers. Arrange on the alighting
board two pieces of 1″ wood, half an inch apart, and with a
lath, or slate on top; so that, to come and go, bees must pass
through a dark passage, which is very discouraging to robbers.
Saturate a cloth with carbolic solution (Recipe 147), and spread
it on the alighting board right up to the entrance, sprinkling
it afresh as required. Add a little carbolic to a large pail of
water, and with a syringe or a watering pot, drench the robbers
as they fly in front of the hive. Set up a piece of glass an inch
from the entrance, and sloping from the alighting board to the
hive front, so that, to stranger bees, the difficulty of finding
an entrance may be increased. If none of the remedies
described prove effectual, close the hive entirely until the evening, opening the doors to full width, covering the entrance
with perforated zinc, and taking care to give all the ventilation
required (228). It may even become necessary to remove the
molested hive from the apiary altogether until the danger is
over. If the robbing be carried on by the bees of only one
hive persistently in spite of preventive measures, some apiarists
deal with it by transferring the hive of the robbers to the
stand of the robbed, and *vice versa*, until the mischief ceases.

" In Germany, when colonies in common hives are being robbed,
they are often removed to a distant location, or put in a dark cellar.
A hive, similar in appearance, is placed on their stand, and leaves
of wormwood and the expressed juice of the plant are put on the
bottom board. Bees have such an antipathy to the odour of this plant,

that the robbers speedily forsake the place, and the assailed colony may then be brought back. The Rev. Mr. Klein says, that robbers may be repelled by imparting to the hive some intensely powerful and unaccustomed odour. He effects this the most readily by placing in it, in the evening, a small portion of musk, and on the following morning the bees, if they have a healthy queen, will boldly meet their assailants. These are nonplussed by the unwonted odour, and, if any of them enter the hive and carry off some of the coveted booty, on their return home, having a strange smell, they will be killed by their own household. The robbing is thus soon brought to a close."
—S. WAGNER.

If it should become necessary to remove the molested hive, it will be well to place an empty hive, of similar appearance, in its place, as otherwise the robbers may attack the neighbouring stocks. Sometimes a useful remedy consists in inserting a " Porter " escape (287), or a double cone (286) in the entrance of the hive that is being attacked—any other inlet being closed—and to leave it so for forty-eight hours, thus confining the bees to the hive, but giving sufficient ventilation over the frames by placing on them a sheet of wire cloth and removing the other coverings. After forty-eight hours, the entrance being opened, robbers and robbed are frequently good friends and work together in harmony; and the stock, weak before, but now reinforced by the robbers, may be strong enough to defend itself. It will often be found that a colony which offers little resistance to robbers, and is overpowered, is either queenless or diseased; and that bees that are being robbed are more than usually difficult to handle (188).

CHAPTER XXIX.

FEEDING BEES: RECIPES.

345. Objects of Feeding Bees.—It is a common notion, and a very mistaken one, that bees, being so well able to forage for themselves, require no artificial feeding. During several months of the year there is little or no nectar to be gathered in the fields: sometimes when natural food might be had in abundance, stress of weather confines the bees to their hives so that they cannot visit the flowers: in winter and early spring, foraging is impossible: and frequently when the bee-keeper has taken his harvest from the hives, the bees are left without sufficient food to carry them through the cold months. In such circumstances, neglect to supply food artificially is often accountable for the death of many stocks. And, by feeding bees, there are other objects to be gained beyond that of staving off starvation. The general desire to obtain a large harvest of honey can be satisfied only by having the stocks as strong as possible before the honey flow opens (268); for, only the bees that have been born at least fourteen days, from eggs laid at least thirty-six days before the honey flow opens, can take full advantage of it. (200). But, it is found that neither will the queen put forth her best laying powers, nor the bees consent to rear brood in quantities, until food begins to come in abundantly (202). Similarly, towards the close of autumn, it is necessary to have a large quantity of bees reared to survive the winter and to carry on the work of the colony in the spring. But, with the cessation of the honey flow, breeding will naturally decrease unless food be supplied; and, even the eggs and larvæ will be destroyed when food becomes scarce, with the result that the stock may come out in the spring too weak to be of any practical use in the season following. Therefore, if good results are to be secured, Nature's supply must be anticipated, and supplemented, by artificial feeding: wise and timely attention to this detail may make all the difference between a good, a bad, or an indifferent honey harvest (212). It goes without saying that sugar is not as good a food for bees as is honey; but feeding with honey except by giving naturally stored combs, is not advisable. It may contain the germs of disease (Chap. XXX.) and it is rather liable to induce robbing (Chap. XXVIII.). Experienced beekeepers are careful not to deprive their stocks of more honey than the bees can afford to give, or, if there is not sufficient stored in the brood combs, they supply the deficiency with syrup made of pure white sugar.

346. Precautions.—The following precautions, as applicable to the feeding of bees, should be adopted as rules for invariable observance : —(1) Use only pure, refined, white sugar. It is quite immaterial whether the sugar be derived from the sugar cane or from the beet, for in either case it is " cane sugar." Mr. D. M. T. Morland, of the Bee Research Institute, Rothamsted, says : " ' Cane sugar,' ' sucrose ' or ' saccharose,' is the name of a definite commercial compound. It is obtained commercially from both the sugar cane and the beet, besides being present in numerous other plants."—(*The Feeding of Bees*, 1929). (2) Never permit the sugar to become burned during cooking : even pure, refined, cane sugar if burned, will do much harm, especially in cold weather when bees are confined to their hives. (3) Contract the entrances of all hives in which feeders are being used, and do not allow robber bees access to the food : robbing is often set up through neglect of this precaution (341). (4) Give the food warm, in the evenings, when the bees have ceased flying : bees will frequently refuse cold syrup in spring and autumn. (5) Keep all feeders warmly covered. (6) Never leave supers on a hive when sugar-feeding is in progress in that hive : syrup stored in sections or extracting supers, will render the honey therein unfit for sale. (7) Do not hesitate to spend money on sugar : it is only quarter the price of the honey you get instead.

347. Spring Feeding.—Bees are fed in spring, and at other seasons, to " stimulate " them (202, 212), and at all times when it is found that their stores are insufficient. Except in winter and early spring, when candy is the food employed, syrup is given. Spring feeding begins when the bees begin to fly freely—in March or April, according to the season and locality. Honey in the combs may have a couple of inches of cappings bruised once a week, exposing the food for use (202). In early spring, when the nights are cold, bees will often refuse to take down syrup. In such a case if there be any liquid honey at hand, a good cake of candy may be made by mixing honey with loaf sugar pounded fine, and the cake may be put on the frames, under the sheet, so that the bees may easily reach it. Liquid food may be prepared according to the directions given at the close of this chapter (Recipe 355). The supply should be regulated according to the season, the needs of the colony, and the objects in view. In spring, for stimulative

purposes, *i.e.*, to induce more rapid brood rearing, the supply
should be very gradual—say a wineglassful given through two
or three holes only (130), and that, during the night, the supply
being cut off in the morning; for, a supply too rapid will lead
to the storing of syrup in the combs required for brood, and
this is to be carefully avoided in the spring. With this object,
feeders are employed which introduce the syrup immediately
over the cluster, and permit the supply to be regulated accord
ing to the requirements (128-133).

348. Summer Feeding.—Feeding in summer becomes
necessary during a spell of bad weather, and is often desirable
between the early honey flow from fruit trees and the main
flow from clover, and also between the latter and the heather
flow. Swarms should be fed for a few nights to the extent
of half a pint of honey or syrup per night, to assist them in
drawing out foundation into comb, and to prevent the danger
of hunger, resulting in the cessation of breeding, the throwing
out of immature brood, and the dwindling of the swarm. But,
swarms to which have been transferred the supers from the
parent stocks (251) do not generally require feeding, and should
not be fed, while the supers are on, except with honey (346).
When the honey flow ceases and supers have been removed
(285), liquid food may be given again, and this may be continued, to the extent of about half a tumblerful per night,
until the middle of September. As a result, breeding will be
continued uninterruptedly, and a large supply of young bees
will be reared to maintain the colony in the winter, and to
begin work in the spring (212). Syrup for summer feeding is
made similar to that used in spring (Recipe 355).

349. Autumn Feeding.—Autumn feeding should be commenced, as a rule, early in September and should be completed
by the end of that month. It is intended to supply sufficient
food to carry the bees through the winter and early spring, if
there be not an adequate quantity in their combs. The syrup
should be given in the evenings, preferably warm, and at a
fairly rapid rate, so that it may be stored and sealed in the
combs before the arrival of cold weather renders the capping
of the cells impossible. (433). Unsealed stores are liable to
absorb moisture and ferment, and such food is highly injurious
to bees (414). The syrup should be thicker than that used
earlier in the year, and may be made according to the directions given later on (Recipe 356). A colony, to winter safely,
should have, at least, 30 lbs. of sealed stores. Six or seven
standard frames (104), well filled, will suffice, and no strong

colony should be considered safe with less. A Duchman, when asked : " How much beer is enough for a man ? " is said to have replied : " Too mush peer is shust enough." More accurately it may be said that too much food is just enough for bees in winter. One should use 1 lb. of sugar for every 1 lb. shortage of honey below 30 lbs. ; *i.e.*, if the stores be estimated as 20 lbs., 10 lbs. of sugar to 2 quarts of water (Recipe 356) should be supplied. As the object of autumn feeding is, not to encourage breeding, but to rapidly supply stores for winter, the feeders used in spring and summer are not invariably suitable in autumn. (131-134). In an emergency, when there is not time for supplying autumn syrup through a feeder, empty combs may be carried into the house, and the warm syrup may be poured direct into the cells, until both sides of the combs are filled. The combs may then be carried out in a comb box (182) and inserted in the hives requiring them. But this method, also, must be adopted, if at all, sufficiently early to admit of the capping of the cells before the arrival of cold weather. It is an excellent plan to use one or more stocks to store and seal the syrup for all the other stocks, as previously advised. (132). It has been found, during the last year or two, that by the addition of a small quantity of Thymol, or Oil of Thyme, and by feeding rather slowly and with somewhat thinner syrup, we enable the bees to make a much better job of the storage and inversion of the sugar syrup, and that, also, fermentation is prevented. Syrup so treated may be fed at any time without danger. Thymol is sold in the form of crystals and is used at the rate of about three grains to 10-lbs. of syrup. Solutions ready for use may be purchased. This treatment prevents crystallization and fermentation and is a valuable discovery put forward by Dr. C. R. Killick, of Somerset.

350. Winter Feeding.—When stocks are short of food in the winter, only sealed honey, or candy, can be given with safety.

" Experience shows that stocks, no matter how well supplied with food below, winter better when they have a cake of candy on top of the frames. The bees use the candy first ; and, when they have consumed a little of it, they have a safe winter passage (433) across the frames. Every beekeeper who is not quite certain that his stocks are sufficiently supplied, should give them ' the benefit of the doubt,' in the shape of a cake of candy—candy not hard enough to require a pickaxe to break it, but candy that is properly made, soft, and palatable, and good. (It may be made according to Recipe 357). Let it cool for half-an-hour. Then, gently slip a cake under the sheet of each hive, so that the candy shall be directly over the clustering bees.

Renew the supply of candy as required. Pressure of the fingers on the sheet will show when the candy has been used. A neater plan for supplying the candy, and one that will repay the little extra trouble, where only a few hives have to be dealt with, may be adopted as follows : Procure for each hive a small, shallow box of wood, or cardboard; remove the lid and cut, in the bottom, a hole to correspond with the hole in the sheet that is on the frames. Put a piece of newspaper over the hole in the bottom of the box, and fill up with candy. Now, set an empty section crate on the sheet that covers the frames; pull the paper off the candy : and set the box on the sheet, so that the bees shall have access to the candy right over the cluster. Place a piece of glass on the box. Fill up the crate with warm stuff, such as tailors' cuttings, cork dust, or chaff; pack all round it with cloth or newspaper; and set the usual quilts on top. Thus, there will be no escape of heat; the candy will be in the warmest part of the hive; and the glass will enable you to see when a further supply of food becomes necessary."—J. G. D. in the *Irish Bee Journal*.

A glass pot, or dish, such as tongue is sold in by grocers, being transparent, is excellent as a receptacle for candy. The discovery of the properties of Thymol (349) has now made winter feeding with liquid food possible without risk of promoting dysentery through the fermentation of the stores which remain unsealed at this season, and candy is no longer the only possible safe winter feed.

351. Feeding for Comb Building.—It has already been pointed out that careful beekeepers make it a rule to have empty combs always at hand when required (203). There are certain weeks in every year when bees are comparatively idle, during a cessation of nectar-secretion in the flowers : the opportunity may then be taken advantage of to procure new combs for future use. If frames of foundation be inserted alternately with the brood combs, and if thin syrup (Recipe 355) be given, the bees will fill the frames with comb in an incredibly short time. Care must be taken to withdraw the new combs before the queen shall have begun to oviposit in them : or, failing this, they must be left in their position for brood rearing, and a corresponding number of broodless combs, if any be there, may be withdrawn and packed up in a dry place until required. Such combs will be of immense service if given to swarms, and will, in other cases also, effect a saving of valuable time in the height of the season.

352. Feeding Bees in Skeps.—Stocks in skeps may be considered safe for winter if the skep, on being weighed, is found to exceed 25 lbs. When syrup feeding in skeps is necessary,

It should be given overhead. An ordinary skep may have a hole cut in the top sufficiently large to admit the mouth of an Economic, or a Bottle Feeder (128-129). When the feeder is placed in position, it should be wrapped round with warm material to prevent the escape of heat, and a cover, such as an empty skep, or a large flower pot with the hole stopped, should be put on to shut out prowling stranger bees. In autumn or winter, a bar of candy may be pushed into the hole and covered up. A better plan is to cut two or three inches off the top of the skep, and to put on, instead, a piece of board with a hole in the centre, over which a bottle and stage feeder (129-130), or a cake of candy, may be placed. The board should be fastened securely by nails passing through it into the skep, and a safe cover should be put on over the feeder. Flat-topped skeps (284), made to take supers, can have feeders placed on them in the same manner as described above for modern hives.

353. **Water.**—Bees cannot carry on their wonderful work without water (9). If they have not access to natural sources

Fig. 150. WATER FOUNTAIN.

close enough to their hives, water should be supplied to them. It is neither necessary nor desirable to add salt. A vessel of water, with corks floating in it on which the bees may alight : a tumbler of water inverted on a plate : or, a bowl of water with a sponge, or a piece of cotton wool in it, through which the bees may suck up what they require, will serve the purpose. Water fountains (Fig. 150) have circular and diagonal grooves in the stand; the grooves hold the water and provide drinking places for the bees. The vessel should be placed in a sheltered, sunny spot. Bees will often resort to dirty pools of stagnant water, rather than take clean but colder water from an artificial source.

354. **Pollen.**—The use of artificial pollen in the form of flour has been referred to elsewhere (202). The practice was formerly thought desirable, but modern research has shown it to be valueless since bees cannot utilise flour, though they will readily carry it to their hives when pollen is not available.

As we have shown (202), the correct management in autumn can alone assure the presence of pollen in the combs in good condition for brood rearing in the spring.

RECIPES FOR FEEDING.

Pure, refined, white sugar only, to be used as follows:—

355. Spring and Summer Syrup (169, 347, 348, 351).—

1 part hot water, by weight, to 1 part sugar, by weight, thus:—

Water	1 pint	1 quart	2 quarts	4 quarts	12 quarts
Sugar	1¼ lbs.	2½ lbs.	5 lbs.	10 lbs.	30 lbs.

Stir incessantly over a slow fire until the sugar is dissolved.

356. Autumn Syrup (349).—

1 part hot water to 2 parts sugar, either by weight or by measure, thus:—

Water	1 pint	1 quart	2 quarts	4 quarts	12 quarts
Sugar	2½ lbs.	5 lbs.	10 lbs.	20 lbs.	60 lbs.

Stir incessantly over a slow fire until the sugar is dissolved, and allow the syrup to boil.

357. Candy for Winter Food (350).—

1 part hot water, by weight, to 5 parts sugar, by weight, thus:—

Water	½ pint	1 pint	1 quart	2 quarts	5 quarts
Sugar	3 lbs.	6 lbs.	12 lbs.	24 lbs.	60 lbs.
Cream	½ Tea-	1 Tea-	2 Tea-	1 Table-	2½ Table-
of	spoonful	spoonful	spoonfuls	spoonful	spoonfuls
Tartar			or ⅓ oz.	or ⅔ oz.	or 1⅔ oz.

Boil the water, withdraw it from the fire, add the requisite quantities of sugar and acid, as above, stirring until dissolved. Return it to the fire and *stir it unceasingly* until it boils; for, if you allow the sugar to burn, through lack of stirring, it will be as poison to the bees (346), and your ingredients, time, and perhaps patience, will be lost. Continue boiling and stirring until the mixture begins to thicken; then test it by dropping a little on a cold plate. It must set soft, but not sticky; if it stick to your fingers, boil it a little longer. When it proves right to the touch, cease boiling it, and without delay stand the vessel in another containing cold water, and stir vigorously until the mixture begins to set, when you must *immediately* pour it into receptacles previously prepared for the purpose; for, the mixture will set quickly, and must be dealt with promptly. The receptacles may be saucers, or soup plates, on each of which a sheet of strong paper must be laid to receive the candy; or shallow boxes may be used (350). If paper be adopted, it will be well to lay upon each cake two pieces of $\frac{3}{4}''$ stick, $1''$ apart, and parallel, pressing them into the candy before it cools, and flush with its upper surface, so that when the candy shall have been consumed, the "winter passage" (433) may be maintained by the sticks *lying across the frames.* If preferred, frames may be prepared with four or five lengths of stout string, after the manner of wires in frames (275), but running vertically, and into these frames, lying on waxed or slightly greased paper, the mixture may be poured. When the candy is cool, a cake may be given under the sheet and quilts, or a frame of candy—the paper having been removed—may be inserted next the brood nest, in any hive requiring it. An alternative method is to use only 5 lbs. of sugar to 1 pint of water boiling *slowly* until the sugar shall have been completely dissolved and until a thermometer, immersed in the mixture, shall show a temperature of 235° Fahr. At that point the vessel is removed from the fire and the contents are cooled to 120° Fahr. and are then stirred briskly until they begin to stiffen and are poured into the receptacles.

358. "Columban" Candy (350).—Brother Columban's recipe, when carefully followed, gives excellent results, thus: 15 lbs. cane sugar (white crystals) and 3 quarts hot water, in an enamelled saucepan or preserving pan—capable of holding twice the quantity—stirred over a *strong* fire until dissolved. When it begins to boil, draw the vessel to one side, and *during slow boiling*, skim off all impurities, after which let it boil as fast as possible, without stirring, for about 20 minutes. Test it as directed above; if it breaks when tested, instead of rolling into a soft ball, it has been overboiled, in which case a little water must be added and boiling must continue up to the right point. When sufficiently boiled, add 5 lbs. of honey, and boil again for one or two minutes, after which remove the vessel from the fire and add 2 tablespoonfuls of Naphthol Beta Solution, or 1 dessert spoonful Izal, if required, then pour the mixture into a large tin, which may be placed in a larger vessel of cold water. *Stirring must not begin until the mixture has cooled so as to admit of the insertion of one's finger for half a minute without scalding,* then stirring must continue until the candy becomes white and hard. Now put it into a vessel standing over another vessel of hot water, and when the candy melts to the consistency of cream, pour it into suitable moulds.

359. **Soft Candy.**—A candy having a higher water content is preferred by the majority of beekeepers. To make it, proceed as follows: Bring 5 pints of water to a boil in a preserving pan. Withdraw it from over the fire and stir into it 12 lbs. of white granulated sugar and ¼ oz. cream of tartar. Stir the mixture until the sugar has entirely dissolved and the mixture has become quite clear. Then replace the pan over the fire and boil until the temperature reaches 235° Fahr. The mixture should not be stirred any more after it begins to boil. It will not burn. When the requisite temperature is reached, remove from the fire and leave it to cool. When the temperature is reduced to about 120° Fahr., begin to stir and the solution will soon begin to thicken and become candy. When almost too thick to stir, pour into suitable moulds. A special thermometer is procurable for the purpose of making candy, and those who are intending to make their own should acquire one as it will save a great deal of trouble. These thermometers are obtainable from the *British Bee Journal* Office, London.

360. **Syrup from Candy.**—To reduce candy (357, 358, 359) to syrup for spring, or summer, feeding (355) add 16 oz. of water, by measure, to each 1 lb. of candy, and stir the mixture over a fire until it boils. For autumn feeding (356) add 10 oz. of water, by measure, to each 1 lb. of candy, and proceed as above.

361. **The Use of Drugs.**—The medication of bees' food with drugs of various kinds, which was practised very generally for many years in the hope of preventing and curing the brood diseases, is no longer recommended by the best authorities, and beekeepers are advised to abandon the use of all medication for those purposes. It may be that some medicament will be made available for the cure of some of the adult diseases, such as *Nosema apis*, but none is certainly known at the present time. It is thought by some persons that Thymol in autumn-fed syrup may have an inhibitory affect upon Nosema apis and other troubles, but nothing is definitely known at present, and the only drugs that are quite surely effective are those used to combat Acarine disease.

362. **Measures.**—

½ Teaspoonful	=	½	Drachm, or 30 Drops.	
1 Teaspoonful	=	1	,, ,,	⅛th Fluid oz.
1 Dessertspoonful	=	2	,, ,,	¼ ,,
1 Tablespoonful	=	4	,, ,,	½ ,,
2 Tablespoonfuls	=	8	,, ,,	1 ,,

1 Wineglass   = 16 Drachms, or   2 Fluid ozs.
1 Tumbler   = ½ Pint,   ,,   10   ,,
2 Tumblers   = 1   ,,   ,,   20   ,,

[NOTE.—The above figures are approximate only, the vessels named varying in size. A graduated glass measure (Fig. 167, p. 277) may be purchased for a few pence.]

APOTHECARIES' WEIGHT.

20 Grains   = 1 Scruple.
3 Scruples   = 1 Drachm.
8 Drachms   = 1 Ounce.

MEASURES OF CAPACITY.

60 Minims (min.)   = 1 fluid drachm.
8 Fluid drachms   = 1 fluid ounce.
20 Fluid ounces   = 1 pint (0.568 *litre*).
8 Pints   = 1 gallon (4.54 *litres*).

CHAPTER XXX.

DISEASES.

363. Diseases.—Bees are subject to various diseases and ailments, among which may be included: Of brood—Addled Brood (364), Chilled Brood (368), Chalk Brood (397), Foul Brood (373), Sacbrood (393), and, Of adult bees—Acarine Disease (399), Nosema Disease (404), Paralysis (409) and Dysentery (412). In the diagnosis and treatment of diseases of the hive bee, modern beekeepers enjoy a distinct advantage as against their predecessors to whom the movable comb was unknown, and to-day it is possible to discern the onset of brood diseases and to deal with them in a manner quite beyond the range of the skeppist. With this object in view, it is important that, when stocks are being manipulated, a sharp look-out be kept for any signs of disease so that when sickness of any kind shows itself, immediate steps may be taken to deal with it.

364. Addled Brood.—This trouble was first described in 1925, by Dr. John Anderson, M.A., B.Sc., and Mr. William Keith. Mr. R. W. Frow has since reported that a case occurred in his apiary in 1924.

365. SYMPTOMS.—An examination of the combs shows quantities of sealed brood which fails to emerge. Upon opening one of the cells, the dead larva or nymph is seen to be lying on its back. The cappings sink. The bees subsequently open some of the cells and endeavour to remove the contents. The colony often dwindles rapidly.

366. CAUSE.—The cause is certainly in the queen; for, upon removing and introducing her to a healthy colony she will continue to produce addled brood there.

367. TREATMENT.—Is to kill the queen and introduce another, when the new queen will produce normal brood. The bees will then remove all dead brood from the cells and the colony will, unless it has become seriously weakened, soon build up to full strength. If a comb or two of healthy brood can be given to it, it will be greatly assisted.

368. Chilled Brood.—This is the name given to the condition of larvæ which have died through lack of the heat necessary for their life and development. It is frequently found after a sudden decrease in temperature out of doors when the bees, under the influence of an early warm spell with a flow of honey, have unduly expanded their brood nest. But chilling is more often than not due to the direct act of the beekeeper.

369. SYMPTOMS.—Chilled brood is sometimes mistaken for brood dead of disease, but, examination of the contents of affected cells will show the dead in all stages of growth, from the newly-hatched larva to the fully-developed bee, and, in the case of chilled larvæ, though not wholly unlike the dead of some of the minor brood diseases, it is very distinct from those which have perished from American Foul Brood (378). Chilled brood is always found at the outer parts of the brood nest and in patches, whereas brood dead of disease is scattered over the brood nest evenly.

370. CAUSE.—Chilling of brood is nearly always caused by one or other of two things:—The act of the beekeeper in "spreading the brood" (203) when, as is generally the case, it would be far better let alone; or by semi-starvation of the stock. A starving colony first loses its heat and contracts its cluster, and the brood is the first to suffer. More rarely, as has been told, a sudden chilling of the weather may cause a contraction of the cluster and consequent exposure and chilling of the outlying brood.

371. PREVENTION.—To avoid the danger of chilled brood, hives should be kept warm during spring and late autumn breeding: spreading the brood should be practised with much discretion, full account being taken of the prevailing weather and of the risk of a sudden drop in the temperature at night (203): manipulations of the brood nest on cold days should be avoided as much as possible, and at no time should combs containing brood be exposed to chill winds.

372. TREATMENT.—If the cause be starvation—feed; if it be brood-spreading or chilling from outside causes—there is little to be done but leave the stock alone until it recovers. As soon as the bees become strong enough, or have food supplied to them, if starving, they will quickly clear the dead brood from their combs, which will be occupied again by new brood.

373. **Foul Brood.**—Under this general title are known at least two distinct diseases. They are called respectively " European Foul Brood " (374) and " American Foul Brood " (378).

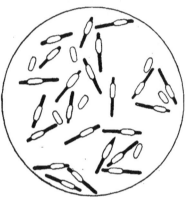

Fig. 151. BACILLUS ALVEI.

The foul brood diseases, as their name implies, have the general symptoms of the death of the brood in the cells and the decomposition of the dead bodies which is accompanied by a more or less offensive odour. These diseases are brought about by the action of specific pathogenic germs, but the causal agents are different in each disease as are the symptoms, except in so far as above described. When Cheshire and Cheyne were investigating the brood diseases of the hive-bee, it was not realised that what was under examination was other than a single ailment which varied in form and virulence in different cases, and these

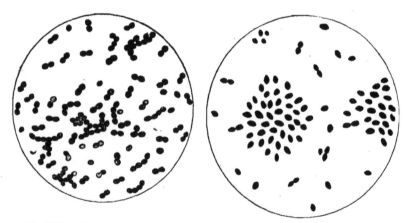

Fig. 152. STREPTOCOCCUS APIS. [Fig. 153. BACILLUS PLUTON.

gentlemen having described *Bacillus alvei*, which they found in larvae dead of the disease, believed it to be the cause of " foul brood." Subsequently, other investigators, notably White and Phillips in America, confirmed the already suspected fact that foul brood in its different varieties is not one disease

Fig. 154.

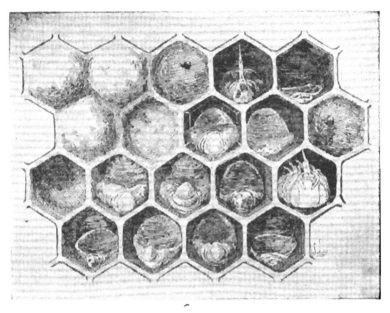

AMERICAN FOUL BROOD.

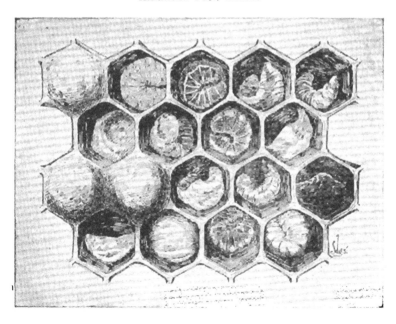

EUROPEAN FOUL BROOD.
Photographs of drawings by R. E. Snodgrass.
By the courtesy of Mr. J. S. Hambleton.

in two forms, but two, or possibly more, distinct ones. Since 1934 systematic research at Rothamsted Experimental Station in England has been carried on, in the course of which a good deal of valuable information concerning European Foul Brood has been obtained, together with full confirmation of the conclusions long since reached in America in respect to American Foul Brood.

374. European Foul Brood (*Strepto-coccus pluton*).—The result of the latest research has shown that true European Foul Brood is caused by an organism named as above which has so far proved uncultivable in the laboratory. *Strepto-coccus pluton* has, however, another form hitherto known as *Bacterium eurydice* which is readily grown in ordinary media, forming very small colonies, in which *S. pluton* subsequently develops. Experiments are being carried on in Switzerland; but results are not yet available. It is, however, now considered certain that *S. pluton* is the actual cause of the rather obscure disease of bee larvæ known as European Foul Brood. The theory of the spread of this trouble, within the hive and from colony to colony, is now believed to be as follows. A proportion of

Fig. 155. STOMACH CONTENTS REMOVED FROM LARVA SICK OF EUROPEAN FOUL BROOD.

Fig. 156. EUROPEAN FOUL BROOD. A to M uncapped, and N to T capped brood ; D, healthy larva at the earliest age at which symptoms of the disease appears ; A E, young larvae showing symptoms of European foulbrood ; B O, larvae partially removed by the adult bees ; C, scales from young larva ; F I, healthy larvae somewhat older than D. G H J, dead larvae of the same age as F and I ; K, healthy larvae slightly older than F, with dorsal side turned toward the observer ; L M, dead larvae about the same age as K ; N, larva dead at the time of spinning ; O, scale of a larva similar to N; P, a punctured cap ; Q R S T, larvae which had assumed the endwise position in the cell before death ; Q, larva partially removed ; S, larva dead of the disease ; R T, end and ventral view, respectively, of European foulbrood scales of larvae of the age shown in S. These scales and those of American foulbrood are quite alike. The caps from N O Q R S and T were removed by the adult bees.

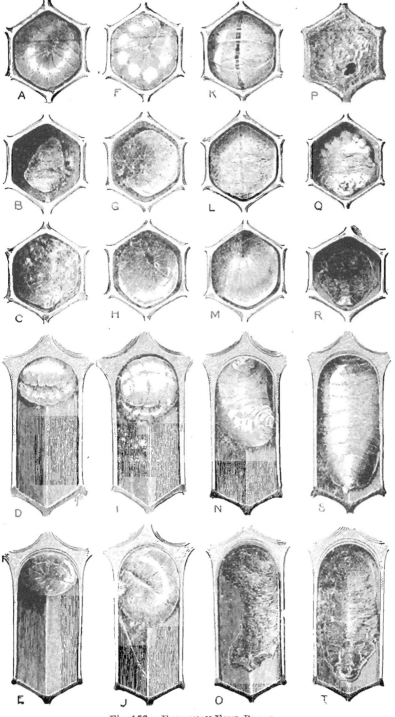

Fig. 156. EUROPEAN FOUL BROOD.

diseased grubs recover, and in the course of gnawing their way out of their cells their mouth parts become contaminated with the germs which lie in the material of the cell walls. When, later on, these young bees, which have become what are known as "carriers," proceed to do the general work of the hive, feeding the young brood, cleaning out the cells, and capping the brood, they in this manner spread the infection rapidly within their own colony, and when they drift into the hives of other colonies they quickly spread the trouble to those also. The disease has not been reported in the British Isles in such a very virulent form as in America, though where it has once obtained a hold it is impossible to get rid of it without resorting to very drastic treatment.

375. SYMPTOMS.—The larvæ are attacked at an early stage; usually while still coiled up in the cells. They may, however, in advanced cases occasionally die just after the cell has been sealed, but death usually occurs before pupation. Irregularity in the brood areas, caused by the removal after death of diseased grubs, is frequently the first sign of trouble. This will be followed by the appearance of dead or dying larvæ, which have become yellow or brown, and finally very dark in colour as they dry into scales. These scales do not adhere to the cell walls, but are readily removed. Larvæ that die after sealing soon become a shapeless brown mass of creamy consistency which gradually dries into an irregularly shaped scale. At a stage of drying this mass of putrid matter may rope slightly, but it will not draw out into a fine elastic thread. Sometimes there is no objectionable smell, but there may be a disagreeable sour smell. In some cases, however, probably through the presence of putrifactive organisms, a most abominable stench may be emitted. It is to this fact that the name "Stinking Foul Brood," which has been applied to this trouble, is due. The disease is not very prevalent in the British Isles at the present time, but its appearance in an apiary should on no account be lightly treated, for there can now be no question that genuine European Foul Brood (S. pluton) is one of the most serious of the brood diseases and should be treated as such.

376. TREATMENT.—When this disease is suspected to be present in an apiary, the owner should *at once* forward a sample of the comb containing the suspected larvæ to a competent authority for diagnosis which can only be carried out by qualified persons. The bee disease research department of the Rothamsted Experimental Station, Harpenden, Herts, will make examination and give a reliable verdict.

Sample comb should never be sent except well packed to avoid
any chance of premature exposure of the contents. Do nothing
about the disease until a reply has been received as there are
other diseases of the brood which may easily be confused
with *S. pluton* by any but those who are in a position to make
proper microscopical examinations. Should it be confirmed
that the disease is in fact *S. pluton*, there is only **one** real
remedy which is to kill the bees and burn bees, combs, quilts
and frames and disinfect the hive as in American Foul
Brood (384).

377. **Unspecified Brood Diseases.**—It seems probable that
a disease or possibly diseases of brood exist which have not
yet been subject to successful research. Brood disease has
for many years been experienced in both this country and in
the United States which in appearance is identical with the
European Foul Brood described above, but which frequently
passes away if the stock be de-queened for three weeks or so,
which would seem unlikely if the cause and method of spread
were that described at attributable to *S. pluton*. In carrying
out this revision it has been thought that the latest research
conclusions should be put before readers, and they are advised,
on confirmation of the presence of *S. pluton*, to destroy the
infected material; but where the symptoms are observed which
coincide with those described for *S. pluton*, but where that
organism is not found to be present in the diseased matter,
it may be wise to attempt its cure by the methods formerly
advised, as follows. In this case, strong vigorous colonies,
headed by good queens, will frequently rid themselves of the
disease which will gradually disappear as the season advances,
the tendency of this disease is, in any case, to be most virulent
in spring and to become less severe later, disappearing to a
great extent in early autumn. When colonies cannot rid themselves of the disease, it is frequently found that they may be
cured by the removal of the queen and the introduction of a
young one about twenty-one days later. In no case should this
disease be treated by shaking from the combs as in American
Foul Brood (382), as this would be both useless and dangerous
because it is the bees themselves that carry infection. In this,
as in all bee diseases, weak colonies should never be treated,
but should be destroyed and their hives sterilized by flaming.

378. **American Foul Brood.** (*Bacillus larvæ*). American
Foul Brood is a specific infectious disease caused by
a bacillus, and is by far the most destructive and dangerous of
all brood diseases. Though it is exceedingly virulent when
once it has gained a foothold in a colony, it is not a disease

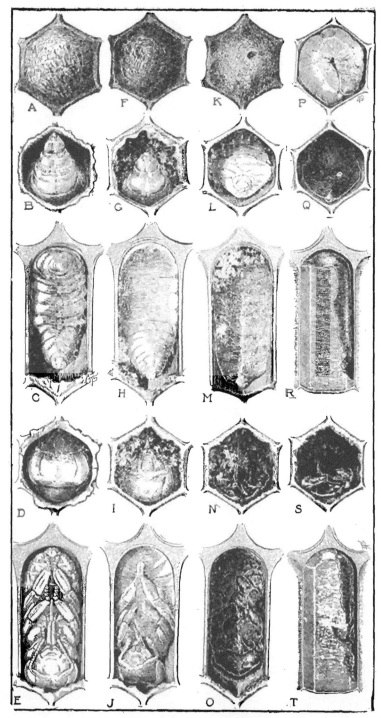

Fig. 157. AMERICAN FOUL BROOD.

that is very readily spread from one colony to another in natural and normal circumstances. The germs of the disease—the spores of *B. larvæ*—are conveyed almost, if not quite, exclusively in food that has been in contact with combs containing the remains of larvæ which have died of the disease. The causes of spread, therefore, from one stock to another in an apiary, are usually traceable to the acts of the beekeeper, such as the manipulation of diseased colonies during a dearth, and thus inducing robbing by other stocks; moving combs from colonies that harbour the disease to healthy ones, or exposing honey which contains the spores of the disease. When a diseased colony has become weak, or has died out from the effects of American foul brood, it will very likely be robbed out; but this will often occur at a time of year when bees are not very active and the robbing is frequently confined to one stock and the range of the disease is thus limited. The beekeeper should, therefore, endeavour to familiarise himself with the appearance of this ailment and thereafter always keep a sharp look-out for the earliest signs of its onset, whenever combs are under examination, so that steps may be taken to eliminate it before it has become widespread.

379. SYMPTOMS.—Except in very advanced cases, when a few deaths may sometimes occur earlier, probably through chilling or through not being properly fed, the brood in this disease always dies after the sealing of the cell; that is, after the grub has ceased to feed, has become fully grown and is stretched at full length on its back ready for pupation. In a proportion of cases death does not take place until after the pupa has formed, and this is one of the most certain signs that the disease under observation is American foul brood and no other. There is a definite physiological reason for this uniformity of late death: it is known that the organism cannot develop and multiply in a medium having a high sugar content; therefore the spores which have been taken into its system by the larvæ with its food are unable to begin the work of destruction until at the cessation of feeding, the sugar content becomes less as it is converted in the process of digestion. As soon as the right condition has been reached the spores become converted into active bacteria which grow rapidly and multiply

Fig. 157.—AMERICAN FOUL BROOD. A to E healthy, and F to T diseased brood A, cap over healthy, and F K over diseased brood. G H larvae and I J pupae dead of the disease. Q M R, scales of larvae, R being cut lengthwise and N O S T pupae dead of the disease, T being cut lengthwise ; K, a punctured cap. L, a partially removed larva which died of American foul brood before reaching the age at which brood is capped. This occurs only occasionally.

at an enormous rate by dividing into two parts. Each of the two divisions again divides into two and so on until, in a short time, the larva dies, overwhelmed by millions of minute organisms. The bi-partitions of *B. larvæ* are said to take place at intervals of about twenty minutes, and a simple calculation will show that a single germ may thus become thousands of millions in the course of twelve hours, and as the original infective dose may, and generally does, contain many germs, the rapid death of the grub attacked is not to be wondered at. Death, then, takes place after the larva has reached its full growth and is stretched along the bottom of the cell, and this gives a very remarkable uniformity to the remains of grubs dead of this disease. The bees of the hive always uncap a great many of the cells in which the dead lie, thus exposing them to the eye of the beekeeper and providing him with his earliest symptom. Later, as the disease advances, bees will neglect to remove the caps, and such cells will be seen with dark-coloured cappings which are sunken and often perforated.

The death of the larvæ is exceedingly rapid and putrefaction quickly sets in, the grub turning brownish first, and later to dark coffee colour. At first, soon after death, the remains are quite liquid, but they slowly dry up and, passing through all the stages from fluid to a hard, dry scale, finally adhere tightly to the lower cell-wall whence they cannot be moved without breaking the cell. *At a certain stage of this drying process* the remains become exceedingly viscous or ropy, and if a match-stick be inserted, this filth may be made to pull out into a fine thread which may stretch for a couple of inches or more. When it breaks the two ends will draw back like elastic. Another symptom is the peculiar smell which is associated with the disease. It is frequently described as like melting glue, bad glue, etc. It is a very characteristic smell, and, once experienced, is not easily forgotten; but it is by no means a powerful odour and never has any affinity to that of putrid flesh, nor is it known to give off the abominable stench that is occasionally found in cases of European Foul Brood. Fig. 157 illustrates this disease very effectively, the reader's attention is particularly called to L. Q. and N. as very typical and distinctive of American Foul Brood.

380. CAUSE.—*Bacillus larvæ* (Fig. 158), described by Dr. J. F. White (U.S.A.), in 1921, who wrote *:

" Scales containing the spores of American foul brood were collected in 1907 and kept in the laboratory until September, 1916. Each succeed-

---

* " Bee Publications," Nov., 1921, p. 106.

ing year, during this period of more than nine years, tests were made, using some of this scale material, and in every instance the spores were found to be alive. It was found also that they were as resistant to heat, and, by the inoculation of the colonies, they were found to be as virulent at the end of this period as at any previous time. It has not yet been determined how long the spores will remain alive in the dry scales, but it is quite probable that they will live much longer than nine years."

Spores, boiled in water (212° F.) remain alive for twelve minutes; boiled in honey, for half an hour or more; exposed in

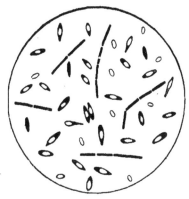

Fig. 158. BACILLUS LARVAE.
GROWING FORM.

Fig. 159.
BACILLUS LARVAE : SPORE FORMATION.

honey to direct sun rays, for six weeks; not so exposed, for more than a year. In a 5 *per cent.* solution of carbolic acid the spores can survive for months; in a 10 *per cent.* solution of formalin, for several hours. Thus the causative agency in American foul brood is seen to have powers of resistance much higher than that in European foul brood (376). The small rod-shaped bacillus is so small, it can be seen only through a microscope after having been magnified 600 diameters. The spores (Figs. 159, 160) are so exceedingly diminutive, "if 20,000 of them were placed end to end, they would measure only about one inch." (*White.*) They are produced in enormous

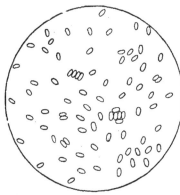

Fig. 160.
SPORES OF BACILLUS LARVAE.

numbers—billions of them in one dead larva, and more exceedingly minute than the dust particles visible in a sunbeam when it shines through a chink in a closed shutter. These spores lie in the scales of the dead larvæ in millions, and when food is stored by the bees in cells containing such remains, it becomes contaminated, and on being fed to healthy larvæ, conveys the disease to them. Their dead bodies, in turn, act as centres of infection, and so on until almost every cell in a hive may contain scales. The colony being by this time weak and unable to defend its stores, these may be robbed out by healthy colonies, and so the disease is spread through a district.

381. PREVENTION.—In order to obviate the chance of his stocks becoming infected, the beekeeper should follow certain rules. He should be extremely cautious in purchasing; only buying bees on combs from reliable men, and whenever possible examining the combs of the stock which he proposes to buy, or getting someone who is familiar with the disease to do so, if he himself is not. He should never under any consideration feed bees upon bought honey or any honey whatever unless he is absolutely assured that there is no possibility of its conveying *B. larvæ*. He should make himself familiar with the disease and its appearance and, when he has done so, may do much to aid his neighbours and to safeguard himself by getting them to allow him to examine their bees occasionally so that an outbreak may be located before much mischief is done. Apart from these things, there is not much that can be done as prevention.

382. TREATMENT.—First of all it is necessary to point out plainly and emphatically that American Foul Brood is not curable in the strict sense of the term. It is not possible to take a diseased stock and, by any treatment whatever so far discovered, to cause the disease to disappear and that stock to become normal once more without the removal and destruction of combs, brood, and honey. The disease is an exceedingly insidious one and, even though there be only a few scattered cells infected when it is first noticed, unless a clean sweep be made of all the combs, brood, and honey, that stock is almost certainly doomed. It should be clearly stated at the outset that no drugs whatever that can by any possibility be used in the presence of living bees or brood will have the slightest effect upon the spores of *B. larvæ*. Therefore all known successful means of elimination are based upon complete elimination of combs.

384. Burning.—It will be well, before describing the method of ridding a colony of bees of this disease, to point out that there is one quite certain way of dealing with a diseased stock. That is by killing the bees and destroying by fire the dead bees, combs, frames, and all fitting, and by thoroughly singeing the interior of the hive by means of a painter's blow-lamp. This is *always* the best plan when a colony is weak, and probably always in the case of an inexperienced beekeeper. To destroy a stock, first smother the bees after sunset or early in the morning before bees are stirring. Prepare a hole in the ground nearby, which may be about 18 inches deep and two or three feet across. Place an armful of dry straw or other combustible material in it and, as soon as the bees are dead, light the straw and place the frames with the comb and honey on the lighted straw, standing them on end propped against one another. As soon as the wax gets alight, the whole will blaze up strongly and quickly consume bees, wood and wax, quilts and anything that is thrown on the fire. The honey will run down and soak into the soil at the bottom of the hole. As soon as all is destroyed the hole should be filled in. Care must be taken not to drop honey anywhere but over the hole; but if by chance any should be so dropped, if creosote or tar be thrown over it, it will be safe for no bee will touch it. It should be dug into the ground in any case. As soon as all frames and combs are removed from it, the hive should be thoroughly scorched out. Fire is the one thing that no spore can withstand.

385. Shaking.—The shaking treatment, or elimination of disease by a form of artificial swarming, is the only known method of dealing with this disease by which the bees can be preserved. It is based on the principle that spores are conveyed effectively in honey only; that honey becomes contaminated by contact with dead larvæ in comb, and that if all comb and stores are removed, the bees will be obliged to assimilate any honey which they carry in their honey-sacs during the process of building new comb or drawing out foundation. In carrying out the plan treat only strong stocks, and treat them only during summer. No stock is worth treating after the honey flow, as it is, after shaking, only equivalent to a lot of driven bees, and it is safer and more profitable to destroy stocks found to be infected late in the year as described (384). When a strong stock is found to be infected with American Foul Brood in the spring, no immediate steps should be taken beyond taking note of the fact and being careful to manipulate as little as possible, and then only after the other bees have ceased to fly for the day, because of all things it is requisite to obviate any inclination to rob on the part of other colonies.

A stock which is strong and not very heavily diseased—and *no other is worth treatment*—should be left alone as much as possible until the first good flow of honey commences and bees are hard at work gathering nectar in the fields. Then proceed as follows: Prepare a clean hive and fit it with frames filled with full sheets of foundation. Also procure another hive, or, better still, a cheap box such as a tea-chest. Have at hand a stiff feather, such as a turkey or goose quill. Lift the hive containing the colony to be operated upon, to one side, and on its stand place the clean hive. Remove four or five of the frames of foundation from the centre so as to leave a space clear for shaking the bees. Have a sack or some such thing to cover over the tea-chest. Now remove the coverings from the diseased stock, and lifting one comb at a time, hold it down between the foundation of the clean hive, giving it a smart shake to throw as many bees as possible into the new hive, and quickly brush off the remainder with the feather. Do not shake the comb anywhere else than inside the clean hive. As soon as all the bees are off the comb place it in the tea-chest or other receptical provided, and repeat the process with the rest of the combs and, having replaced the frames of foundation, cover up the new hive, leaving the bees, now an artificial swarm, to draw the foundation out into new combs. A feeder should be placed on the hive in the evening and the bees fed, unless there should be a very heavy honey flow, in fact feeding is never out of place as it greatly helps the quick building of new comb. As soon as this operation is finished the box of combs should be removed and placed out of reach of bees, and the whole thing—combs, frames and box, quilts and feather and sack—burned in a hole and the ashes buried. This should be done after flying has ceased for the day, or else immediately after the job is done. In a good honey flow bees will not try to rob, and this *shaking* treatment *should be done at no other period than during a flow of nectar*.

Properly carried out, this treatment will result in a clean, healthy colony which will quite frequently give a good surplus of honey, especially should the season be a fairly late one.

At one time it was thought necessary to place the shaken bees on foundation starters and later remove these and substitute full sheets; but this is now known to be unnecessary. Success depends upon meticulous care in removing the combs without allowing the bees of other stocks access to the diseased combs for, if this should occur, we effect the spread of disease to other hives, while clearing it out of one. The shaking should be done in the middle of the day, when the honey flow is at its height, because at this time the bulk of the bees will be out in the fields, and also bees of other hives will not try to investigate the proceedings and carry away honey.

387. Infected Honey Dangerous.—Honey taken from the supers of infected stocks, although perfectly safe for human use, should never in any circumstances be fed to bees, not even if previously boiled. It is certain that the spores of *B. larvæ* can resist boiling for some time, or even freezing and boiling, such as would readily destroy many disease germs. Honey should never be extracted from brood combs that contain American foul brood in any circumstances, but should be destroyed with the combs.

388. Disinfecting.—After the shaking treatment has been completed and combs, frames, quilts, etc., have been destroyed by fire and buried, the hive itself should be thoroughly sterilized. The one really satisfactory agent for the destruction of *B. larvæ* spores is fire, which accordingly should be used. Scorch the interior of the hive with a painter's blowtorch until it is singed to a light brown shade. This will effectually destroy any stray germs that may adhere to the hive and prevent them from becoming transferred to honey and so to the digestive system of some larva. After handling colonies with this disease, the hands should always be well washed in order to remove any trace of honey that may have contaminated them. It is frequently advised to use disinfectants of various kinds, but these, like drugs, are of little or no use; in fact they may be indirectly dangerous through giving the user a false sense of security. The thing the beekeeper should keep always before him in regard to American foul brood is that the germ is carried *in honey* and probably in no other way. The infected honey is fed to larvæ, these die and their remains adhere to the cell. Then honey is stored in that cell and becomes infected and is, in turn, fed to other larvæ, and so *ad infinitum.*

389. The differing symptoms, as already described, may be here stated :

EUROPEAN.	AMERICAN.
Not so widespread.	Very prevalent.
Usually found early in the season.	Equally prevalent at all seasons when bees breed.
Larvæ die before pupation, usually before sealing, but never after pupation.	Larvæ die after feeding has ceased, or even after pupation.
Bees clean out the dead.	Bees cannot move the dead.
Matter does not rope to a fine thread.	Matter ropes to a fine thread at a particular stage of drying.
Scales irregular in shape, size and position.	Scales almost uniform in size, shape and position.
Cause—*B. pluton.*	Cause—*B. larvæ.*

390. Disinfecting Combs.—The possibility of effectively sterilizing combs taken from colonies treated for American Foul Brood was for many years under consideration, and various attempts have been made to render such combs safe for use by bees. Though some measure of success has been from time to time announced, notably by Dr. Hutzelman's formalin in alcohol treatment, and by the subjection of the combs to formalin gas under pressure, results have not been found reliable, and beekeepers are strongly advised to have nothing to do with attempted comb sterilization where such combs have ever been used for breeding. When, however, a large number of stocks are involved it may be worth while to subject the super combs, if these have never contained diseased larvæ, to formalin gas under pressure; but for this purpose a special gas-tight container must be used and all combs must be thoroughly rinsed in two or three changes of water before being given to bees. This last treatment is required to wash away the formalin deposited on the combs which, if left, would poison the bees. All who cannot obtain a suitable gas chamber will be well advised to destroy all combs as being in most cases both much safer and in the end the cheaper method. Few readers of this GUIDE will be likely to be in a position to make disinfection of combs in any shape or form worth while.

393. Sacbrood.—Sometimes erroneously called " Pickled Brood," was investigated by Dr. G. F. White in 1913, and named Sacbrood by him because of the sack-like appearance

BEES, SEALED BROOD AND NATURALLY-BUILT QUEEN CELLS.

of the dead larvæ.† The disease is not prevalent in these countries nor is it nearly so contagious, infectious or destructive as either European or American foul brood.

394. SYMPTOMS.—As in other diseases, this disease is frequently mistaken for foul brood; but, the symptoms are too distinct to admit of any doubt upon the part of a careful observer. The brood dies about, or after, the time of the capping of the cells. Some cappings may be removed by the bees from cells containing dead brood; other cells may be punctured. The dead larva, generally much swollen, lies on its back, with its head, or both ends, upwards: it is first white, like healthy brood, afterwards changing to yellow, gradually darkening until it is nearly black: it is never sticky or ropy. Eventually scales are formed, but these do not adhere to the cell walls; they may be easily removed and may even be shaken from the combs.

395. CAUSE.—The disease, which is infectious, is due to a filterable virus not yet demonstrated or named—"a micro-organism which is so small or of such a nature that it has not been seen, and which will pass through the pores of fine clay filters." Dr. White estimates that the quantity of virus in a single larva dead of this disease is sufficient to p oduce infection in and death of at least 3,000 larvæ, which means a possible increase of the virus contained in one larva, to the extent of three-thousand fold in one week. In less than two weeks, therefore, theoretically it would be possible to produce a sufficient amount of virus to infect 9,000,000 colonies, and within three weeks to infect every colony in existence.

396. TREATMENT.—The treatment commonly adopted is to transfer the bees to clean hives, feeding them with medicated syrup. (Recipes 355, 356). But it is pointed out that, rapid as may be the increase of the virus, its capacity for infecting is limited in point of time, so that if left in the combs for one month it ceases to be infectious and colonies may recover quickly and the percentage that die be small and that without any special treatment.

397. Chalk Brood.—This disease is very common in these Islands. It seems to be in some way influenced by the strain or variety of the bees, for it is much more prevalent in colonies of black bees than in those of Italians. Drone brood is more

---

† G. F. WHITE—"Sacbrood." Bulletin, No. 431, p. 30.

often attacked than worker, though the latter is often destroyed in large numbers. The grubs, when attacked, die at about the time of sealing and after they are stretched at full length. They dry up into a hard, greyish-white body which may, at a superficial glance, be mistaken for mouldy pollen. These dried-up larvæ are often to be seen at the entrances of diseased colonies. The cause is a mould or microscopical fungus. The disease is not usually very serious and will some-times disappear on re-queening the stock with an Italian queen.

398. " Isle of Wight Disease."—This disease made its first appearance in the Isle of Wight in 1904, and was first described in the *Irish Bee Journal* (1906) by Mr. H. M. Cooper, **Hon. Secretary of the local Beekeepers' Association**, who said that the symptoms of the disease were exactly as described in this Guide (1910 Edition), under the heading of " Paralysis." At that time ninety per cent. of the stocks in the Island had perished.—

" In some cases several hundreds of bees are to be seen on the ground near the hive, often crawling rapidly, but quite unable to fly,

CONFERENCE AT MENTONE, FRANCE, MARCH 21, 1927.
Left to Right : M. Baldensperger, Dr. Bugnion, Dr. Poutiers, Rev. J. G. Digges, Dr. Morgenthaler.

their abdomens greatly distended and containing a large amount of ropy, yellowish-brown matter. The stocks affected rapidly dwindle, and usually succumb in about a month or six weeks, leaving their stores, and often a quantity of brood. The queen appears to keep healthy and survives to the last. Although re-queening and other remedies have often been tried, the results have always been fatal."— *Irish Bee Journal*, June, 1906.

It is now known that "under the original and now quite properly discarded designation, 'Isle of Wight Disease,' were included several maladies having analogous superficial symptoms." (*Rennie*.) *

399. **Acarine Disease.**—This disease which, since 1904, wrought almost indescribable destruction among colonies, devastated whole apiaries, ravaged and laid waste the domain of Beekeeping in every part of the Three Kingdoms, preserved its secrecy and anonymity for sixteen years—until researches in Aberdeen University unmasked it in 1920. All that harassed and unfortunate beekeepers knew was that their bees suddenly left the hives, were unable to fly, crawled about and died, colony after colony succumbing. The cause being unknown, prevention and cure were impossible.

400. SYMPTOMS.— The symptoms have been described above (398): to those must be added a dislocation of the wings of affected bees, and, in advanced cases, diarrhœa.

401. CAUSE. — In 1920, a report was made of the result of investigations carried out by Dr.

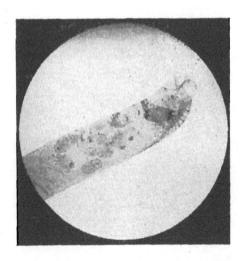

Fig. 165. INITIAL STAGE OF ACARINE DISEASE. Mites (*Acarapis woodi*) in thoracic trachea of hive bee. Magnified 160 times. *Photo by R. W. Frow.*

---

* For Reports of Investigations (1907, 1909, 1912, 1916) see this Guide, **sixth edition, p. 275.**

Rennie, Mr. Bruce White, and Miss Harvey, of the University of Aberdeen. A discovery had been made of the existence of a type of parasitism in bees, which had been hitherto unknown—an extremely diminutive mite (Figs. 165-166), which invades the respiratory system, and belongs to the genus *Acarapis*. This mite (*Acarus*), bred within the bee, was confined to a limited, but important, region of the breathing system. The mites blocked the air tubes, cut off the air supply from surrounding organs, seemed to feed on the blood of the bee, and possibly to affect the blood with a specific virus, and, by the investigators, were believed to be the cause of what had hitherto been known as "Isle of Wight Disease," for which name it was decided to substitute the title "Acarine Disease." The mite was named *A c a r a p i s w o o d i*. From a scholarly scientific Report by Dr. Rennie, published in 1927,[*] we learned that the mite, which cannot be seen with the naked eye, measures .007 inch, or one-fourth the length of the familiar cheese mite. The mites pass from the spiracles to the outside of the bee and from bee to bee; they may be found on frames and

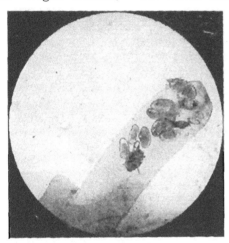

Fig. 166. ADULT FEMALE MITE (*Acarapis woodi*) in thoracic trachea of hive bee, with the whole of her progeny, eggs and larvae. Magnified 160 times. *Photo by R. W. Frow.*

on old combs; they may be deposited on blossoms by foraging bees to be picked up by other bees; they may be carried from hive to hive by drifting bees and robber bees; they may be introduced on the bodies of swarms, stocks, and driven bees, purchased in the ordinary course of trade.

402. PREVENTION.—If absolute prevention be not possible, some useful precautions may be taken. Purchase of bees should be made, if at all, with extreme caution: if possible, there should be microscopical examination and, in every case, a certificate of absolute freedom from infestation should be

* "Acarine Disease in Hive Bees," by JOHN RENNIE, D.Sc., 1927.

required from the vendor. Only young, vigorous queens should be permitted in the hives. Every possible effort should be made to breed robust bees suited to the climate. Combs and frames from diseased colonies should not be used until they have been unoccupied for a couple of weeks in order that any stray mites present may die in the interval; otherwise combs, etc., are non-infectious. There should be regular systematic microscopical examinations of bees taken from colonies apparently healthy, the samples being sent for diagnosis and advice to one of the well-known microscopists who undertake such work. As bees carry this disease, robbing should be particularly guarded against.

403. TREATMENT.—In his last report Dr. Rennie said that to introduce amongst the bees some specific to kill the mites "ought not to be done." The idea appears to have been that any specific which would kill the mites would kill the bees also, or, at least, would seriously injure them.

THE FROW TREATMENT.—In 1927-1928, Mr. R. W. Frow announced in the Beekeepers' journals of Great Britain and Ireland that, having experimented for a number of years, he had discovered a form of treatment by which to kill the mites within the bees without injuring the latter. In a most generous manner he presented this—an invaluable free gift—to his fellow-beekeepers throughout the world. For several years the treatment has been in use at home and abroad. Many thousands of affected stocks have been cured. Judiciously applied, with strict observance of the following instructions and careful attention to details, the treatment will succeed, provided that the degree of infestation be not too high. The beekeeper must not assume that if there be no crawling bees all is well; nor should he defer treatment until mass crawling begins, when the disease will probably have advanced beyond remedy. He should have specimen bees from his stocks microscopically examined from time to time—at least once a year—and should apply the treatment, where necessary, before the percentage of bees per stock affected becomes too high. Sample bees for examination should be flying bees, say, thirty from each stock, and may be forwarded in ventilated match boxes, numbered for identification and secure against bruising or other damage in transit.

THE PRESCRIPTION is made up of Nitrobenzene (Nitrobenzol, or Oil of Mirbane), 2 parts; Safrol oil, 1 part; Petrol, 2 parts. The petrol should be of first-grade quality; none of the mixtures in general use is suitable for this purpose. It is to be noted that this Nitrobenzene-Safrol oil-Petrol mixture is of a poisonous nature and also highly inflammable, and should not be sniffed at, nor tasted, nor brought near to a flame; it should be prepared and kept in a coloured bottle having a close-fitting stopper, and should be plainly marked—POISON.

THE DOSE.—Much experimenting has been done during the last few years to ascertain the best possible method of application and the correct dosage in using the Frow treatment. There is no question that this mixture will readily rid a stock of acarine disease, but to do so effectively while reducing risk of injury to the bees as much as possible is not an entirely simple matter. The obvious aim is to use the smallest effective dosage, but this is affected by several factors such as atmospheric conditions, temperature, size of hive, and strength of stock. Mr. Frow himself now recommends the giving of six daily doses of 20 minims, and this will certainly be effective for almost any stock or hive in times of moderate temperature. It seems

Fig. 167. A, PEN FILLER. B, PAD. C, MEASURE GLASS.

probable, however, that much less tedious methods will be found sufficiently effective. Experiments in 1933 and 1934 in several apiaries showed that when a single dose of 60 minims was given to Modified Dadant stocks and the pad removed at the end of about ten days, mites were killed equally as quickly and surely as in the case of six daily doses. In fact, several whole apiaries were treated in each way as a trial, and it was found that the mites in bees treated with the one dose were actually dead more quickly than those in bees which had been subjected to six doses.

This treatment is for use during the resting period; late autumn, winter or early in the spring. The method of application is to take a small pad of porous material such as felt (Fig. 167), upon which a measured dose is placed, and thrust it under the frames or lay it on the top bars. When applied under the combs, the pad may be fastened to a piece of wire to facilitate insertion and withdrawal or, better still, it may be placed in a shallow tin lid such as that of a cocoa tin, having a string attached. This can be pushed in with a rod and removed by means of the string; it prevents contamination of the hive floor which otherwise is apt to retain the smell for a long time and by this means tempt robbers to try to get in. The pad should usually remain in the hive for about ten days in all. In the case of six daily doses, being removed three days after the last dose is given, and in the case of fewer doses, being still left in place for the full ten days. The effect upon the mites is that, after from three to ten days, according to temperature, humidity and other factors, they die off, shrivel up, and turn yellow. Eggs, larvæ, and mature mites, all are destroyed.

The effect of the treatment upon the bees is to stupify them slightly, especially when heavy dosage is used. They do not defend their hive and, since the individual odour of the colony is masked by the smell of the drug, and that smell appears to be very attractive to bees of other hives, robbing is exceedingly liable to occur while treatment is being carried out. This is the greatest difficulty to be overcome in the administration of the Frow mixture. In fact, robbing is almost inevitable in an apiary undergoing treatment if the weather favours or even permits flight, unless the precaution be taken of confining the bees by means of a piece of perforated zinc arranged to allow plenty of ventilation and retained in position until the bees shall have so far recovered from the effects of the drug as to be able again to defend themselves. If, however, during treatment, weather conditions permit flight, the perforated zinc may with advantage be removed for a very short time just before sunset and the bees allowed a short flight. They will quickly return and may be secured as soon as all are inside.

Probably, at present, there is no better method for the small beekeeper to adopt in regard to acarine disease than the following. Have a sample of bees from each hive examined microscopically every year in August or towards the close of summer. If light infestation is reported, wait until activity ceases with the advent of cold weather, or even until the following February and treat with the entrances securely guarded with perforated zinc. There is little inclination to either flight or robbing at this time of year, and such stocks will generally be cured safely and without much trouble or risk. If severe infestation be reported, it is better to proceed at once to destroy the mites or they will spoil the colony before it settles for winter. In this case, if possible, carry the hive into a dark room or cellar. Let the place be quite dark, and administer the treatment there. When treatment is over the stock may be replaced on its outdoor stand and the bees released. It is wise to heap some grass over the entrance when first brought out and contract the entrance as for robbing.

Methyl Salycilate. *Acarapis woodi* attacks only young bees. The reason for this is probably that the mites are only able to pass the fringe of *setae* which guard the spiracles while these are still in a soft and pliable condition. At any rate this fact has been ascertained by investigators, notably by Dr. Morgenthaler, who considers that by far the greatest part of the bees attacked are under four days old, and that after ten days from emergence from its cell a bee may be considered immune. The implications of this fact are obvious. These mites breed and multiply within their hosts at all times and seasons, but cannot spread from one bee to another except during the breeding season. Therefore treatment should take place in early spring or towards the close of the breeding season, otherwise young bees will be infested as fast as they emerge in spring, and in autumn the late hatching brood which will have to carry the colony through the winter, having become infested, will fail to do so satisfactorily if, indeed, they are able to do so at all.

Experiments with *methyl salycilate* carried out in recent years have proved very successful. This drug has the very great advantages of not in any way inducing robbing; in fact it has, if anything, the opposite tendency. Unless used in very large doses it appears to have no noticeable effect on the bees or their brood, and a stock under treatment acts in a completely normal manner. Very serious cases of acarine disease have with certainty been completely freed of infestation which shows that it is effective, and it appears that the disease may be entirely controlled by biennial routine treatment. Some experimenting is still required to determine the most suitable method of administration and the amount of the drug most effective, but if a small bottle with a rather narrow neck, preferably of a squat shape as being less liable to be knocked over, be fitted with a small piece of soft cotton wick, such as may be purchased in balls in ironmongers' establishments, and half an ounce of *methyl salycilate* put into it, and then stood on the hive floor behind a dummy, one frame having been removed to make room, this will be found effective; but it must be left in place for several weeks.

It seems that Dr. Rennie's idea that migrating mites are unable to establish themselves in the tràchæ of new hosts in the presence of *methyl salycilate*, which is synthetic oil of wintergreen, is correct, and it will thus be understood that its presence in a hive for any considerable period, especially in spring or autumn, must, if this is so, be effective. The older bees which carry the mites do not live long at these stages of the breeding cycle, and if the mites cannot transfer themselves they must perish with the old bees as these wear out, leaving the colony free of infestation. That is the theory, and practical experience appears to confirm its correctness.

404. Nosema Disease.—The investigators appointed by the Board of Agriculture, London, in 1912, reported upon *Nosema apis* as the agent responsible for what was then known as " Isle of Wight Disease "; but, four years later (1916) Dr. Rennie and Dr. John Anderson showed that that report was wrong. The protozoan, *Nosema apis*, had been found by Zander (1909) in the mid-intestine of bees and had been described by him as an organism that was responsible for the death of thousands of colonies. The disease is infectious.

405. SYMPTOMS.—A badly infected colony soon shows signs of failing prosperity; bees appear in the hive and on and under the alighting board with much-swollen abdomens; the colony dwindles, especially in the spring and even during the season of the honey-flow, and gradually perishes. The larger number of attacks, however, are quite mild, not more than a small percentage of the bees being infected; in such cases there is usually a rapid recovery. Brood is not susceptible to this disease.

406. CAUSE.—*Nosema apis*, a minute protozoan animal parasite, produces spores and increases rapidly. Voided in the excrement, it becomes a source of infection, especially if it should fall on food or water that is used by healthy bees. The infection may be spread by robber, or by drifting, bees.

407. PREVENTION.—Prevention may be aimed at by encouraging the bees to collect pure water from fountains arranged in the vicinity of the hives (353)—which fountains, or drinking places, should be protected from pollution by flying infected bees—and by rendering stagnant, or slow-flowing, water resorted to by the bees, as unpalatable as possible by the addition of small quantities of tar products, creosote, or paraffin.

408. TREATMENT.—A satisfactory treatment of affected bees has not been discovered, but it is always desirable that all colonies should be kept strong, since very strong and vigorous stocks are more able to resist attack and even to throw off the diseased condition. It is now thought that *Nosema apis* is endemic in the hive-bee and may possibly be present in all colonies at all times, developing into malignance when circumstances favour it. In this disease bees, hives, frames and everything that has had contact are infectious.

409. Paralysis.—This disease is common in our country, but its cause is not certainly known. It appears to be more prevalent in the South than in the North. It seems to be carried by certain strains of bees, and a new queen will sometimes assist in clearing it up.

410. SYMPTOMS.—Bees are at first noticed about the entrance of the hive or running over the frame tops when the hive is opened, which have a shiny appearance. Dead bees are seen outside and these are also shiny and appear hairless. Both dying and dead have a bad smell. Contents of intestines are watery and will usually squirt out if the bee is squeezed. The healthy bees may constantly be seen dragging the diseased from the hive. In severe cases the stocks will dwindle rapidly and may even die out entirely. The queen is occasionally affected and when this is so she dies quickly.

411. TREATMENT.—First a new queen from a healthy strain should be introduced. Sometimes this alone will effect a complete cure; but several remedies have been put forward as effective, though none has been with certainty proved to be so. Colloidal Sulphur fed in syrup has been suggested, also dusting with flowers of sulphur. Feeding with thymolised syrup has been tried and recommended by some, but it cannot be said that this has been proved effective.

Apart from the administration of drugs, it has been suggested that by exchanging the positions of a healthy stock and a stock suffering from paralysis, the diseased bees can be got rid of; but it does not cure. Another plan tried is that of placing the hive in such a position that paralysed bees cannot regain the entrance, once they have left it and fallen to the ground. So little is known of this disease that really effective treatment must wait on further research, but any or all of the above seem to do good in some cases.

412. Dysentery.—Properly speaking, this is not a disease, but is a condition consequent upon a retention of fæces which, in the ordinary course, should be voided regularly. When bees are suffering from dysentery, the ailment will show itself at the close of winter, or early in spring.

413. Symptoms.—On examining the stock affected, it will be seen that the bees have discharged their excrements over the combs, and on the sides, floor, and alighting board of the hive, as they never do in a healthy state, being scrupulously clean in all their habits (11). The fæces have a very offensive smell, and vary in colour from a red-brown to a mud-black, according to the nature of the food that has been used. The bees move about languidly, and the colony rapidly dwindles.

414. Cause.—When bees have been long confined to their hives, and unable to take a cleansing flight: when they have, from any cause (434), such as untimely manipulations, consumed an excessive quantity of food: or, when their food has consisted, to any considerable extent, of sour, or unripened honey (349), honey dew (66), fermenting stores, or of syrup made with unsuitable sugar (346), they become subject to dysentery; and, being unable to retain the excrements, they void them anywhere (433).

415. Prevention.—To guard against this complaint, late manipulations, causing undue excitement and consumption of food, and late feeding with syrup, when evaporation and sealing of the food are impossible, should be avoided: none but pure, refined cane sugar should be used for syrup and candy feeding.

416. Treatment.—When an attack of dysentery has set in, the bees should be transferred to a clean hive, contracted to the space accupied by the cluster; very soiled combs should be removed and washed clean, and their places should be occupied by clean combs; candy, or sealed honey should be given; and, the bees should be kept warm, and as free as possible from excitement. A few warm days generally put matters right, by giving the bees opportunities for cleansing flights.

RECIPES.

417. Carbolic Solution, for Subduing Bees (136).—

Calvert's No. 5 Carbolic Acid	... ...	1 part.
Water	... ...	10 parts.

Shake the bottle. Thoroughly damp the cloth, and keep it in a tin box.

418. Solution, for Disinfecting Hives (384).—

Calvert's No. 5 Carbolic Acid	... ...	1 part.
Water	... ...	2 parts, or
Izal	... ...	1 teaspoonful.
Water	... ...	1 quart.

Paint the hive thoroughly with the solution, and set it in the open air until the smell disappears.

419. Solution, for Disinfecting Clothing, etc. (388).—

Calvert's No. 5 Carbolic Acid	... ...	1 part.
Water	... ...	15 parts, or
Izal	... ...	1 teaspoonful.
Water	... ...	1 quart.

422. Solutions, for Acarine Disease (403).—

Chloropicrin	... ...	1 part.
Camphor	... ...	1 part.
Methyl salycilate	... ...	12 parts.
		(*Rennie*)
Nitrobenzene	... ...	2 parts.
Safrol oil	... ...	1 part.
Petrol	... ...	2 parts.
		(*Frow*)

CHAPTER XXXI.

ENEMIES OF BEES.

423. Enemies.—Bees, like every other living thing, have their natural enemies; and, in some countries, it is very necessary to protect them from a variety of foes. In our country, however, all that is required is to keep the stocks strong enough to protect themselves, and to give them hives that do not offer special facilities to the attacks of dangerous intruders.

424. Ants.—These insects (66) sometimes make their nests about the hives, and give a little trouble. But healthy bees are very well able to cope with them. Naphthaline (381) in the hives and among the quilts discourages ants. To stand the hive-legs in saucers of tar will keep out these insects. If they become very troublesome, the nest should be destroyed by making a hole a foot deep through the centre of the nest with a pointed stick, and two or three similar holes around it, when ½-oz. of bi-sulphide of carbon (384) may be poured into each hole, and the clay may then be closed in. Bi-sulphide of carbon is highly inflammable, and must not be brought near fire or lamp.

425. Birds.—Sparrows, Starlings, Chaffinches, Blue Tits, and even Swallows, occasionally prey upon bees. In hard winters, birds may sometimes be seen on the alighting boards, picking up venturous bees. It is not reasonable to declare war upon, and to destroy these beautiful things for obeying their instincts in search of food, when frost has dried up the earth, and berries are no longer in the hedgerows. All that is necessary is to arrange a yard of old herring netting in front of the hive; thus, at the expense of a penny, protecting each colony until the opening of spring shall offer other provender to the songsters of the woods.

426. Woodpeckers.—These birds will sometimes attack beehives in frosty weather, boring holes in them to get at the combs. Newly erected scares of strings of white feathers will keep them off for a time—until a change to mild weather, in fact.

427. Mice.—When winter drives the bees away from the entrance, mice will creep into hives and make their nests in the warmth if the space at the doors be more than $\frac{3}{8}''$ high. They eat honey and chilled bees, and set up a stench which is so highly objectionable to bees, colonies will often forsake such hives in the spring and, if returned, will refuse to remain. Bees have been known to completely cover up a dead mouse with propolis, in order to suppress the smell (80), and they will refuse to occupy supers that have been visited by mice when carelessly stored away in winter. Entrances that are too high should be reduced to $\frac{3}{8}''$ by means of a strip of perforated zinc, or a wire stretched tightly from side to side. All hives, hive fittings, foundation, etc., should be protected from the visits of mice.

428. Parasites.—*Braula Cœca.*—Often called the " Blind Louse," is a very remarkable parasite upon the hive-bee. In reality it is a minute wingless fly which has the habit of living on the bodies of the bees where it clings by its wonderfully specialized feet. It does not actually feed upon the bees' bodies, nor does it injure them, but it obtains its nourishment in its adult state by the method of taking food directly from the mouth of the bee. Usually, if there are any of these parasites present in a colony, a number will be found upon the queen. This is probably because the queen is constantly being fed by workers and consequently much greater facility is thus offered to the parasite to obtain food as it is passed to the queen. When a stock is heavily infested by braula, its queen may be almost covered with these little creatures, which cling to every part of her, though they prefer the thorax so long as there is standing room thereon. As many as 133 have been removed from a single queen in England. These creatures are of a bright red colour when mature, but almost white when newly hatched. They are about the size of a very small pin's head. But, though when numerous they are a great source of irrita-tion, especially to queens, the worst damage they do is done while in the larval stage. The adult females lay their eggs upon the cappings of the honey, and the tiny grub which hatches from each egg, burrows in the thickness of the cappings, leaving small whitish lines to show where its burrows are. Much damage is frequently done to sections by the dis-figurement of the cappings by this creature. While it is practically impossible to remove the mites mechanically, they may be made to drop off a queen if the latter is placed in a match-box and a little strong tobacco smoke is blown in with her. The box should be covered with a piece of glass while this is done so that it can be seen when the parasites fall off. The queen should never be kept under the influence of the fumes longer than is necessary. It is said that if strong tobacco smoke be blown into the hive entrance by means of a smoker, that the braula present will fall to the floor and may be removed and destroyed while stupified. It is also stated that naphtha-line or camphor have the same effect if placed under the combs. There is, however, no known means of destroy-ing the larvæ. The Pollen Mite—This insect is often found in pollen cells in weak colonies. Not actually harmful to the bees, strong stocks quickly clear them out of their hives. The Maggot (*Stylops*)—This maggot is commonly found in the abdomens of *Andrenæ* (59), and other wild bees. It has not been reported as appearing in the honey bee.

429. **Wasps.**—In autumn, wasps sometimes struggle hard to gain access to the honey in hives and, as these insects are both stronger and more active than bees, they can do a great deal of mischief in weak colonies. When their attacks become troublesome, a " dark passage " may be constructed on the alighting board, as advised for robber bees (344). Bottles, with a little beer, or sugar and water, if left beside the alighting boards, will attract and catch these enemies. Their nests should be destroyed whenever found and queen wasps should get short shrift. To destroy wasps' nests, place small pieces of cyanide of potassium at the entrance of each nest; or, better still, dissolve ½ oz. of the cyanide in 1 pint of water and pour the mixture into the nest, closing the opening immediately with a sod. Cyanide of potassium is a deadly poison and its fumes are highly dangerous; the mixing of it with water should be done out-of-doors only. In the morning, the nest should be dug out and burned. Never interfere with a wasps' nest during the day: mark it with a piece of stick and white paper, and do the killing by lantern light.

Fig. 168. LESSER WAX MOTH AND LARVA. (*Magnified*).

430. **The Wax Moths.**— There are two species of moth which are serious enemies to the bees whose combs their larvæ devour. The Greater Wax Moth (*Galleria mellonella*) is about ¾" long and is easily recognised by its fore wings, which are scalloped

out at their ends which gives a very distinctive effect. The eggs are deposited in masses on the frames or interior of the hive and the resulting grubs tunnel into the combs, spinning a silken gallery as they go. When fully fed they spin a white cocoon, and these are usually found grouped together and placed on the hive walls or on frames. The larvæ, before pupation, almost always gnaw a shallow groove in the wood in which the pupa lies. This insect is fairly common in these countries, but not nearly so destructive as in America and many other places. The Lesser Wax Moth (*Achroia Grissella*) (Fig. 168)

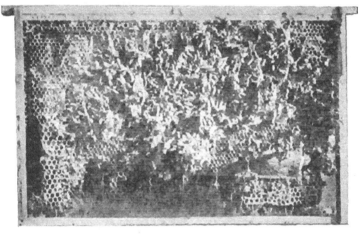

Photo by A. S. *Rowse.*

COCOONS OF THE LESSER WAX MOTH.

is much more common in these Islands. It is much smaller than the other, being about half an inch in length. Its wings are rounded at the ends and not concave. These moths breed two or three times in one year. They are very fleet in their movements—" the most nimble-footed creatures that I know."— *Reaumur.* They may sometimes be seen flying in front of a hive on a cloudy afternoon in summer. At night, if she can gain admission, the female deposits eggs in the hive (104). The worms from these eggs devour wax, brood, pollen, and the cast-off skins of bee larvæ, during from fourteen to twenty days, according to the temperature. They spin around their bodies white, silken cases, and further fortify themselves with a coat of wax and their own excrement. They expose only their heads and necks, and these are so strongly helmeted with scales as to be impenetrable to stings. They perforate the combs and cover them with webs, cocoons, and excrement, speedily working ruin in the hive, and emerging as perfect winged moths. Bees seem to realize fully the danger of admitting the wax moth (80) and, unless the colony is weak or queenless, the moth will stand but a poor chance of getting into the hive (52). But, beekeepers often introduce the mischief to their colonies; for, combs out of use when left lying about attract the moths, and become fruitful sources of danger when given to the stocks. When the danger threatens, weak colonies, if not united to strong colonies, should be confined to the combs which they can cover and defend; for, if the outer combs be left vacant, the moth, on entering, will be able to work her mischief unhindered. The larvæ of wax moth should be destroyed when found; and comb infested by this enemy should be removed and the wax extracted. Combs that are not beyond saving may be placed in hive bodies, or super boxes, piled up on an empty box in which some ounces of sulphur have been placed and kindled. The receptacles being properly covered, the sulphur fumes will ascend and will kill the moths and grubs. This treatment should be renewed after a few weeks.

CHAPTER XXXII.

WINTERING.

431. Successful Wintering.—So much depends upon the successful wintering of bees, some general advice may, perhaps, be usefully given here. The main points to be attended to are—(1) To winter only strong stocks. (2) To provide a sufficient quantity of wholesome food. (3) To keep the bees as quiet as possible. (4) To supply sufficient ventilation. (5) To avoid damp, and the ill-effects of storms.

432. Winter only Strong Stocks.—Small stocks of bees consume more food, proportionally, than do strong stocks, and are seldom profitable in the following year. Frequently such stocks die out altogether before the spring opens, from inability to keep up the necessary heat of their cluster, and from excessive consumption of food, leading to dysentery **(412)**. Stocks that do not cover at least six frames in the middle of September should be either strengthened by the addition of healthy, driven bees **(262)**, or should be united to each other, or to stronger stocks.

433. Provide a Sufficient Quantity of Wholesome Food.— This has been dealt with under the heading of " Feeding " **(349)**. The bees cluster on the empty parts of the combs, just below the honey, the head of each bee under the abdomen of the bee above her ; and the food is passed down from one to another until, during a warm hour on some sunny day, the lower bees find opportunity to move up to the food. As the bees on the outside of the mass become chilled, they pass into the warmth of the cluster. But, when the food in the immediate vicinity of the cluster is consumed, the bees, in very cold weather, are unable to move to distant combs and will often starve to death in the midst of plenty. Therefore, the food required should be given rapidly, towards the middle of September. Candy, if given, should be placed right over the cluster ; and, when candy is not supplied there, " winter passages " **(357)** should be provided, to permit the bees to pass from comb to comb without having to go under or around the frames in cold weather, when many of them would become chilled, and the remainder, refusing to leave the warmer portion of the hive, would perish from hunger. Two pieces of stick, ¾″ thick, laid across the frames, say 1″ apart, provide a winter passage under the sheet. Entrances should be sheltered from direct sun rays while snow is on the ground, lest bees, attracted by the light and heat, should fall on the snow and die; and lest those within, encouraged to break up the cluster, should continue in a state of activity throughout the winter, consuming extra food, exhausting their vitality, and, probably, falling victims to disease (414). Towards the end of February, or the beginning of March, if the weather permit, a corner of the sheet may be raised for a moment, when, if it is seen that food is required, a cake of candy should be given at once.

434. Keep the Bees as Quiet as Possible.—Sudden changes of temperature lead to increased activity in the cluster, and this means increased consumption of food, with the frequent

Fig. 169.   THATCHED SKEP.

result of filling the intestines with digested food which, the bees being unwilling to void it in the hive (11), promotes dysentery (414). Therefore, unnecessary, empty combs should be removed, and the nest should be reduced to the size required by the bees, the dummy being moved up for the purpose. Warm coverings should be placed over the frames. A section crate, with a piece of stuff tacked underneath, and filled with cork dust, dry chaff, or torn paper, may be set upon the quilts (103). With hives constructed for the purpose, the riser (92) may be inverted over the body box, thus supplying additional walls; and the porch may be transferred from the body box to it. (Fig. 172, a). It is necessary to point out that all the above-mentioned proceedings must be carried out when bees are being prepared for winter, and that on no account must any interference with the brood frames, dummies or other fittings be done in winter, after the cluster has been formed.

435. Supply Sufficient Ventilation.—When danger of

robbing is over, the bees having ceased to fly freely, the doors of all hives should be opened to a space of about six inches; and, frequently during the winter, a bent wire should be used to draw out any dead bees which, accumulating near the entrance, might prevent ventilation and lead to the smothering of the living bees within.

436. Avoid the Ill-effects of Damp and Storms.—Care should be taken to make all hive roofs thoroughly water-proof, because, damp entering is very unhealthy. Damaged roofs should be repaired and well painted before the winter sets in; and, where necessary, water-proof covers should be put on in anticipation of severe rain and snow. A durable paint may be prepared by mixing $1\frac{3}{4}$ pints of milk and $2\frac{1}{4}$ lb. of cement, to be laid on the roof with a brush. Only sufficient for immediate application should be mixed. Colour may be added if desired. A defective roof can be made rainproof by giving it a coat of thick paint, then laying on, while the paint is wet, a piece of canvas or calico to cover the roof top. This material should have a good coat of paint, and a second coat when the first has dried. Skeps require special attention in this respect. They should have a thick covering of straw, tied securely at the top, and held to the skep by hoops (Fig. 169). Storms sometimes make havoc of stocks by upsetting, or unroofing, the hives. A stake should be driven into the ground close to the hive, and a rope, carrying a heavy stone, or a couple of bricks, and tied to the stake at one end, should be passed over the hive as a protection against storms (Fig. 170). Where there is no danger of the overturning of hives by storms, but some danger of their being unroofed, they may be made safe by the application of a spring hook, as illustrated. (Fig. 171). Ten inches of brass wire, or bull wire, bent in spiral spring (A) by passing it three times round a lead pencil, giving a turn at (B) for a handle, a hook (C) and a loop (D), is attached at (D) by a brass screw to the body box, or lift, and grips at (C) a brass screw in one side of the

Fig. 170. HIVE SECURED AGAINST STORMS.

Fig. 171 SPRING HOOK

roof. It costs a penny. Snow should be brushed off the hive
roofs before it melts. Apiaries, in situations exposed to

Photo by   *J. G. Digges.*

Fig. 172. Hives prepared for (a) Winter and (b) Summer.

severe storms, should be protected by substantial storm-breaks.
Hedges of either privit or beech grow rapidly and, if clipped
regularly, give the necessary shelter.

CHAPTER XXXIII.

THE YEARLY ROUND.

437. January.—Towards the end of this month—sometimes earlier—the queen will be commencing to breed, but only a few eggs will be laid daily. Food consumption is small at this time and, if bees have been properly attended to in the autumn, there will be no danger of starvation. In case of there having been neglect, and bees are known to be short of food, a couple of pounds of candy may be laid on the frames directly over the cluster, but unless it is known to be needed, it is better to leave bees completely alone during January.

438. February.—What has been said for January applies equally to this month, but towards the end, if it is found necessary, Frow mixture may be administered to colonies known to require it. In all winter months, from November to February, inclusive, damp quilts, if found, may be profitably replaced by dry ones, dead bees may be gently cleared from entrances if they have accumulated there, the apiary may be tidied up from time to time and equipment may be prepared for the coming season. Apart from these things, almost any interference with bees in winter will be to their injury.

439. March.—Breeding becomes much more active now, and stores are accordingly more rapidly consumed. The bee-keeper may gently lift the corners of the quilts to see if there are stores present. If sealed stores are seen to be present in two or three combs it is better to close the hive and leave quite alone until April. If stores appear to be wanting, candy may be given as before, or warm syrup, preferably containing Thymol, may be given rapidly. Remember that all interference with the bees in March is to be regarded as injurious and only to be undertaken through necessity. Good autumn management should obviate all need for any such interference before April.

440. April.—Breeding is now rapidly going on and stores are quickly reduced. More bees starve in April and May than in all the other months put together. In early districts feeding may be undertaken for stimulative purposes, though there is much doubt as to the value of this proceeding. In less early districts, mid-April is time enough to commence feeding. It should be emphasised that a great deal of damage is frequently done by beekeepers to their stocks by impatience to see how they have wintered. The early opening of hives should be rigorously avoided. Every year hundreds of queens are lost through too early interference with the brood nest. Bees, when so disturbed, are very apt to ball their queens for some reason, and the last week in April will, in nine cases out of ten, be early enough for the first opening of the brood chamber, and, apart from feeding, no work is required to be done to the stocks before that time.

441. May.—This is the month for spring cleaning in most places, and the first week the most suitable time. When no honey is being gathered, this is the month of all others when it pays to feed bees. The queen is now laying at a great rate and the resulting brood is consuming large quantities of honey and pollen. It will always pay to feed in May unless there is a honey flow. In May, after spring cleaning, when stocks are found to be very strong, brood may be spread if caution is exercised, in order to lessen the inclination to swarm. It is better to place the outer comb of brood in the centre, rather than an empty comb thus early in the year, for May is apt suddenly to turn bitterly cold and a completely divided brood nest may then be a great danger to the progress of the stock. Towards the end of May, stocks may be doubled or " Demareed." The reader must remember that things in the apiary move fast in May and June. There is far more change in one week in May than in three months of winter. Whereas, at the opening of the month, we may be only getting bees spring cleaned and into summer order, by the end all strong stocks should occupy at least one super, whether there is a honey flow or not. Super in May and prepare for swarming. Proceed with queen-rearing.

442. June.—Work for this month consists of giving supers as required; attending to swarm control and making increase. Also queen-rearing should be in full swing, when practised. In early districts honey may be removed if needed for sale or use.

443. July.—The work is much the same as for June, but towards the end of the month, the first supers of sections should be removed, if ready, and extracting may be begun from the earlier sealed combs, if honey is wanted for sale. Contract all entrances at the end of the honey flow.

444. **August.**—Remove the supers and extract honey. When bees are to go to the heather they should be now taken to the moors. Guard against robbing, for this is the month of all others when this is a danger. Do not attempt to feed, except in cases of absolute necessity, until September. This will give bees time to settle down peacefully after the close of the honey flow. If feeding is commenced in August, as is sometimes recommended, robbing will very often be started and may be very difficult to suppress.

445. **September.**—The principal work for this month is to feed the bees for winter and to requeen all those stocks that require it.

An Apiary of Modified Dadant Hives in an Oxfordshire Orchard, some worked for section and some for extracted honey.

446. **October.**—Any last manipulations to the brood chamber, such as reducing the number of combs, should, if not done, as it ought to have been, before feeding up, be carried out now. See that all roofs are waterproof and that the hive is secure against the gales and rains of winter. Wrap well with warm quilts so that all is snug for the time of rest to come. By October 1st every stock should be fully fed for winter and have at least 30 pounds of honey or syrup sealed in its combs. If, however, this has not been attended to, feeding must be undertaken directly. Though late, it will be

effective if done at once; but syrup should be thick, and preferably be impregnated with Thymol in case bees fail to seal it
so late.

447. November.—This is the first real winter month and
bees should be left strictly alone. Entrances should be set at
about six inches wide and left so throughout the winter.

448. December.—Leave the bees completely alone. If
properly prepared, only harm can result in any interference
with the hives. There is plenty of work for the beekeeper in
making appliances, hives, etc., painting and repairing.
Preparation and marketing of honey should be undertaken at
this time, for the Christmas trade should be catered for.

GENERAL NOTE.—*In considering monthly work, we
must always bear in mind that different localities have, of
necessity, different times for bee work, and readers must allow
for local peculiarities when reading the foregoing notes. Work
described as suitable for May in a general work of this kind,
may be applicable to April for a Cornish beekeeper, or for June
in the Highlands of Scotland. Every beekeeper must learn
his own district if he is to be successful*

CHAPTER XXXIV.

BEE FLOWERS AND PLANTS.

449. Spring.—Among the garden flowers which are most useful to bees are those which bloom before the field flowers, and after the Clover and Lime:—of the former, Aconite, Crocus, Hellebore, Scilla, Arabis, and Aubretias, in which bees revel during every sunny hour from January to April; and Limnanthes Douglasii, a prime favourite in May. Of trees and shrubs, Pyrus Japonica, Cotoneaster, Box, Sally, Gorse, Willow, Broom, Ribes Rubra, and Gooseberry yield largely in the opening months of the year, and are followed by Sycamore, Hawthorn, and fruit trees, which usher in the honey flow, and usually give bees continual employment until White Clover and Sainfoin begin to yield. Of the foregoing, those which produce honey in quantity, and of a distinct type, are:—Sycamore—honey heavy, somewhat green in tint, and lacking in flavour. Hawthorn—honey heavy, amber coloured, flavour and aroma delicious. Fruit trees—honey excellent, in colour and consistency resembling that from Sycamore.

450. Summer.—The main honey flow, which occurs in summer, is from quite a small number of plants in most districts. While in a few special localities the trees which flower early in the year may give a flow equal to that which comes later from the more generally important plants, in nearly every part of these islands White Clover is the most important source of honey. In places where the subsoil is limestone or chalk, Sainfoin and Charlock are extremely valuable and, in some seasons, may give most of the honey. In some places, where woodlands have been cut down, large areas of Rose Bay or Willow Herb give a heavy flow of excellent honey during the latter half of July and the first half of August, or even later. An important honey plant in many agricultural districts is the Field Bean which furnishes a beautiful light honey in good quantities. The Lime trees, where numerous, are generally in full yield, when there is hot weather during their flowering, from the end of June for about a fortnight. White Clover gives one of the finest of all honies. In colour, density and flavour, it is doubtful if any unblended honey equals it. Sainfoin honey is of a somewhat deeper yellow colour and usually not so dense. Lime honey has a slightly green tint and is much appreciated by some. When present, Wild Thyme and Marjoram yield some honey of very fine flavour which is an improvement to almost any natural blend stored by bees. Willow Herb honey is pale in colour and very mild in flavour, if pure. The colour of the wax from White Clover is white; from Sainfoin, a pale straw colour, and from Willow Herb a pure, dead white. Pollen from Willow Herb is of a peculiar

a   ⌈*b*   *c*

Fig. 173.

HEATHER BLOOMS.

a, Calluna vulgaris (Ling Heather) ; *b, Erica cinerea* (Bell Heather) ; *c, Erica tetralix* (Cross-leaved Heather).

saxe-blue colour and very distinctive. Sainfoin has a light tan coloured pollen, and white clover a brown. Between Lime and Heather, besides numerous garden flowers, we have Blackberry, a good yielder of both honey and pollen; Wild Clematis, a good yielder where plentiful, and late growths, after being cut for hay, of Red Clover, Lucerne and Sainfoin. Mustard, where grown late, often gives a good yield at this time. Ragwort or Benweed, which flowers in profusion through July and into August, gives a strong flavoured honey which is distasteful to many. Its wax is of a deep yellow colour. Blackhead blooms at the same time as Heather, and, being a prolific source of nectar, is often preferred by bees. Its honey is thin, of a rich amber colour, and acrid in flavour. Heather (Ling) honey is quite distinct from any other; its colour is deep amber, and it is strong and slightly bitter-sweet in flavour. It is of a somewhat gelatinous consistency and cannot be extracted by means of the centrifugal extractor, but must be pressed from the combs. It should, as far as possible, always be produced in the form of comb honey in sections. Ling Heather (*Calluna vulgaris*) (Fig. 173, *a*) is a small evergreen shrub. Leaves and flowers are small, the latter are purple-pink in colour, while a white spot is not uncommon. It is a heavy yielder and is specially valuable on high moors and mountain sides. When growing in low-lying bogs its honey is inferior. Bees at heather should be left to themselves as much as possible, for they are always inclined to become bad tempered while working this source of nectar. The wax of heather is of a pure, dead white. Bell Heather (*Erica cinerea*) (Fig. 173, *b*) is more bushy than the former; its flowers are larger and oval shaped. Its honey is quite different from that of Ling and can be extracted in the ordinary way. It is not classed as " Heather Honey " in the market. Cross Leaved Heather (*Erica tetralix*) (Fig. 173, *c*) is short, with leaves growing in fours, crossways, up the stem; its flowers grow in clusters at the top of the stem and are pale pink in colour. The plant is of little value to the beekeeper.

451. Autumn.—Ivy, which, if left to grow of its own sweet will on walls and trees, blooms profusely in October, is eagerly sought after on sunny days. The honey it yields is very inferior, but it makes a useful addition to winter stores in the hives.

452.—COMPARATIVE LIST OF BEE PLANTS AND FLOWERS.

(Yield :—G, good ; M, medium ; P, poor.)

NAME	Date		For Pollen	For Honey
	From	To		
Aconite	January	April	P	M
Box	February	March	G	M
Crocus	,,	April	G	P
Dandelion	,,	October	G	P
Hazel	,,	March	G	Nil
Hellebore	,,	May	G	M
Sedum Major	,,	April	M	G
Snowdrop	,,	March	P	M
Aubrietias	March	July	P	M
Barberry	,,	April	G	P
Cotoneaster	,,	May	P	M
Gorse (Furze-Whin)	,,	June	G	P
Mallow	,,	,,	G	M
Poppies, Single	,,	,,	G	Nil
Ribes Rubra	,,	May	M	G
Sallow	,,	,,	G	G
Scilla	,,	,,	P	G
Violet, Sweet	,,	,,	P	G
Wallflower	,,	,,	M	G
White Rock	,,	June	P	M
Willow	,,	May	G	G
Cherry	April	,,	G	M
Gooseberry	,,	,,	P	M
Pyrus Japonica	,,	June	M	M
Pear	,,	May	M	M
Plum	,,	June	M	M
Sycamore	,,	May	M	G
Apple	May	June	M	G
Bird Cherry	,,	,,	M	M
Broom	,,	,,	G	P
Cabbage	,,	July	G	M
Forget-me-not	,,	,,	M	G
Hawthorn	,,	June	M	G
Field or Tick Bean	,,	,,	M	G
Holly	,,	July	M	G
Limnanthes Douglasii	,,	June	M	G
Mignonette	,,	November	G	M
Ragweed	,,	August	G	G
Raspberry	,,	June	M	G
Strawberry	,,	,,	G	M
White Clover	,,	July	M	G
Bokhara Clover	June	September	M	G

NAME	Date		For Pollen	For Honey
	From	To		
Borage	,,	November	M	G
Buckwheat	,,	July	P	G
Charlock	,,	,,	G	G
French Honeysuckle . .	June	September	G	G
Mustard	,,	August	M	G
Sainfoin	,,	,,	G	G
Thistle	,,	,,	M	M
Vetch	,,	,,	M	G
Blackhead	July	September	M	G
Lime	,,	August	M	G
Willow Herb	,,	,,	G	G
Meadowsweet	,,	,,	P	M
Saxifrage	,,	,,	M	M
Thyme	,,	,,	M	G
Marjoram	,,	,,	M	G
Blackberry	,,	September	G	G
Heather	,,	,,	G	G
Poppy	,,	,,	G	P
Canterbury Bells . . .	August	November	G	P
Devil's Bit (*Scabiosa Succisa*)	,,	September	M	M
Ivy	October	December	M	M

INDEX

BEEHIVES, APPLIANCES
AND EVERY BEE-KEEPER'S REQUIREMENT
FOR THE MODERN PRODUCTION OF

HONEY

Wholesale and Retail

Buyers and Marketers of Honey
and Wax. Current Prices on
request, also Honey Grading Rules

Specially appointed Distributors of
DADANT'S FOUNDATIONS
ALL GRADES and

**JONES-WEED PROCESS COMB
FOUNDATIONS**

Both recognised as the World's best

M. Rowan & Co. Ltd.

Bee Hive and Bee Appliance Merchants

51 & 52 CAPEL STREET, DUBLIN
and at 1 & 2 Westmoreland Street, Dublin

Telegrams:
"*Rowan, Dublin*"

Telephone: 75105
(3 Lines)

Everything for the Bee Keeper

C.D.B. Hives, National Langstroth Hives, Dadant Modified Hives, Sections, Bar Frames, Excluders, Super Clearers, Gloves and Gauntlets, Honey Bottles, Honey Labels, Extractors, Section Holders, Waxed Papers, Cellophane.

SPRAYERS, DISINFECTANTS, ETC.

For Foul Brood and I O.W. Disease

Naphthaline, for using in hives as a preventive of infection. **IZAL,** for I.O.W. Carbolic, Calvert's— **No. 5. Isle of Wight Cure. Control Fluid. Sprayers.**

SUNDRIES.

Awls for use in wiring frames. **Control Fluid,** with instructions, for use in quieting bees. **Control Cloth,** made of stout transparent linen scrim, very durable. **Drone Traps** (Dunboyne Porch). **Embedder,** for Wiring Comb (Woiblet Spur). **Embedder,** The "O'Bryen" pattern. **Candy**—Candy specially made for feeding in cold weather. Flour Candy, specially prepared for Spring feeding. **Grimshaws' Apifuge,** for preventing the attacks of bees, midges, and all other winged insects. **Knives** for uncapping combs (W.B.C.) **Labels,** Irish, Oblong. **Labels,** Irish, Oval.

Papers, Cellophane. Petroleum Jelly. Packing Boxes (folding). **Queen Cage,** to press on the comb. **Queen Cage,** Abbott Pattern, etc. **Quilts,** thick wool felt, 16 ins. sq. **Quilts,** strong jute, 16 ins. sq. **Quilting** wool felt. **Scrapers Section Holders.** Card boxes, glass both sides. **Waxed Papers,** for wrapping sections. **Wiring Outfit,** consisting of board on which to lay frame and foundation, boring and embedding awls, and card of tinned wire **Wiring Board. Wire** (Tinned), for comb foundation, pull through cards

Catalogue free.

M. Rowan & Co. Ltd

Bee Hive and Bee Appliance Merchants

51 & 52 CAPEL STREET, DUBLIN
and at 1 & 2 Westmoreland Street, Dublin

Telegrams :
"Rowan Dublin"

Telephone : 75105
(3 Lines)

307

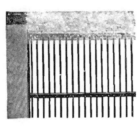

THE ALTON AUTOMATIC VENTILATOR.

Prov. Patent 1013/43

INCREASES HONEY YIELD

The World's first Thermo controlled Ventilator for use on all Types of Beehives, so sensitive that the heat given off by the palm of the hand will operate it.

12/6 each

Fits over Brood or Super Box, on Quilt, or Coverboard.

Size, 14" x 14"

Northumberland :- Must say it works very well indeed and is very sensitive.

Lancs : Temperature control equipment will become a standard feature in hives.